Constitutional Self-Government

Constitutional Self-Government

CHRISTOPHER L. EISGRUBER

HARVARD UNIVERSITY PRESS

Cambridge, Massachusetts
London, England   2001

Library of Congress Cataloging-in-Publication Data

Eisgruber, Christopher L.
    Constitutional self-government / Christopher L. Eisgruber.
        p.   cm.
    Includes bibliographical references and index.
    ISBN 0-674-00608-9 (cloth : alk. paper)
    1. Judicial review—United States.   2. Representative government and
    representation—United States.   3. Legislative power—United States.
    4. Democracy.   I. Title.

    KF4575 .E37 2001
    320.973—dc21   2001024319

for Lori

Preface

WHEN I BEGAN WORK on this book six years ago, I planned to describe a distinctive blend of American history and political theory that would enable interpreters to unlock the Constitution's meaning. My reflections took me in unexpected directions, and I have ended up writing a book far different from the one I envisioned. Democratic theory has displaced interpretive method as the central topic. My germinal intuitions about the relationship between history and theory survive in Chapters 4 and 5, but most of the book argues for no particular interpretive protocol. On the contrary, the book maintains that jurisprudential technique is less important to good judging than lawyers and scholars commonly suppose, and that, at least in constitutional cases, what matters most is moral conviction and practical judgment.

As the book evolved, I received more collegial support than I can adequately acknowledge. For comments and discussions pertaining to portions of the manuscript, I am grateful to Sot Barber, Vicki Been, Yochai Benkler, Mary Anne Case, Norman Dorsen, Ronald Dworkin, John Ferejohn, Marty Flaherty, Jim Fleming, Barry Friedman, Lewis Kornhauser, Helen Hershkoff, Sam Issacharoff, Lori Martin, Andy Moravcsik, Liam Murphy, Tom Nagel, Dan Ortiz, Stephen Perry, Pasquale Pasquino, Rick Pildes, Robert Post, Ricky Revesz, David Richards, Carlos Rosencrantz, Larry Sager, and Peter Schuck. Larry Kramer and Bill Nelson read the entire manuscript at a critical stage in its progress, and they responded with extensive comments and much-needed encouragement. Sandy Levinson prepared an unusually thoughtful and detailed review letter for the Harvard University Press; his advice was a great help. I was fortunate to be able to present portions of the manuscript to multiple sessions of the New York University School of Law's Colloquia in Law, Philosophy, and Social Theory and in Constitutional Theory, where rigorous questioning from conveners Dworkin, Nagel, and Sager, and from other workshop participants, led me to make numerous revisions. I presented related papers to faculty audiences at the Fordham Law School, the Hofstra Law School, Princeton University, the University of Chicago Law School, and the Yale Law School, and I am grateful for the comments I received at all those workshops (in some cases, their comments prompted changes so extensive that the chapters published here bear little resemblance to the drafts I once presented). I am also thankful to my editor, Michael Aronson, for his counsel and support, and to my copyeditor, Kate Brick, for her improvements to the manuscript.

I have other debts of a more general character. The book was completed while I was on the faculty of the New York University School of Law, where Dean John Sexton and the entire administrative staff have created a special community in which scholarship flourishes. NYU's support was provided partly through grants from the Max and Filomen D'Agostino Greenberg Faculty Research Fund, and I thank the fund for its assistance. During my first years at NYU, Lewis Kornhauser, Bill Nelson, and Larry Sager provided mentorship of the best kind. My interaction with Sager grew into a rich scholarly collaboration, and conversations with him have influenced my thinking immeasurably. Still earlier in my life, I benefited from many gifted teachers. Of those who taught me constitutional law, Will Harris, Dennis Hutchinson, and especially Jeff Tulis were exceptionally generous with their time and insight, and they deeply shaped my thought. I have tried to follow their example in my own teaching, and have been rewarded by, among other things, many wonderful students who have challenged me and enriched my thinking. Finally, Lori Martin commented upon the entire manuscript, provided all variety of support, and patiently tolerated my brooding when I believed the project was not going well (which was most of the time). To her this book is dedicated.

◈ CHAPTERS 1 AND 4 include material originally published in "The Living Hand of the Past: History and Constitutional Justice," 65 *Fordham Law Review* 1611 (1997). Chapter 1 also includes material originally published in "Early Interpretations & Original Sins," 95 *Michigan Law Review* 2005 (1997). Chapter 6 includes material originally pubished in "Democracy, Majoritarianism, and Racial Equality: A Response to Professor Karlan," 50 *Vanderbilt Law Review* 347 (1997). I thank the publishers for their permission to reprint portions of those articles here.

Contents

Introduction

THE UNITED STATES SUPREME COURT intervenes in many political controversies. Abortion, gay rights, term limits, legislative apportionment,
affirmative action, gun control, and school prayer have all found their
way onto the Court's recent docket. Most scholars and judges assume
that the Court's power is justifiable (if at all) on the basis of its special
legal expertise. More precisely, they suppose that the Constitution is a
set of binding constraints which Americans inherit from their past, and
that legal craftsmanship is essential to decode the meaning of that inheritance. This view is common ground among people who disagree
radically about the *kind* of constraints embodied in the Constitution
and the *nature* of legal craftsmanship. Some think that the constraints
are rules, and that history is the only guide to their meaning. Others
believe that the constraints are principles or aspirations, and that philosophy is a better guide to their significance.

Scholars have refined these basic alternatives in imaginative ways,
yielding a dazzling variety of interpretive approaches. "The Constitution must be construed according to the intention of the framers,"
some say, "and that is the essence of legal craftsmanship."[1] "No," say
others, "the key to the Constitution is legal precedent; lawyers know
what it means to preserve the integrity of precedent, and that skill
is what gives them special insight into the Constitution's meaning."[2]
"No," says yet another group, "to read the Constitution responsibly,

1

one must take text and structure seriously in a way that lawyers know best."[3] And so it goes. Beneath this variety, though, the consensus remains clear: the Constitution is a sacred and obscure legal text, and lawyers are the high priests of American politics specially entitled to pronounce its meaning.[4]

Like most widely held views, this one has important elements of truth. The Constitution obviously does contain rules that Americans inherit from their past. It provides, for example, that "[t]he Senate of the United States shall be composed of two Senators from each State." This provision, and others like it, do constrain the choices that Americans can make: even if most Americans think that the Senate's apportionment scheme is unfair or silly, they will find it almost impossible to change. But this is not the sort of provision the Supreme Court is called upon to interpret. Moreover, you need no legal training to say what it means. The real question is what to do with the Constitution's abstract provisions. The Constitution declares that "[t]he executive Power shall be vested in a President of the United States of America." What does the Constitution mean by "executive power"? Does that power include the controversial prerogative of "executive privilege," which might permit the president to withhold information from courts or Congress? People disagree vigorously about such issues. They also disagree about the meaning of many clauses that guarantee individual rights. What does the Constitution mean when it prohibits states from denying "the equal protection of the laws"? Does that phrase rule out any kind of discrimination, or is it limited to certain historically important forms of discrimination—such as race discrimination? Does it rule out affirmative action programs, or does it instead apply only to forms of discrimination that disadvantage minorities?

The conventional view assumes that the Constitution's abstract provisions operate in a way parallel to the specific ones. On this view, the Constitution's abstract clauses (like its specific ones) state principles or standards or rules that restrict the ability of Americans today to govern themselves on the basis of their own best judgments about political justice. The effect of the Executive Power and Equal Protection Clauses is to put certain questions about presidential power and equality "outside of the political process"—to "take them off the table" and settle them on the basis of decisions made in the distant past. Unlike the Constitution's specific clauses, however, the abstract clauses state norms in ways that are difficult to understand. Legal skill is the key that cracks the code. For that reason, legal competence is essential to making sense of the Constitution's most controversial passages. That (according to the conventional view) is why we permit the Supreme Court, a body of nine unelected judges, to interpret the Constitution: by applying their legal expertise, the justices can give precise content to norms approved generations ago.

In this book, I suggest a different way to reconcile the Supreme Court's prominent political role with democratic ideals. I deny that the Constitution's purpose is to constrain American democracy on the basis of rules or principles laid down long ago. Instead, I interpret the Constitution as a practical device that launches and maintains a sophisticated set of institutions which, in combination, are well-suited to implement self-government. More specifically, I argue that the Constitution's specific provisions should be understood to serve, rather than constrain, the freedom of later generations: those provisions endow later generations of Americans with useful political institutions that make democratic ideals easier to achieve. And I argue that we should regard the Constitution's abstract provisions not as coded messages from the past which deprive Americans of the power to govern themselves, but as invitations which call upon Americans to exercise their own best judgment about moral and political principles. I treat judicial review in a similar spirit: I argue that it, like the Constitution, should be regarded as a practical mechanism which implements a subtle form of democratic rule. I deny that the Supreme Court's power of judicial review depends upon the Court's legal expertise; I also deny that judicial review interferes with democratic decision-making. Instead, I maintain that the Supreme Court should be understood as a kind of representative institution well-shaped to speak on behalf of the people about questions of moral and political principle. What distinguishes the justices from the people's other representatives is their life tenure and their consequent disinterestedness, not their legal acumen.

This argument invites an obvious objection. Supreme Court justices are unelected and almost impossible to remove from office. What basis can there be for regarding them as representatives of the people? To answer that question, we will have to articulate a theory of democracy: we will, in particular, have to say what counts as a good representative institution. Executing that assignment will be the task of later chapters, but it is possible to suggest now the course we shall pursue. When people point out that Supreme Court justices are not elected, they highlight an important fact—but they conceal something else that is equally important. Though the justices are not chosen by direct election, they are nevertheless selected through a process that is both political and democratic. They are not, for example, chosen by a competitive civil service examination. Nor are they selected by a bipartisan panel of distinguished lawyers. Instead, they are chosen by elected officials: they are nominated by the president and confirmed by the Senate. Not surprisingly, presidents pay attention to the political views of the judges they appoint. Republican presidents appoint Republican judges, and Democratic presidents appoint Democratic judges. Conservative Republican presidents try to appoint conservative Republican judges.[5]

The justices have what I shall call a democratic pedigree: they owe their appointments to their political views and their political connections as much as (or more than) to their legal skills. Once they reach the Court, however, the justices have an advantage that makes them unique in our political system. They do not have to worry about losing their jobs, and they do not have to struggle to get better jobs—they stand at the apex of their profession. For that reason, they are able to pursue politics in a fashion that is principled rather than partisan.

Supreme Court justices will, of course, disagree along political lines. For example, we know that Justice Scalia is more likely to hold affirmative action laws unconstitutional than is Justice Ginsburg. Disagreements of this kind correlate visibly with the political views of the justices and (less reliably) with the views of the presidents who appointed them.[6] Despite the political nature of these disagreements, they nevertheless differ from the kinds of disputes that are most common in the elected branches. They usually reflect real differences of political principle, rather than an effort to pander to voters, campaign for higher office, engineer an interest-group deal, or honor a party platform. Indeed, although the contested presidential election of 2000 split the justices along with the rest of the nation,[7] the Court behaved much differently in two earlier political imbroglios. When President Nixon sought to frustrate the Watergate investigation, and when President Clinton sought immunity from the Paula Jones sexual harassment suit, the resulting cases presented the justices with obvious opportunities for crass partisanship. Yet, in neither *United States v. Nixon*[8] nor

Clinton v. Jones[9] did the justices divide along party lines: on the contrary, in both cases they ruled unanimously, basing their decision on the principle that the president is not above the law. Indeed, a conservative justice wrote the opinion in *Nixon*, and a liberal justice wrote the opinion in *Clinton*.

If we reflect for a moment on the psychology of political communities, we can see how the judiciary's institutional characteristics make it a valuable representative institution. The psychology of a community, like the psychology of an individual, is complex. People have views about how they ought to behave, and views about what they want or desire. These views sometimes tug in different directions. Our interests are not always in harmony with our values: we sometimes desire things that we ought not to have. Under these circumstances, most of us hope that we will be faithful to our values, not our interests; we hope, in other words, that we will do the right thing. A good representative government must take these complexities into account. It must be able to represent the people's convictions about what is right and what is in their interest, and it must also reflect the people's judgment that values should take priority over interests. Congress and the president, because they must please voters to get re-elected, are likely to represent people's interests. But Supreme Court justices, because they have both a democratic pedigree and the freedom to behave disinterestedly, are better positioned to represent the people's convictions about what is right. The justices thereby make a distinctive contribution to representative democracy.

That, in any event, is one of the conclusions I will defend in the chapters that follow. I hope, though, that the brief summary offered in this Introduction will suffice to illustrate the character of this book's arguments: they view the Constitution and judicial review as practical mechanisms for coping with the complexities of self-government in a large, modern nation. These conclusions affect the scope and format of this book. People sometimes suppose that books about constitutional adjudication should aspire to the model of John Hart Ely's great work, *Democracy and Distrust*.[10] In fewer than two hundred tautly reasoned and lucidly written pages, Ely covered the whole of constitutional law. He surveyed existing justifications of judicial review, provided his own, and announced principles to guide the Court in the resolution of almost every constitutional case. Conceived according to Ely's model, the job of constitutional scholarship is to supply an easily grasped theory that tells judges how to decide every issue that comes before them.

Ely's ambition was to "fill in the Constitution's open texture."[11] As may be apparent from what I have already said, I think such a venture both impossible and undesirable. The Constitution's open texture invites judges to engage in principled argument about moral and political issues. Such argument enables judges, especially Supreme Court justices, to speak on behalf of the American people about justice. The judiciary thereby makes a distinctive contribution to a political system that might otherwise be overly sensitive to the people's desires at the expense of their values. Open texture is thus useful to constitutional self-government. It helps to establish an institutional structure that implements democracy more effectively than a purely legislative system could do.

This is a recipe for political contention. Liberal and conservative judges will have different convictions about justice, and, as a result, they will produce different interpretations of the American people's best judgment about justice. There is no getting around those disagreements. One hopes that, over time, moral progress will occur. People will develop new political theories and institutions; judges and other Americans will reconsider their views (or, more likely, new generations will reconsider the prejudices of their parents). Over the long run, we must hope, more people will come to accept the better view and reject the worse one. But that is over the long run. In the short run, Supreme Court justices will disagree vigorously and quite legitimately on the basis of deeply held, divergent convictions.

This book does not attempt to settle these disagreements. Instead, it endeavors to legitimate them by explaining how they contribute to democratic self-government. Chapter 1 examines the purpose behind the Constitution itself. The chapter attempts to debunk the widespread idea that the point of a rigid, written Constitution is to enhance the power of past generations, or to diminish the ability of present and future generations to govern themselves. The chapter maintains that barriers to constitutional amendment can actually increase the capacity of later generations to govern themselves freely. The next two chapters explain how judicial review can make a valuable contribution to the democratic pursuit of justice. Chapter 2 defends the democratic legitimacy of judicial review: I argue that judicial review is reasonably regarded as a version of democratic decision-making, rather than a constraint upon it. Chapter 3 takes this argument one step further. It contends that judicial review is not merely democratically legitimate, but that in American circumstances it may be democratically desirable: it may help democracy to flourish.

Taken together, the first three chapters address *whether* judges in constitutional cases should make independent judgments about justice. I conclude that when judges interpret ambiguous constitutional provisions, it will often be their duty to speak on behalf of the American people about justice. The book's final three chapters consider *how* judges should pursue that task. Chapter 4 considers the implications of my argument for jurisprudential methodology. It emphasizes how judges have distorted the Constitution's meaning by relying too heavily on various kinds of legal craftsmanship and by pretending that constitutional questions can be decided in apolitical ways. Chapters 5 and 6 develop a conceptual framework through which to analyze the limits of judicial competence. These chapters focus on the strategic questions that complicate judicial efforts to enforce moral principles. Chapter 5 uses the Supreme Court's controversial cases about privacy and sexual autonomy to underscore the need for judges to distinguish carefully between the moral and strategic components of their decision-making rationales. Chapter 6 identifies a set of especially profound strategic problems that arise under various constitutional doctrines, including those that pertain to federalism, the separation of powers, and the electoral process.

Throughout these chapters, I will pay special attention to three prominent disputes in American constitutional theory. The first dispute is about whether judges should be free to draw upon their moral and political convictions when deciding constitutional cases. I shall argue that Supreme Court justices have a constitutional duty to speak about justice on behalf of the American people. There is no way for them to do that without making controversial judgments about justice. American judges have never been able to avoid taking contestable stands about political issues. I doubt that they could do so; in any event, I shall argue that they ought not even to try. Professors and judges have disserved the American political system by promulgating theories that call upon judges to aim for neutrality or to suppress their moral convictions when deciding cases.

The second dispute is about how judges should mix historical interpretation and philosophical argument. In recent years, this issue has
spawned a flood of law review articles. Some professors insist that the
historical record holds the only true key to the Constitution's meaning.
Others have heeded Ronald Dworkin's call for "a fusion of constitutional law and moral philosophy."[12] Professors likewise debate how
judges should balance abstract generalization against detailed study.
Most people favor a complicated mixture of history, philosophy, abstraction, and detail. They put great value upon getting the mix just
right. They suppose that this mix is the essence of legal craftsmanship,
and that judges cannot decode the Constitution's hidden meanings unless they practice this craft with surgical precision. As I have already
said, however, I do not think that the Constitution consists of opaque
messages from the past, and I do not think that lawyers have any special claim to interpret it well. I accordingly believe that much of the
debate about the role of history and philosophy in constitutional interpretation is a red herring. I will argue that the Constitution requires Supreme Court justices to construct the American people's best
judgment about justice; either philosophical argument or historical reflection might aid that task, and which works best is probably a matter
of personal style and preference. What matters is not whether judges
use historical and philosophical argument, or even how much they
do, but rather that they understand the point of such argument: it
should assist judges in their effort to speak about justice on behalf of
the people. Although this view can accommodate a wide variety of approaches to constitutional interpretation, it has at least one crucial consequence. It implies that judges who invoke history in order to deflect
attention from justice are shirking the responsibility the Constitution
assigns to them.

The third dispute is about how judges should conceive of constitutional issues. Some people write as though the practice of judicial
review is, or should be, principally about choices among *ends* or *objectives*. On this view, the core of constitutional adjudication will be the
identification and application of moral principles. Another school of
thought maintains that judicial review is, or should be, principally
about choices among *means*. On this view, constitutional adjudication
is a form of pragmatic policy-making, more concerned with strategy
than with morals.[13] These apparently inconsistent positions in fact have

more to offer one another than people commonly suppose: I will argue that constitutional adjudication involves a complex mix of moral principle and institutional strategy. In one respect, however, I will join forces with the camp that regards adjudication as a domain for moral judgment rather than strategic policy-making. In Chapters 5 and 6, I maintain that judicial review becomes most problematic when certain kinds of strategic issues predominate over moral ones.[14]

My focus throughout the book will be upon the American constitutional system. My argument requires, however, a general theory of democracy that has implications for the analysis of all constitutional systems. Political theorists have often assumed that democratic government is defined by its reliance on certain institutions, such as legislative assemblies and majoritarian elections. They have used these institutions as benchmarks against which to evaluate the democratic credentials of other practices, including judicial review. One of my principal objectives in the first three chapters of this book, and again in Chapter 6, is to argue that it is a mistake to regard any particular set of institutional arrangements as presumptively democratic. Democracy means government by the people, and that is not the same thing as government by a majority of the electorate, or government by the legislative assembly, or government by any other specific institution.

This insight poses special challenges for large polities. In small city-states, the people might govern directly, by assembling in town halls or public squares. In large nations, that is impossible. The people can govern only through institutions, and any institution will tend to misrepresent the people in systematic ways. In order to understand how self-government is achievable in modern circumstances, we must first appreciate the wide variety of institutions—including judicial review and super-majoritarian amendment rules—that nations might harness to democratic purposes. Americans and others around the world will better be able to govern themselves if they come to see their constitutions in that light—not as undemocratic (if perhaps beneficial) inheritances from their collective past, but as differentiated arrays of institutions that combine to make self-government meaningful in vast, populous nations.

1

The Democratic Functions of Inflexible Constitutions

Constitutionalism and the Dead Hand of the Past

IN TWO DIFFERENT WAYS, Americans organize their politics around a written constitution that is more than two centuries old. First, the Constitution contains specific language that settles some important features of the American political system. It stipulates, for example, that states with vastly different populations must have equal representation in the Senate. Americans believe that they must honor that rule even if they think it inconsistent with basic principles of justice, such as the principle of "one person, one vote."[1] Second, the Constitution also contains abstract concepts that frame public political debate. That is obviously so with regard to issues, such as abortion and affirmative action, that make their way onto the Supreme Court docket, but it is also true of other important political questions. For example, when Americans argued about whether Bill Clinton should be removed from office for concealing his affair with Monica Lewinsky, they did so by debating whether he was guilty of "high crimes and misdemeanors."[2]

This textualist form of government is so familiar that many Americans never give it a second thought, but on reflection it begins to seem mysterious. What sense does it make for Americans to do what the Constitution says, rather than what they think is right? What purpose is served by arguing about what the Constitution means, rather than about what justice requires? These practices are hard to justify. Indeed, thoughtful scholars have charged that America's constitutionalism is undemocratic and therefore undesirable. These critics sometimes make their point by alleging that the Constitution empowers "the dead hand of the past."[3] The concern is easy to understand. The Constitution entrenches institutions and principles against reform. Constitutional amendments must be proposed either by two-thirds majorities in both houses of Congress or by a special national convention, and they must then be ratified by three-quarters of the states.[4] As a result, political parties and coalitions that dominate Congress may find their agendas frustrated by constitutional rules enacted long ago. Would not the United States be more democratic (and better off) if it had a flexible constitution, rather than one that allowed generations long dead to constrain the behavior of people alive today?

Constitutional theorists have developed sophisticated theories to answer the "dead hand" charge. Some commentators have suggested that American constitutional practice is more democratic than it appears because the Constitution is more easily amendable than it seems. For example, both Bruce Ackerman and Akhil Amar have argued that Article V of the Constitution, which specifies procedures for constitutional amendment, is subject to implied exceptions derived from principles of popular sovereignty.[5] Other theorists have contended that the Constitution presupposes a novel and somewhat literary conception of democracy, pursuant to which Americans and other peoples use a written constitution to narrate their collective political identity into existence.[6] Still other scholars have conceded that the Constitution is undemocratic but have defended it on the ground that it promotes justice.[7]

All these defenses of the Constitution share something in common with the "dead hand" accusation: like the accusation itself, they assume that the demanding super-majoritarian procedures specified in Article V cannot be reconciled with ordinary conceptions of democracy. If that is so, then we can justify the Constitution only by interpreting Article V in surprising ways, or seeking out radically new conceptions of democracy, or conceding that good government may be undemocratic. In this chapter, I will argue that there is a simpler and better way to understand the Constitution's relationship to democracy. In particular, I will contend that we should regard inflexible written constitutions, including the American one, as practical, procedural devices for implementing relatively ordinary, albeit non-majoritarian, conceptions of democracy.[8]

My argument aims to expose a misleading half-truth at the core of the "dead hand" accusation. That accusation rightly recognizes that constitutionalism imposes boundaries upon democratic choice. It over-looks, however, that constitutionalism shares this attribute with every other form of democratic government. People can speak only through institutions, and any set of institutions will simultaneously enable and constrain political action. As Stephen Holmes has observed, we cannot sensibly compare constitutionalism to some utopian state of affairs in which the people magically speak for themselves unfettered by institutions or procedures.[9] If Americans abandoned super-majoritarian amendment rules, they would have to replace them with some other set of political procedures, and it is an error to suppose that those arrangements would have no costs from the standpoint of democracy.

We must therefore compare an inflexible constitution to some alternative scheme of government, and we must ask what opportunities for self-government exist under each of these systems. When we undertake that comparison, we discover three reasons why democracy might suffer if the Constitution were easier to amend. First, flexible amendment procedures might make it difficult for a nation to develop and sustain a stable institutional foundation for democratic policy-making. Second, flexible amendment procedures might encourage improvident reforms that would, as a practical matter, encumber later generations. Third, majorities might use amendment procedures to consolidate power at the expense of the people as a whole. Through an exploration of these points, we will discover that barriers to amendment may actually enhance the capacity of people to govern themselves, and that the Constitution is best understood not as a departure from democracy but as an effort to implement it.[10] As we shall see, these insights have important implications for how Americans should interpret their Constitution.

Establishing Stable Institutions

In order for a people to govern itself, it must possess stable policy-making institutions. Creating such institutions requires making detailed decisions. To establish a legislature, for example, a nation must decide how many representatives will serve in the legislature, how long they will serve, what qualifications they must have, how they will be elected, and so on. These details will often have substantial and complex policy consequences. Large legislative bodies will behave differently than small ones, and a legislature elected through a system of proportional representation will perform differently than a legislature chosen through first-past-the-post elections in single-member districts.[11] Yet, even though institutional design is a high-stakes affair, it is more important that a people have some stable, reasonably good set of institutions than that it have the best possible institutions. If a polity is consumed with endless debates about how to structure its basic political institutions, it will be unable to formulate policy about foreign affairs, the economy, the environment, zoning, and so on.[12]

Constitution-makers who are committed to democracy therefore face a delicate challenge. On the one hand, they will want to ensure that later generations will be able to reform unsatisfactory institutions. Flexible amendment procedures make reform easier. On the other hand, democratic constitution-makers will also want to guard against creating a system in which the people are unable to form a stable government. For that purpose, inflexible amendment procedures have clear advantages. If constitutional amendment is easy, then groups disappointed with the outcome of the ordinary political process will have the incentive to campaign for institutional reform.

Some people might suppose that democratic principles require constitution-makers to resolve this tension in favor of flexibility. After all, democracy does not guarantee good outcomes; if the people choose to spend all their energy revisiting basic institutional questions, then why not respect their choice? But to say that "the people" have chosen to focus on institutional reform begs the question. "The people" cannot act except through institutions. If amendment is easy, then it is hard to see what institutional device would allow "the people" to stand back from the amendment process and decide whether to debate another round of constitutional reforms. Suppose, for example, that a coalition begins to agitate for an amendment. Imagine that some citizens are sympathetic to the coalition's proposal, but would gladly bypass it if they could thereby secure political stability. Unfortunately, these citizens have no guarantee that their willingness to give up a reform now will induce anybody else to do likewise in the future. They may accordingly fear that unless they support the proposed reform, they will have the worst of both worlds: they will get neither stability nor the reform they desire. To use the language of rational choice theory, the citizens confront coordination problems which prevent them from settling upon the practices or policies that would best serve their interests. One purpose of constitutional institutions in general, and super-majoritarian amendment rules in particular, is to enable democratic citizens to coordinate their behavior more effectively.[13]

There are at least two strategies that constitution-makers might use to achieve the right mix of flexibility and stability. They might search for some medium degree of unamendability, in which constitutional amendment is more difficult than ordinary law-making but not so difficult as to frustrate reform. Or, alternatively, constitution-makers might make amendment arduously difficult, but constitutionalize a minimal number of decisions. The constitution-makers might hope that the constitution's unamendability would ensure a stable institutional foundation for democratic politics and also hope that most reforms and adjustments could be made through non-constitutional channels.

The United States Constitution exemplifies the second strategy. By comparison to other constitutions, the American one is short and hard to amend.[14] To be sure, despite the American Constitution's brevity, it addresses some matters that could have been left to the ordinary political process. For example, it stipulates minimum ages for representatives, senators, and presidents. A constitution could establish a government without imposing such restrictions. Indeed, if voters can decide whether a candidate is too stupid or too inexperienced to hold office, why not also trust them to decide whether a candidate is too young? Still, the American Constitution leaves much to be filled in through legislation and political practice. And if judged against the objective of establishing a stable foundation for democratic politics, the American constitutional strategy appears to be a success.[15]

Political Inertia and Institutional Quality

Those who charge that constitutionalism perpetuates the "dead hand of the past" often seem to suppose that in the absence of formal barriers to amendment, the people would legislate upon a blank slate, selecting policies and implementing reforms unimpeded by any legacy from the past. A moment's reflection, though, should explode that notion. In fact, a nation's history always defines the choices available to it.

To begin with, any change will involve, as the economists say, "transaction costs." Major reforms frustrate settled expectations and disrupt learned patterns of behavior. New institutions require people to test and develop strategies of political cooperation and to overcome opposition from dissident bureaucrats who wish the old institutions were still in place. But the "presence of the past," as Sheldon Wolin has called it,[16] runs far deeper than these obvious, albeit substantial, transaction costs. First, when a nation debates institutional reform, certain people will be in power and others will be marginal. Who speaks how in the debate about a nation's next government will depend upon the composition of its present one. Some people will have the right to vote and others will not; some people will have prestigious titles, such as "Senator," or resources, such as the power to reward allies with desirable jobs, and others will not. Second, even if people agree that the existing system of government is unsatisfactory, they may find themselves unable to agree upon any particular alternative. It is thus possible that no reform will occur even when everybody thinks the transaction costs would be worth bearing. Third, the existing system of government will affect citizens' ability to analyze alternative political schemes: it will determine what information they have (about how institutions work and what people think); it will determine what problems occupy their attention (those that loomed largest in the existing system); and it may even determine their values and interests.

Examples are legion. Nothing in the Constitution, for example, prohibits Americans from abolishing the Department of Energy, or from cutting back the Social Security program, or from abandoning single-member House districts in favor of multi-member districts. I do not mean to disparage the Department of Energy or Social Security or single-member districts; perhaps you think they are all wonderful institutions. We should hope so, I suppose, because they undoubtedly have a staying power independent of their merits. Once established, institutions entrench interests, invite reliance, and define perspectives. Only a fool could believe that political majorities can eliminate a bureaucracy as easily they created it.

Consider, too, how closely state institutions conform to the national model. For example, many people have complained that America's presidential system tends to produce "gridlock": because the president is elected independently of Congress and has the power to veto legislation, there is a risk that the president and Congress will stop one another from implementing a coherent policy agenda.[17] Americans could not alter the relationship between Congress and the president without running the gauntlet of Article V. Many state constitutions, however, are more easily amended; some can be changed by a simple majority vote. In fact, however, no state has a parliamentary system of government.[18] Is that because every state has concluded, after careful deliberation, that the American separation of powers is a superb political invention? Perhaps. It seems plausible to think, however, that the status quo has limited Americans' political imagination: the separation of powers looks so good partly because it is what we have.[19]

"So what?" you might reasonably ask. Even if the past inevitably constrains the political choices of future generations, super-majoritarian amendment rules seem only to exacerbate the problem. For example, doing away with the Department of Energy might be hard, but doing away with presidential government or the United States Senate is virtually impossible. Those institutions, unlike the Department of Energy, are constitutionally entrenched, and so we must overcome not only the inertial forces that inevitably privilege the status quo, but also the additional demands of Article V.

Yet, once we recognize that the past inevitably constrains present choices, we can no longer afford to ask only about how Article V affects the obduracy of the institutions we inherit. We must also ask how it affects the quality of those institutions. If the institutions we inherit are very much like the ones we would design for ourselves, then we have little reason to complain about them. Indeed, far from being a burden the past imposes upon us, good institutions are an inheritance for which we should be grateful. We get what we want without having to do the work to create it. Such an inheritance does not stand in the way of self-government; it makes self-government easier.[20]

That is why the problem of political inertia might help to explain the democratic function of super-majoritarian amendment rules: such rules may tend to improve the quality of the institutions a nation creates. People easily overlook or underestimate the informal resilience of political institutions; they assume that if a policy works out badly, it can always be fixed in the future. Formal constitutional rigidity forces decision-makers to acknowledge the long-term consequences of institutional reform. By contrast, when formal constitutional barriers to change are modest, people may pursue various "experiments" in the mistaken belief that subsequent majorities can painlessly terminate the experiments if they go awry.[21]

As a result, flexible amendment procedures may have two undesirable effects. First, they may induce people to constitutionalize a greater range of policies and decisions, and so constrict the range of choices available to later generations. We have already observed, for example, that the Constitution's restrictions on the age of legislative and presidential candidates are unnecessary; they may also be unwise. People writing a more easily amended Constitution might have been tempted to include other qualifications, ones related to wealth, education, professional experience, and so on.

Second, easy amendability may encourage a short-term perspective. Lawrence G. Sager has pointed out that the Constitution's amendment procedures discipline reformers to take into account interests different from their own.[22] Because Article V insists upon a broad geographic coalition, it ensures that any successful constitutional amendment will represent more than regional interests. And—most important for our present topic—Article V's promise of durability encourages constitution-makers to think about the interests of future generations. Constitution-makers act with the knowledge that their decisions will affect their children and grandchildren. Article V thereby focuses attention upon the long-term effects of institutional reform, effects that would exist even in the absence of Article V, but might easily be underestimated or overlooked by decision-makers who too quickly assume that later generations will be able to undo their work.

Sager treats abstract individual rights as paradigmatic subjects of constitutional concern, and he emphasizes that Article V provides constitution-makers with an incentive to make sound, justice-driven choices about "first-order, constitutional principles."[23] Yet, the bulk of the Constitution consists not of abstract principles but of detailed provisions that fix certain features of national political institutions.[24] That is hardly surprising: the principal function of the American Constitution and most other constitutions is to establish political institutions,[25] and one cannot define institutions on the basis of abstract principles alone.[26] Any successful written constitution must therefore incorporate specific choices about institutions, and the most direct consequence of barriers to amendment is to make it difficult for later generations to change those decisions. If Sager is right about the incentives created by

Article V, the most important application of his argument is not to the Constitution's abstract rights-protecting provisions, but rather to the detailed institutional choices that are the inevitable stuff of constitutional design.

Of course, Sager's claims about Article V are contestable. Perhaps he is wrong; perhaps politicians drool at the prospect of shackling later generations to their most partisan agendas, and care not a whit for the freedom of unborn children who will live in different times and circumstances. Still, those tempted by such cynical conclusions owe us specific examples. The quality of debate about institutional design at the Constitutional Convention was remarkably high, and most subsequent reforms have been at least competent.[27] Ordinary majoritarian politics invites a number of unfavorable comparisons; for example, when state legislatures reapportion House seats every ten years, we see majoritarian, short-term institutional reform in action— and it is a shameful pageant of partisan self-interest.

Democracy vs. Majoritarianism

Suppose that we wanted to establish a stable, effective, and maximally democratic system of government for a large and diverse nation like the United States. What would that system look like? People who criticize the American system's inflexible amendment procedure seem implicitly to favor a British-style system, in which a national parliament enjoys ultimate legislative power over all matters.[28] Britain, of course, lacks a written constitution, but it is easy to imagine a marriage of written constitutionalism and parliamentary omnipotence. We need only consider a written constitution which stipulates that the national parliament shall have the power to amend the constitution by simple majority vote.[29]

As a formal matter, such a constitution would be very flexible, and it would permit majorities to do whatever they wish. Does it follow that this constitution would be ideal from the standpoint of democracy? Not at all. The constitution's thoroughly majoritarian character should worry democrats. Democracy is not the same thing as majoritarianism. On the contrary, a majority is by definition merely a fraction of the people. It seems impossible to quarrel with the proposition that the people should govern themselves, but it is easy to deny that the majority should be able to dictate terms to minorities.[30] Majoritarianism, after all, is a principle that permits 51 percent of the people to govern 100 percent of the time, and no presumption of fairness can attach to so imbalanced a result. Suppose, for example, that a country is debating whether to spend tax dollars upon art museums or parks. Sixty percent of the population prefer museums, the remainder prefer parks. Would anybody think it desirable, from the standpoint of democracy, if all the money went to pay for museums, and none for parks? Would anybody think it unfortunate, from the standpoint of democracy, if the country adopted a rule designed to ensure that tax dollars were shared among majority and minority interests?

Popular sovereignty is an attractive idea only if we interpret "the people" to refer to "the whole people," and not just a majority, or any other part, of the people. It demands a government that is inclusive enough so that all people (and not merely the majority) can associate themselves with the project of self-government.[31] To qualify as democratic, a government must respond to the interests and opinions of all the people, rather than merely serving the majority, or some other fraction of the people. I will refer to this goal as *impartiality*.

If constitution-makers want to establish a democratic system of government, they should design institutions that are impartial rather than majoritarian. They might therefore reject the British model of an omnipotent national Parliament. They might choose instead to fragment power in order to increase the likelihood that the government will be responsive to the interests of minorities as well as majorities. To that end, they might wish to set up a variety of institutions with differing constituencies and responsibilities. Rather than locating all power in a single national legislative body, they might create a federalist structure, or a bicameral legislature (in which differently constituted majorities could check one another), or an independent executive with policy-making responsibilities, or (as we shall see in the next two chapters) an independent judiciary with special responsibility for protecting individual rights.

Of course, constitution-makers might choose to share power among multiple institutions but nevertheless create a majoritarian system of constitutional amendment. They might, for example, establish a federal system in which the national legislature has a limited set of powers, but in which the constitution is amendable by a majority of that legislature or by a majority of the national electorate. Yet, the risks in such a scheme are obvious. Precisely because the amendment process is sensitive to majority will, national majorities might use it to consolidate power in the national legislature.

We can generalize the point: it is an error to look at constitutional amendment rules in isolation from the other democratic institutions that compose a political system. If amendment processes are vulnerable to capture by factions, then they may be used to degrade institutions that are valuable to the people as a whole. If so, then any increase in democratic freedom brought about by more flexible amendment rules would be nullified by the destabilization and corruption of other institutions that make democracy possible.

People sometimes conflate democracy and majoritarianism, and we might therefore summarize our argument by saying that inflexible constitutions do indeed limit democracy, and justifiably so, if by "democracy" one means "majoritarianism." But that is a misleading way to speak. As we have seen, majoritarianism and democracy are not the same thing. Majoritarian institutions are only one among many imperfect procedural devices for pursuing democratic principles. Constitution-writing is a way to insist upon, and institutionalize, the distinction between democracy and majoritarianism. Constitutionalism therefore limits majority power not only in the interest of justice, but in service of democracy.

How Much Constitutional Obduracy Is Optimal?

We have now identified three reasons why constitutionalists might use super-majoritarian amendment rules to implement democracy. First, constitutionalists might want to produce institutions sufficiently stable for democratic politics to flourish. Second, constitutionalists might wish to discipline reformers to appreciate that changes to the political system will be difficult to reverse and hence will limit the choices of later generations. Third, constitutionalists might use super-majoritarian amendment rules to guard democratic institutions against majoritarian encroachments.

These pro-democratic justifications for constitutionalism have a pragmatic cast, and they can be resisted on comparably pragmatic grounds.[32] Inflexible amendment rules have obvious disadvantages. To begin with, even if barriers to constitutional amendment bring with them some pro-democratic benefits, those benefits must be weighed against the fact that super-majoritarian amendment rules impose real restrictions on political choice. In addition, there is no guarantee that an inflexible amendment process will have significant pro-democratic effects. For example, no matter how good the incentives created by the constitutional reform process, there is always a risk that constitution-makers will attempt to consolidate and entrench their own power. Moreover, even if constitution-makers do their best to design institutions that will benefit later generations, they will sometimes err, and they may err badly. Finally, institutions that work superbly for many decades may eventually become obsolete. For all of these reasons, barriers to amendment might end up protecting a political system that unfairly advantages one sector of the population or that is grossly inefficient. If so, super-majoritarian rules would be an impediment to democracy.

Inflexible amendment rules also have more subtle disadvantages. I have suggested that one benefit of such rules is that they can discipline reformers to consider the long-term consequences of their actions. If so, barriers to amendment may enhance the quality of political institutions that later generations inherit. Yet, as Stephen Griffin has pointed out, if constitutional amendment is very difficult, reformers will have a strong incentive to claim that their proposals do not require an amendment.[33] Such claims may lead people to underestimate the long-term consequences of the proposals. Thus, ironically enough, high barriers to constitutional amendment might actually encourage casual reform by fostering a belief that most reforms are "non-constitutional" and hence not fundamental. For example, if the United States Constitution were easier to amend, politicians and citizens might have been more inclined to believe that the creation of new bureaucracies—such as the Department of Energy—required a constitutional amendment. If such decisions were classified as "constitutional," it would have been harder to establish the new departments, and people might have been inclined to deliberate more seriously about the implications of such a choice.

On the basis of considerations of this kind, reasonable constitutionalists might ultimately decide that super-majoritarian amendment rules are undesirable, and that the best way to pursue democracy would be to create a British-style constitution, in which all laws would be revisable by majority vote of a national legislature. After all, Britain is one of the world's most successful democracies. On the other hand, not every country can be Britain. Few nations, if any, can boast a legal and customary tradition as stable as Britain's, and many nations have populations more ethnically diverse than Britain's.[34] Moreover, British democracy is not unblemished (just ask the Irish, the Scots, or the Welsh!). Indeed, although American constitutional theorists have long worried about the divergences between the American and British system, it is now the British model, rather than the American one, that seems anomalous by world standards.[35]

Of course, there are many degrees of unamendability, and if Britain is at one end of the spectrum, the United States is arguably at the other extreme.[36] It is hard to measure the barriers imposed by Article V. Their impact will turn upon a number of cultural considerations, such as the extent to which state politics differ from national politics and the extent to which people are receptive to or skeptical about the general idea of constitutional amendment. If we scan the list of successful amendments, we will find at least two—the Eighteenth and the Twenty-Seventh—which suggest that Article V's procedures may sometimes have proven too easy to satisfy. Still, even constitutionalists who are convinced that super-majoritarian amendment rules have pro-democratic benefits might conclude that American procedures are too demanding.

Indeed, it has become fashionable for American constitutional theorists to suggest that Article V's amendment procedures are undemocratic, mediocre, or even "stupid."[37] Perhaps these theorists are correct to think that the United States would be better off in some way if Article V's procedures were more flexible, but it strikes me as odd to express a confident judgment one way or the other. As we have already seen, majoritarian amendment rules are not inherently more democratic than super-majoritarian procedures. The case for flexible amendment rules must therefore be made out on the basis of an all-things-considered practical judgment about whether the American people would be better able to govern themselves if their constitution were more easily amendable. That involves guessing what sort of institutions and political experience the United States might have had if Article V had been written differently. Such counterfactual historical speculation is cheap, fun, and completely unreliable. What we know best is how the United States developed under Article V. And, of course, the United States as we know it has substantial problems, including (to name only a few) persistent racial divisions, huge wealth disparities, low voter turn-out, a failing system of public education, and so on. Yet, the United States is also undoubtedly one of the freest, most economically successful, and most politically stable democratic regimes in world history. It has implemented a more or less democratic system on a scale once thought impossible. It pioneered political institutions—including a written constitution adapted to the needs of a large nation-state—that have been imitated by democracies throughout the world seeking similar success and stability. Under these circumstances, it would be peculiar, if not downright arrogant, to assume that the United States would have done significantly better if Article V had been drafted differently.

In any event, questions about the optimal degree of constitutional inflexibility should be pursued in practical context, not in the abstract. It is almost incoherent to ask what amendment rules should exist in the ideal democracy. Constitutional institutions, including amendment rules, are practical devices to meet practical challenges. Different nations will face different problems and hence will need different institutions; therefore, when we assess Article V or some other set of amendment rules, we should ask questions that are sensitive to the challenges facing a particular nation. These practical questions divide into three categories.

First, we might ask a question about constitutional design: we might ask what amendment rule would best serve the democratic goals of some country that is drafting a new constitution. When a constitution is first established, one crucial objective of its framers will be to secure widespread, durable commitment to the new political system. Rarely will that be easy. Constitutions are usually, among other things, deals among parties who distrust one another. New constitutions are therefore fragile. After the constitutional system is launched, winners in the political process will be tempted to consolidate power, and losers will be tempted to reopen questions about the legitimacy of government institutions. If a constitution is to endure, its makers must strive both to create institutions that seem fair and to provide institutional guarantees that the deal will be honored. The American founders, for example, needed to contend with the distrust that the states felt toward one another. Whatever else Article V accomplished, it had to allay citizens' fears that other states would collude after ratification to unravel the constitutional bargain. Perhaps a less demanding amendment rule would have produced a better balance of stability and flexibility, but that fact would carry no weight if the rule made it impossible to establish a stable system of government in the first place.

Second, we might ask a question of constitutional reform: we might ask whether some mature constitutional regime would be well advised to change its rule of constitutional amendment, and, if so, what sort of change would be most desirable. In this context, the practical considerations will be different. On the one hand, there may be little or no need to worry about whether revising the amendment rule will lead significant portions of the population to reject the constitution's authority: if a set of constitutional institutions have been operating for a long period of time, political inertia will help to protect them. On the other hand, when dealing with a mature constitutional system, we must consider whether improvements to an amendment rule might disrupt stable and useful political practices. So, for example, even if we would not recommend the demanding procedures of Article V to the framers of new constitutions in other countries, we might nevertheless think that it would be a mistake to change the rule in the United States, where institutions have developed against the background of Article V. If the United States Constitution were made easier to amend, legislators and citizens would have to revisit judgments about what sorts of decisions required constitutional amendment; judges would have to consider whether they could afford to exercise their power of review more boldly, since unpopular or unsuccessful rulings could be more easily revised;[38] and so on. Perhaps these new challenges would be revitalizing and desirable, but they might also turn out to be costly disruptions of the political system. We might accordingly conclude that Article V was worth keeping even if we thought that it sometimes frustrated useful reforms.

Third, we might ask a question of constitutional interpretation: we might ask how, if at all, the super-majoritarian character of an amendment procedure ought to affect our interpretation of other provisions in the constitution. As a practical matter, this interpretive issue may be the most important question we can ask about the amendment procedures in the United States and other mature constitutional regimes, where the stage of constitutional design is long past and where major constitutional reform may be undesirable or impracticable.[39] People commonly suppose that constitutional language ought to be interpreted in light of its purpose. Specific provisions will of course have specific purposes, but to the extent that a constitution as a whole has a purpose, that purpose will inform our understanding of all its provisions. A constitution's amendment procedures will play an important role in shaping our conception of a constitution's purpose.

In the preceding pages, I have argued that super-majoritarian amendment rules, including those contained in the United States Constitution, can best be understood as pragmatic devices for implementing democracy. As we shall soon see, that conclusion has substantial entailments for interpretation of the United States Constitution.

Originalism and the Constitution

The Constitution contains many abstract moral and political concepts. For example, the First Amendment protects "the freedom of speech"; the Fourteenth Amendment guarantees "the equal protection of the laws"; and Article II declares that the President shall have "the executive power." If we are worried about whether the Constitution allows dead generations to govern at the expense of their successors, then we should welcome the abstraction of these provisions. Abstract principles are not so confining as specific rules. Insofar as the Constitution insists only that Americans must honor their own best understandings of "the freedom of speech," "the equal protection of the laws," and "the executive power," it leaves a great deal of room for democratic choice.

Many people contend, however, that the Constitution's abstract language ought to be read pursuant to the doctrine of "originalism": it ought, in other words, to be read as a reference to the moral and political views of the people who drafted or ratified the Constitution, and not as an invitation that calls upon interpreters to make their own best judgments about the ideals referenced in the constitutional text. According to originalists, when the Constitution instructs states to provide "the equal protection of the laws," it does not mean that states must comply with what we, today, would consider "equal protection"; states must instead afford what the framers of the Fourteenth Amendment thought of as "equal protection," even if their theories of "equal protection" now strike us, in retrospect, as benighted or silly. So, for example, if the framers thought that segregated schools were consistent with "the equal protection of the laws," we might have to interpret the Constitution to permit segregation, even if we now believe that segregation is inconsistent with the best conception of equal protection. And, likewise, if the framers thought that affirmative action programs were inconsistent with "the equal protection of the laws," then we might have to interpret the Constitution to prohibit such programs, even if we now believe that those programs are fully consistent with the idea of "equal protection."

Originalism comes in a bewildering variety of colors and flavors. Most originalists warn, for example, that we should not interpret the framers' intentions too concretely. Judges, they say, need not honor the framers' most specific expectations. On this account of originalism, judges need only be faithful to the theories that the framers embraced, or to political and moral values that were popular when the framers acted. As a result, originalists can reach some surprising conclusions. Robert Bork, for example, says that originalists should construe the Fourteenth Amendment to prohibit racial segregation even though the framers of the amendment "did not think that it outlawed segregated education or segregation in any aspect of life."[40] On the other hand, most originalists are equally insistent that we should not interpret framers' intentions too abstractly. Neither too specific nor too general: it is not easy to fix such a mid-level of abstraction, and, as a result, originalists and their critics joust endlessly about how specifically to describe the intent of the framers. Moreover, many originalists permit exceptions to their doctrine. So, for example, Justice Scalia has confessed to being a "faint-hearted originalist"; he says that he subscribes to originalism, but that, if originalism ever required him to reach a truly abominable result, he would disregard it.[41] Michael McConnell, a prominent academic defender of originalism, writes that he does not "think that the 'original understanding' exhausts the resources available to the interpreter," and he suggests that in some "hard cases" it may have to yield to other "sources of wisdom."[42]

Analyzing originalism is thus a treacherous business. The academic literature is filled with counter-punching between originalists and their critics, much of it devoted to definitional battles about what counts as "originalism." Fortunately, for purposes of our inquiry, we can avoid these rhetorical skirmishes. We can define originalism in an abstract way, a way that will (I hope) be broad enough to encompass any meaningful version of originalism. My proposal is this: a theory should count as "originalist" if and only if, in some cases involving ambiguous moral and political concepts in the Constitution, it dictates that we must comply with a certain moral view because it was held in the past (when the Constitution or a relevant amendment was ratified), even though we now think the view erroneous. In short, any originalist theory worthy of the name will permit historical fact to trump moral judgment in one or more controversies about the meaning of the Constitution's abstract moral and political concepts.[43]

In principle, one might imagine softer versions of originalism. Somebody might say, for example, that originalism requires only that we reflect carefully upon the lessons of history before forming a conclusion about justice.[44] We will consider recommendations of this kind in Chapter 4. For the moment, though, I want to put aside such ultra-soft versions of originalism because, whatever else one might say about them, they will not stand in the way of self-government. If Americans practiced ultra-soft originalism, they would have to consult history when forming their judgments about such ideals as "the equal protection of the laws," but if, after careful reflection, they found historical practice wanting, they would remain free to govern themselves on the basis of their best current view about justice.

Matters are different if originalism makes the meaning of the Constitution's abstract moral and political concepts depend upon historical fact rather than contemporary judgment. Originalism then magnifies the power of the "dead hand of the past." If interpreted pursuant to originalist methods, the Constitution's abstract moral and political concepts, which seemed at first to be especially congenial to the exercise of democratic judgment by later generations, turn out to be among the Constitution's most undemocratic features. By virtue of their abstraction, those concepts apply to a vast range of political issues, and by virtue of the originalist protocol, they preclude present-day Americans from exercising their own moral and political judgment.

It is far from obvious why we would want to adopt a doctrine like originalism, which radically increases the Constitution's rigidity. On the contrary, it is plausible to suppose that wise constitution-makers would want later generations to disavow originalism. Suppose, for example, that we discovered a previously unknown letter from James Madison to Thomas Jefferson, in which Madison said something like the following: "We have done our best to protect the freedom of speech, and I think we have done well. Nevertheless, I am sure that later generations will disagree with us about liberty, just as we disagreed with our fathers. When they do, I hope they will have the courage to act upon their convictions, rather than meekly deferring to our practices and understandings." Would any of us think ill of Madison for harboring such a hope? Would we think, for example, that he lacked the courage to defend his own ideas about the freedom of speech? I doubt it. On the contrary, most of us would admire Madison all the more. Madison commits no solecism by admitting that liberty might differ from his own best understanding of it. The hypothetical letter reveals a man who cares more about what is right and good for his posterity than about his own pride or reputation. Why, then, should we approach the Constitution in the spirit recommended by originalism rather than in the loftier way recommended by the hypothetical letter from Madison? Would not originalism dishonor the framers as well as impair our government?

Originalism as a Theory about What Words Mean

Sometimes people defend originalism as a semantic theory: they say that unless we adhere to originalism, the Constitution's language will become infinitely malleable and hence meaningless.[45] Is that a plausible argument? I think not. To begin with, some of the Constitution's language is very precise. For example, Article II, Section 1 declares that the president "shall hold his Office during the Term of four years." It would be bizarre to think that this phrase is meaningless or "infinitely malleable" unless conjoined to evidence about framers' intent. Indeed, if somebody managed to produce evidence that many framers thought that presidents would occasionally serve five-year terms, we could quite properly dismiss this view on the ground that it contradicted the patent meaning of the rigid language they ratified.

Those who believe that originalism is necessary to render constitutional language meaningful must therefore restrict their argument to the Constitution's abstract phrases, such as "the equal protection of the laws" or "the executive power." Even here, however, the view does not have much to recommend it. Begin with a non-constitutional example. Suppose that Grandpa is on his deathbed, and he whispers to Sonny, "Just promise me this Sonny: eat only healthy food." Sonny, eager to grant this modest request, makes the promise. Grandpa dies, confidently believing (as Sonny well knows) that raw fish and red wine are bad for you and that whole milk is good for you. Now suppose Sonny becomes convinced, on the basis of subsequent scientific studies, that sushi and Chianti are part of a healthy diet but that whole milk is not. We can argue, I suppose, about whether Sonny, if he wishes to honor his promise, should eat or refuse sushi. But we should in any case be able to agree that the concept "healthy" does not become meaningless if divorced from Grandpa's outdated beliefs about what is healthy. If Sonny decides to eat sushi, he will still be acting on the basis of a promise to eat healthy food. It would be wrong to say that Sonny had substituted a different promise, such as a promise to eat only delicious food or expensive food.

Why should the concept of "the equal protection of the laws" or "the executive power" be any different from the concept of "healthy"? Why should they be meaningful only if defined by specific applications rather than by reference to a general ideal? Why, in other words, should we think that the framers' instructions to their posterity are any different from Grandpa's instructions to Sonny? A skeptic might say that the difference is that there are better and worse views about what is "healthy" but that there are only different opinions, not better or worse ones, about what constitutes "the equal protection of the laws" or "the executive power." For that reason, the skeptic would say, we cannot ask what "equality" or "equal protection" really means in the way that we can ask what "healthy" really means; all we can ask is what some person meant when they used those words. I do not find such skepticism very attractive. Nor, I think, do most Americans who care about how the Constitution is interpreted. On the contrary, they care about the Constitution precisely because they believe the differences between injustice and justice, between inequality and equality, and between tyranny and democracy, are meaningful and real, not the product of word games or definitions.

In any event, I do not propose to pursue the merits of radical skepticism here. For our present purposes, it suffices to point out that such skepticism requires the originalist to answer the following questions.

Are there better and worse understandings of concepts like "constitutional interpretation," "democracy," and "judicial restraint"? If all understandings of these concepts are equally good, what is the argument for originalism? If, on the other hand, these concepts admit of better and worse interpretations, why is "the equal protection of the laws" any different? I see no way out of this conceptual tangle: even if skepticism were a defensible doctrine in general, it cannot be a good justification for originalism, because originalism is not a skeptical doctrine. Originalism, like any other theory about the judiciary's proper role, "must depend upon a political philosophy that is taken to be true."[46]

All of this might be quite unsatisfying to originalist readers of the Constitution. "It seems," they might complain, "that your argument makes the Constitution's meaning entirely independent of what the framers thought it meant." That would be a peculiar conclusion indeed, and, if it were true, I agree that it would be good reason to doubt the validity of my argument. But it is not true. The framers' understandings of their words do matter, but they matter in a way different from what originalism supposes. Consider again Sonny's promise to Grandpa. In one sense it does matter what Grandpa means when he advises Sonny to eat healthy. Suppose that after Grandpa dies, the word "healthy" becomes a synonym for "cool" or "awesome." When skateboarding teenagers perform a difficult maneuver, their pals shout, "Healthy, dude!" And they say the same thing when given a heaping plate of bacon nachos: "All right! Healthy!" Gladdened by this development, Sonny interprets his earlier promise to mean, "Eat only cool foods," which he cashes out as, "Eat what you like." At this point, Sonny has departed from his original promise to Grandpa. He is not interpreting the ideal or value of "health" at all; he has substituted an entirely different ideal.

Ronald Dworkin has developed a distinction that captures the ways in which Grandpa's understandings about healthiness do and do not matter. Dworkin distinguishes between *linguistic* intentions and *legal* intentions.[47] Linguistic intentions are intentions about what statements one wishes to make. Grandpa intends to invoke the concept of "health," not the different concepts of "delicious" or "cool." Likewise, the framers of the Eighth Amendment intended to invoke the concept of "cruelty," not (for example) the different concept of "expensiveness."[48] Legal intentions are expectations about the consequences of particular statements. Grandpa's legal intentions with regard to the promise he extracts from Sonny are that Sonny should drink whole milk but avoid raw fish and red wine. The framers' legal intentions regarding the Eighth Amendment may have included, for example, an expectation that the death penalty would be permissible.

Dworkin says, "We make constant assumptions about the framers' linguistic intentions, and we never contradict these in our views about what the Constitution says. We assume, for example, that the framers of the Eighth Amendment meant by 'cruel' roughly what we mean by 'cruel,' and that they followed roughly the same linguistic practices we do in forming statements out of words."[49] Yet, "if, incredibly, we learned that 'cruel' was invariably used to mean expensive in the eighteenth century," then we would have to change our reading of the Eighth Amendment.[50] Likewise, Sonny, if he wishes to honor his promise to Grandpa, must honor the linguistic practices that Grandpa (and Sonny himself) used when discussing the promise. The connection between "healthy" and "cool" is an accident of later linguistic practice, not a dispute about the best application of the concept Grandpa and Sonny invoked in their conversation together.

As Dworkin points out, the argument over originalism has nothing to do with whether interpreters must honor the *linguistic* intentions of the framers or ratifiers.[51] Everybody agrees that interpreters must respect the framers' *linguistic* intentions. Originalism is controversial insofar as it urges us to abide by the founders' expectations as to how their language would be applied—that is, to abide by their *legal* intentions.[52] It is therefore impossible to defend originalism by reference to our obligation to respect constitutional language. When a lawmaker chooses to invoke abstract concepts, discrepancies between the lawmaker's *legal* intentions and later applications are a natural (and often desirable) consequence of the lawmaker's decision to use abstract language. For example, the fact that Sonny rejected Grandpa's views about what foods were "healthy" was not some freak of linguistic practice; on the contrary, "healthy" is an abstract concept that invites competing interpretations of what is, in fact, healthy. No doubt Grandpa understood this feature of the word; over the course of his lifetime, he probably changed his own views about which foods were healthy. Indeed, if Grandpa genuinely cared about Sonny, he probably used the concept "healthy," rather than asking Sonny to swear off raw fish and red wine and so on, precisely because he wanted Sonny to be able to act upon the best understanding of what was "healthy." Likewise, we have no reason to doubt that the framers understood that their own understandings of "the equal protection of the laws" might be imperfect or that they wanted us to be able to act on the best understanding of that ideal.

The semantic argument on behalf of originalism thus founders on a fundamental difficulty. The argument recommended originalism as a way of taking the Constitution's text seriously. It suggested that the Constitution's words would become meaningless unless we respected the framers' views about the legal implications of those words. But respecting the Constitution's words means respecting the distinction between what was included in the text and what was not. The framers drafted and ratified the text, not their intentions. Originalism inverts this relationship. It substitutes unratified intentions in place of the abstract concepts actually ratified by the framers.

Originalism as a Theory about What Constitutions Do

Dworkin's argument explains why originalism cannot succeed as a *semantic* theory—that is, as a theory about how words get their meaning. Dworkin's case against originalism is, however, incomplete. There is another way in which originalism might be defended. It can be defended as a *political* theory—that is, as a theory about how constitutions do their job. An originalist might concede that when speakers or writers invoke moral ideals, they may wish to refer to the best understanding of those ideals, even if that understanding differs from their own. Nevertheless, the originalist might insist that we should interpret the Constitution's moral language in light of its context. More specifically, we must interpret the Constitution's language in a way that is consistent with the Constitution's function or purpose.

In this respect, interpreting a constitution is no different from interpreting a poem or a recipe: we have to keep in mind the different purposes served by constitutions and poems and recipes when we interpret the words they contain. So, for example, if we ran across a reference to a "hot oven" in a recipe, it might be perfectly sensible to hope for a technical convention that would enable us to translate "hot" as 400 degrees Fahrenheit, or 450 degrees, or something else very specific. Without that translation, we would have a hard time executing the recipe. Yet, if we ran across the phrase "hot oven" in a poem, it might be perverse to worry about which temperature the poet had in mind; indeed, it is even possible that, in the poem, "hot" might mean "whatever seems hot to you."

Does the Constitution have some purpose or function that should make originalism attractive to us? Surprisingly enough, originalists sometimes try to justify their interpretive theory by reference to the Constitution's democratic aspirations. For example, Michael McConnell contends that the "force of the originalist argument is that the people had a right to construct a Constitution, and that what they enacted should therefore be given effect."[53] Defending originalism by appealing to the people's "right to construct a constitution" for themselves is an odd project. The Constitution's most important provisions—the first six Articles, the Bill of Rights, and the Reconstruction Amendments—are one or two centuries old. The people who voted on them are all dead. If we care about democracy, we should care about giving effect to the will and judgment of living Americans, not to the views of their dead predecessors.[54]

There is another, equally fundamental objection to be made against McConnell's appeal to democracy. Even if we concede that people in the past "had a right to construct a constitution," McConnell's argument begs the question of what the people constructed. Did the people constitutionalize abstract ideals, or did they entrench their own, more specific understanding of those ideals? If the framing generation had a right to construct whatever constitution it thought best, it might have instructed later generations to act on the basis of their best judgment about "the freedom of speech," even if that judgment was inconsistent with the framing generation's own. If "the people" chose to constitutionalize abstract ideals, then originalism would defeat, rather than respect, their intent.

Did the people make such a choice? You might think that the answer to this question would depend heavily on historical inquiries into what the framers and ratifiers of the Constitution said they were doing. I doubt, however, that such inquiries could ever, even in principle, provide any solid ground for rejecting the hypothesis that the framers intended to constitutionalize the best understanding of whatever moral ideals or political concepts they mentioned. The reason is simple: the best evidence we have of the super-majority's intent is the language it put into the Constitution, and, in all the cases that most concern us, the super-majority chose to use ambiguous moral and political language rather than specifying its views concretely.

Suppose, for example, that we discover that the framers of the Fourteenth Amendment all shared some ugly prejudice that would have kept them from respecting equality in full measure. Perhaps this prejudice led them to support unjust statutes in the course of their political careers. Could we say that, in light of this prejudice, it makes sense to attribute to the framers some dilute or truncated principle of equality consistent with their prejudices? No, for we will then be confronted with the fact that the framers could have made their prejudices explicit, but chose not to. It is possible that the principle they enacted embodied their prejudices, but it is also possible that the framers enacted a broader principle which—while they might have hoped and believed it to be consistent with their opinions and expectations—transcended the particularities of their views. All other things being equal, why not select the more flattering characterization?

For all practical purposes, the only way to avoid associating an exceptionally broad moral principle with the sweeping, enigmatic phrases of the Fourteenth Amendment is to identify some consideration that would lead the framers, at their moral best, to refrain from writing full, robust principles of equality and liberty into the Constitution. What might that consideration look like? Here is one possibility. We noticed earlier that a people cannot establish a government without making some specific decisions about, for example, how to apportion legislators. A constitution that invited endless re-examination of these nuts and bolts questions might well prevent a people from creating a government sufficiently stable to serve the needs of its citizens. Suppose somebody were to suggest that the point of the Constitution is to settle potentially disruptive controversies, and that we should therefore regard the Constitution's abstract provisions, like its concrete ones, as efforts to provide definitive resolutions to political and social disputes. On this view, originalism might be desirable precisely because it tended to constrain the judgments of later generations: if questions about the "equal protection of the laws," "the freedom of speech," and "the executive power" were settled by past generations, then people would no longer have to spend time arguing about them.

Some serious and thoughtful commentators—not all of them originalists—have in fact suggested that the primary purpose of American constitutional law is to settle controversy, and that having settled answers to moral disputes is more important than pursuing the right answers.[55] Such accounts of the Constitution do not appeal to me. Indeed, I argued earlier that one benefit of inflexible amendment procedures is that they provide reformers with an incentive to refrain from constitutionalizing too many specific judgments. And although it seems obvious that citizens can never get down to the business of policy-making if they are always arguing about how to count the votes, it is far from clear that there is any comparable disadvantage to an ongoing, durable argument about (for example) what equality requires. On the contrary, sustained public argument about the meaning of equality and other ideals might plausibly be regarded as the essence of democracy.[56]

Yet, even if we thought that a good constitution should settle as many basic moral controversies as possible, that belief could not justify an originalist reading of the American Constitution. Specific constitutional provisions settle controversy precisely because they are specific. The rule apportioning two senators to each state, for example, describes a standard that means the same thing to every American who reads it. Some people disagree with that provision, but nobody argues that it authorizes some states to have, say, three senators.[57] That is not true about abstract clauses, such as the Equal Protection Clause. Whatever the Equal Protection Clause accomplishes, it does not save us from argument about the topics it addresses. On the contrary, it virtually compels us to have such arguments. People differ now—and they differed when the Fourteenth Amendment was drafted[58]—about the meaning of that clause. Originalism does not solve that problem. Not only do Americans disagree about whether originalism is an attractive doctrine, but originalists disagree with one another about what their doctrine requires.[59] Of course, if everybody were to accept originalism, and if everybody were to agree upon what originalism entailed, then originalism would have the power to settle political controversies. But that banal observation does not distinguish originalism from any other controversial theory about the constitution's meaning: if we all agreed on *any* determinate theory about the Constitution, that theory would settle all the disputes to which it spoke.

The "Dead Hand" Problem Revisited

If originalism is to succeed as a political theory, it cannot do so either on the ground that the people have a right to construct a constitution for themselves or on the ground that we should want the Constitution to settle as many fundamental disputes as possible. Is there some other account of the Constitution's purpose or function that might justify originalism? Justice Scalia has articulated a theory that might do the job. He has written that the Constitution's "whole purpose is to prevent change—to embed certain rights in such a manner that future generations cannot readily take them away."[60] According to Scalia, "A society that adopts a bill of rights is skeptical that 'evolving standards of decency' always 'mark progress,' and that societies always 'mature,' as opposed to rot."[61] This theory at least has the right character to justify originalism. If Scalia's theory were true, then he and other originalists could reasonably urge us to interpret the Constitution's language in the way that would best protect past practices and values. And they could recommend originalism as a good way to do that job: originalism prevents change. It privileges ideologies and practices that were popular with generations now dead.

Yet, why should we believe that a constitution's purpose is to prevent change? Scalia assumes that skepticism about the likelihood of moral progress is somehow intrinsic to constitutionalism. That is far from obvious. Indeed, as an historical claim about the American Constitution, Scalia's argument comes close to palpable falsehood. Thomas Jefferson was one of the most ardent proponents of the Bill of Rights;[62] he also believed that the Constitution should be rewritten every nineteen years.[63] Jefferson wanted the Bill of Rights because he distrusted political officials in general (including those who were his contemporaries), not because he feared that later generations would rot. Moreover, although the framers created amendment rules that made it hard for future generations to engage in constitutional reform, the framers subjected themselves to restrictions at least equally formidable. Not only did the founding generation's own amendments (including the Bill of Rights itself!) have to survive the process specified in Article V, but the super-majoritarian standard of Article VII, which governed ratification of the Constitution, is arguably even more demanding than its counterpart in Article V.[64] Finally, at least some of the framers knew the compromises they had made with slavery were unjust and perhaps unstable.[65] Almost a century later, when Abraham Lincoln addressed the relationship between slavery and the Constitution, he insisted that the framers were able to approve the Constitution only because it "placed the institution of slavery where the public mind rested in the hope that it was in the course of ultimate extinction"[66]—only because, in other words, the framers expected that society would mature rather than rot.

We cannot, however, evaluate Scalia's theory by reference to history. The relevant question is a matter of political theory. We must ask how Americans today should understand the Constitution's purpose. Is there any reason for Americans to regard the Constitution as protection against the possibility that present-day moral and political judgments would be rotten by comparison to those of the founding generation? "Preventing change" might be a sensible goal to attribute to the Constitution if we thought the framers' society nearly perfect, but we do not. Their society had horrible faults. Most of the founders tolerated slavery and many practiced it. They were racist, they were sexist, and many of them were religious bigots. They denied poor people the right to vote and to travel freely.[67] They censored the press in ways few modern officials would dream of doing. To be sure, the founding generation included many great people. They achieved extraordinary things in the face of huge obstacles. We have much to learn from them—but we *can* learn from them, and that fact underscores another reason why it is unattractive to suppose that the Constitution's purpose is to "prevent change." Americans today can learn not only from the framers' wisdom but also from the framers' mistakes; from leaders (Franklin Roosevelt and Martin Luther King, Jr.) who post-dated the framers; from two centuries of American political development; from events and experiences elsewhere in the world; and from advances in economics, political science, jurisprudence, and political theory. In light of all these advantages, and in light of the patent injustices of the framers' society, Americans have no reason to want a form of government organized around the fear that their society is, or will become, so corrupt that it must operate under the benevolent paternalism of eighteenth-century moral and political judgments.[68]

Admittedly, not everybody will agree with this assessment of contemporary America. Some Americans take a gloomy view of their society. There are people who affirm that America is prone to rot, or that societies in general decay as they age[69] (of course, even people who take this pessimistic view do not seem worried that their own judgments are corrupt—it's the rest of the population that is the problem!). Still, such thorough-going pessimism is probably rare, at least among Americans.[70] Insofar as Scalia's argument has widespread appeal, its power almost certainly stems from a different kind of judgment: not that "preventing change" is a desirable goal, but that it is the only way to make sense of what the founding generation actually did. After all, the framers made a number of very specific decisions, predicated upon the moral judgments of their own generation, and they made those decisions almost impossible for later generations to change. The Constitution's most obvious effect is thus to prevent change. And since "preventing change" appears to be the Constitution's principal effect, it is natural to infer that "preventing change" must also be the Constitution's purpose.

The temptation to draw such inferences can be especially strong if one focuses on the Bill of Rights. In its most specific provisions, the Bill of Rights comes close to establishing government by the dead. Why should today's political majorities, faced by a handgun problem that the framers could scarcely have imagined, be limited in any way by the Second Amendment? Why should Congress, concerned about the ability of juries to assess damages in complex cases unlike any familiar to the framers, be constrained by the Seventh Amendment's embrace of common-law tradition? Why should modern juries, far removed from the particular abuses that prompted enactment of the Fifth Amendment's self-incrimination clause, be prohibited from drawing any inference from the unwillingness of a criminal defendant to testify on his or her own behalf?

Indeed, the anti-democratic character of the most specific provisions in the Bill of Rights may help to explain why so many people pay obeisance to originalism. It is probably no accident that when Justice Scalia offered his defense of originalism, he elided the difference between the Constitution and the Bill of Rights: he suggested that "the *Constitution's* whole purpose is to prevent change" because "a society which adopts a *Bill of Rights* is skeptical . . . that societies always 'mature,' as opposed to rot."[71] Scalia's casual identification of the Constitution with the Bill of Rights is by no means uncommon. Most of the great constitutional controversies of the last half-century have raged around matters of individual right. As a result, people often assume that the Constitution's most important provisions are the ones that protect individual rights, and the Constitution's most famous rights-protecting provisions are included in the Bill of Rights.

If the Second Amendment, the Seventh Amendment, and the self-incrimination clause of the Fifth Amendment were exemplary of the Constitution as a whole, then perhaps we would have some ground for supposing that the Constitution's purpose was to prevent change. The Constitution, however, is not principally a list of specific rights. On the contrary, the Constitution is fundamentally concerned with questions of institutional structure, and its most important rights-protecting provisions—such as the Free Speech Clause and the Equal Protection Clause—are framed in abstract terms. The Constitution's structural provisions undoubtedly limit the government, but they also bring it into existence and enable it to act. Article V's super-majoritarian amendment rules make it difficult for people to change the Constitution, but, as we have seen, they also address threats that might undermine the institutional foundations of democratic politics. Taken as a whole, the Constitution is best regarded as a device for implementing democratic self-government, not as a means to "prevent change."

I suggested earlier that in the American political system today, the pro-democratic justifications for the Constitution would matter even more to questions of constitutional interpretation than to questions of constitutional reform. It should now be clear why that is so. Originalism, a prominent and controversial approach to constitutional interpretation, is sustained in part by the supposition that the Constitution's purpose is to prevent change. That idea is profoundly mistaken. As we have seen, it is an open question whether, on balance, the Constitution's *effect* is to empower the "dead hand of the past" rather than to implement democracy. Perhaps Article V's procedures are more restrictive than they need to be. Yet, it does not follow that the Constitution's *purpose* is to "prevent change" rather than to facilitate democracy. The Constitution's purpose may be to facilitate democracy even if the Constitution does not do so very well. It would be perverse to suggest that if we conclude that the Constitution or Article V is flawed from the standpoint of democracy, we should then take those flaws to be the defining feature of the Constitution and interpret it to maximize them. But that perverse strategy is what originalism recommends.

The Democratic Functions of Ambiguous
Constitutional Text

Justice Scalia's defense of originalism thus fails, as have all the other arguments for originalism that we have considered. No doubt there are other arguments that might be made on originalism's behalf, and perhaps devotees of originalism will feel that I have neglected some powerful argument for their position. I hope not, but, in any event, it should now be obvious that any attempt to defend originalism as a political theory will have to contend with severe problems. To begin with, originalism lacks normative appeal. If somebody were to propose, as a matter of abstract political theory, that the best form of government is one in which citizens are required to subordinate their own political judgments in deference to the values and decisions of men dead for a century or more, few of us would agree. Any argument on behalf of originalism will therefore have to fall back on the idea that, like it or not, "government by the dead" is what America has got. Yet, once we appreciate the Constitution's pro-democratic functions, there is no reason to regard it as some mysterious form of "government by the dead." Originalism is thus neither normatively attractive nor necessary to make sense of the Constitution we have. It is hard to see any ground on which the doctrine might be recommended.

We should therefore reject originalism and construe the Constitution's ambiguous language in a way that is consistent with the goal of facilitating self-government. More precisely, we should interpret the Constitution's ambiguous moral and political concepts as requiring Americans to exercise their own best judgment about the matters to which those concepts refer. On this reading of the Constitution, the Equal Protection Clause demands that Americans use their own best judgment about what it means for states to respect equality under law, and the Executive Power Clause demands that Americans employ their own best judgment about what prerogatives should inhere in the executive power.

At first that might seem a rather empty interpretation of the Constitution's abstract phrases. Surely Americans would argue about matters like equality or executive power even if the Constitution said nothing about them—or even, for that matter, if the United States had no written constitution. What sense does it make to have a constitution that tells you to do precisely what you would undoubtedly do anyway? And if it makes no sense, might that not be a reason to take a second, more sympathetic look at originalism?

A theory that rendered constitutional language pointless might still be preferable to originalism, which maximizes the power of dead generations at the expense of living ones—better a pointless provision than an unjust one! But we need not pursue the comparison, for the inclusion of abstract language within the Constitution serves at least two pro-democratic functions. First, it marks the seriousness of some issues. The Constitution does not simply say, "use your own judgment in politics." It calls upon Americans to exercise their best judgment about a variety of named issues, such as what counts as "the equal protection of the laws" and the scope of "executive power." The Constitution thereby induces Americans to treat some issues, and not others, as posing questions about the foundation of the polity. If somebody says, "I think that this policy raises questions about the scope of executive power," she thereby implies, "I think that this policy raises constitutional questions, and we should offer our positions as interpretations of this country's constitution." That posture, in turn, puts certain pressures upon the interpreter: if you offer an argument in the name of the Constitution, you implicitly warrant that you have made a good faith effort to transcend partisan, short-term goals and produce a long-term, impartial assessment of what is good for the country.[72]

Identifying particular issues as matters of "constitutional interpretation" therefore functions in a way analogous to characterizing some issues as matters of "constitutional amendment." We saw earlier that a key feature of the amendment process is its tendency to focus participants' attention upon distant consequences of political reform. In the case of constitutional amendment, this focus resulted from Article V's demanding amendment rules. Those rules do not apply to the activity of constitutional interpretation. Legislators or presidents who claim that their positions are predicated upon the Constitution do not thereby trigger any special voting requirements. Still, by describing their position in constitutional terms, they invite their fellow citizens to take a particular attitude toward the stakes of an argument and toward the sort of considerations that should bear upon its resolution.

Of course, in the United States today, describing an issue as a matter of "constitutional interpretation" also carries with it important institutional consequences: people usually suppose that the Constitution is judicially enforceable. That brings us to the second specific function of the Constitution's abstract provisions. Since the Constitution is itself law, the provisions in it that invite arguments about abstract topics (such as equal protection and executive power) are possible bases for the adjudication of legal rights. As a result, it becomes possible that judges will play an important role in the country's collective effort to make judgments about the principles named in the Constitution.

At this point in the argument, however, that is only a possible consequence, not a necessary one. I have thus far said nothing to justify an aggressive, independent judicial role. I have suggested only that the Constitution calls upon Americans to exercise their own best judgment about the principles it incorporates. We can easily imagine at least two very different constructions of that formula. One person might believe that in order for "Americans" to exercise their judgment about, for example, "the equal protection of the laws," American *legislators* must be free to act on the basis of their own opinions about that ideal. Another person might believe that American *judges* have special title to speak on behalf of the American people with regard to issues mentioned in the constitutional text. If we accepted the first position, the Constitution's interpretive ambiguity—its "flexibility," if you will—would benefit legislatures. We would have to say either that legislatures have the primary responsibility to enforce the Equal Protection Clause, or that the clause imposes only modest requirements, so that judicial enforcement of it would not greatly constrain the legislature's choices. If, on the other hand, we accepted the second position, the Constitution's "flexibility" would benefit judges. We would say both that judges had the principal authority to decide what the Constitution means and also that they might legitimately interpret it to impose substantial restrictions upon legislative options.

Originalism and Judicial Review

Having now approached the topic of judicial review, we should notice one last argument that is offered on originalism's behalf. I have thus far discussed originalism as though it were derived from some thesis about constitutionalism—such as the idea that the constitutional language is meaningless unless interpreted in light of the framers' expectations, or the idea that the Constitution's purpose is to prevent change. One argument in favor of originalism justifies it differently, by reference to judicial review rather than constitutionalism. Originalism, according to this theory, is a desirable method of constitutional interpretation because it constrains the discretion of judges.[73]

We cannot assess what sorts of constraints upon judges are feasible or desirable until we have a theory about what role judges should play in implementing American democracy. The next two chapters begin to develop such a theory, and in Chapter 4 we will take up questions about how history should figure in judicial interpretations of the Constitution. There is, however, no need to leave incomplete this chapter's case against originalism. The argument that originalism is desirable because it constrains judges turns out to be stunningly weak. Originalism is a lousy source of constraints. The claim that originalism can constrain judges is in essence a claim that originalism can settle arguments among judges, and is hence a variation upon the argument (which we considered earlier) that originalism can settle controversies among the American people in general. It therefore fails for the same reason: there is simply too much legitimate disagreement within originalism, to say nothing of legitimate disagreement about originalism, for it to constrain judges effectively.

But in fact the argument that originalism constrains judges is even worse than the argument that originalism can settle disputes among the American people. I suggested earlier that people who want to put an end to principled argument among Americans are simply out of luck: Americans do, in fact, disagree strongly about such matters as what equality requires, and no methodology of constitutional interpretation will change that fact. If, however, our goal is simply to constrain judges, then there is in fact an obvious alternative to originalism: we can advise judges that they ought to defer to legislatures. There are a variety of ways in which judges might put this judgment into practice. They might, for example, adopt a "clear statement rule," pursuant to which they defer whenever the legislature makes clear that it has considered and resolved the relevant constitutional issue.[74] Or judges might adopt a "clear mistake rule," in which they defer to any reasonable interpretation of the Constitution even if they themselves would read the Constitution differently.[75] None of these protocols will be fully mechanical in character, and so judges will continue to produce controversial decisions. Yet, if constraining judges is our goal, isn't it obviously more sensible to counsel that they defer to legislatures rather than that they defer to original intention?

Conclusion

Constitutions are properly understood and assessed as practical instruments for self-government. Like other institutions, they define pathways for action.[76] Such pathways facilitate democratic politics, since one can act authoritatively by proceeding through them, but they also limit democratic politics, since one cannot act authoritatively except through them. It is therefore a mistake to suppose, as people sometimes do, that constitutionalism is usefully characterized as "limited government." Constitutions do not merely limit government; they also establish it. And although constitutions do indeed limit government, they share that feature in common with all other political institutions.

The right way to assess constitutional government is by asking how government should be limited, not whether it should be limited. A democracy that adopts a written, inflexible constitution is creating a distinctive channel for political action, one that simultaneously permits and requires the nation to single out certain issues as fundamental and hence subject to super-majoritarian voting rules. This institutional strategy can benefit democracy in three ways. First, by settling certain basic structural questions, the constitution can establish a stable foundation for democratic policy-making. Second, by establishing a separate and difficult track for some political issues, the constitution may focus public attention upon those decisions and improve deliberation about them. Third, by prohibiting majorities from amending the constitution to consolidate their power, super-majoritarian amendment rules increase the likelihood that a nation will respect the distinction between democracy and majoritarianism.

Americans thus should not assume that their constitution would become more democratic if it were reformed to be more majoritarian. Majoritarian institutions and super-majoritarian institutions bear the same relationship to democracy: they are both pragmatic devices for achieving democratic goals, such as the goal of impartiality. It is possible to argue that, as a matter of pragmatic institutional strategy, American government would operate more impartially if it were more majoritarian. But if a case is to be mounted against Article V, it must be made in that sort of consequentialist fashion, and not on the basis of the simple but inconclusive observation that Article V limits the power of legislative majorities.

The Constitution's pro-democratic justifications have crucial implications for constitutional interpretation as well as constitutional reform. If we understand the Constitution as a practical instrument for self-government, we should construe the Constitution's abstract language in a way that permits Americans to improve and implement their judgments about justice and public policy. The Constitution's purpose gives us no reason to shackle the Constitution's ambiguous language to old conceptions of right and wrong that no longer seem defensible. To describe constitutional interpretation in further detail, we must ask what it means for Americans to exercise their best judgment about such matters as equality and executive power. That will require us to study, among other things, how judges can best contribute to that process. The next chapter begins that project.

2

Judicial Review and Democratic Legitimacy

⌇

The Presumption in Favor of Legislatures

THE PRECEDING CHAPTER concluded that the Constitution calls upon Americans to exercise their own best judgment about the abstract principles referred to therein. That recommendation reinforces the democratic character of the Constitution, but it might seem to presage difficulties for judicial review. Judicial review is usually regarded as a constraint upon the American people's ability to act on their own judgments. If the Constitution authorizes the American people to decide among competing conceptions of "equal protection" or "the executive power," then how can unelected judges claim authority to make such choices for the people?

Questions of this kind have, of course, been the principal focus of American constitutional theory. The Supreme Court's critics have attacked judicial review as undemocratic, and the Court's defenders have fretted about how to answer the charge.[1] Their justifications for judicial review have generally fallen into two categories. The first strategy tries to show that judicial review is necessary to secure rights that are constitutive of a well-functioning electoral and legislative process.[2] On this view, for example, judicial enforcement of free speech rights is justified because unfettered political discussion is an essential precondition to competitive elections and accountable legislative policymaking. An alternative strategy concedes that judicial review and democracy are inconsistent with one another. This second approach

46

attempts to justify judicial review on the ground that it limits democracy in ways that promote justice and protect individual rights.[3]

Few people find either approach fully satisfactory. Most people believe that judges should enforce some rights that bear little or no relation to the electoral process, such as the right of persons to decide whether to have children and how to raise them.[4] Even free speech rights, which at first seem to fit the political process rationale for judicial review, would have to be curtailed sharply if the rationale were rigorously followed. It is easy to see why the electoral process might malfunction if citizens could not criticize public officials. It is more doubtful, however, that democracy would be unachievable if citizens lacked the freedom to burn flags or crosses,[5] to say nothing of the liberty to advertise low prices or publish raunchy novels.[6] Of course, if we make the idea of democracy sufficiently nuanced and demanding, we can argue that all sorts of rights are essential to the democratic process. Some theorists have done exactly that; they have suggested, for example, that rights of sexual autonomy must be protected in order to enable citizens to develop fully the identities and values upon which they will draw when engaged in political activity.[7] One way or another, though, justifying judicial review on the ground that it reinforces electoral democracy is a procrustean endeavor: either popular constitutional rights must be hacked off to fit our understanding of democracy, or else our understanding of electoral democracy must be stretched to accommodate popular constitutional rights.

The second strategy, which suggests that judicial review is about promoting justice and protecting rights, fits better with Supreme Court doctrine and most people's understanding of the scope of judicially enforceable rights. That strategy, however, fails to explain why justice and individual rights should not be subjects for democratic deliberation. If there existed some uncontroversial algorithm for deciding moral controversies, and if judges applied that algorithm reliably, then perhaps it would make sense to recommend judicial review on the ground that it limited democracy in the service of moral principle. But there is no such algorithm. Thoughtful people disagree about what justice requires and about what rights individuals should have. For example, some people believe that it is unjust for the government to prohibit abortions; other people believe that it is unjust for the government to permit abortions. Some people believe that affirmative action programs are inconsistent with the principle of racial equality; other people believe that affirmative action programs are one of the best ways to pursue racial equality. Why should these disagreements be resolved non-democratically? If we characterize judicial review as a limit on democracy, it becomes hard to explain why the people's judgment about contested moral issues should yield to the Supreme Court's.[8] One might instead suppose that the essence of democratic government is, in Jeremy Waldron's words, that "the people are entitled to govern themselves by their own judgments."[9]

There is a simple reason why the two conventional defenses of judicial review run into trouble. Both of them unwisely concede a crucial point to judicial review's critics. They both accept that legislatures (or, more generally, elected officials) are the only institutions which can plausibly claim to speak on behalf of a democratic people. This shared premise defines the three available positions in conventional treatments of judicial review. Judicial review unquestionably constrains the power of legislatures. If legislators are uniquely well qualified to speak on the people's behalf, then judicial review is presumptively suspect, and we can defend it only by arguing that it reinforces the legislative process or by compromising our commitment to democracy.

Yet, the presumption in favor of legislative supremacy, like the presumption in favor of majority rule, which we considered in the last chapter, rests upon an over-simplified conception of democracy. Government by the people cannot be reduced to government by legislatures any more than it can be reduced to government by electoral majorities. If we deepen our understanding of democracy, it becomes possible to understand the Supreme Court as a sophisticated kind of representative institution.[10] We can thus reconceive judicial review in much the way we did constitutionalism in the last chapter: we can view it not as a constraint upon the democratic process, but as one institutional mechanism for implementing a complex, non-majoritarian understanding of democracy.[11]

The next two chapters elaborate the case for regarding judicial review as a democratic institution. This chapter argues that judicial review is democratically legitimate. Chapter 3 goes one step further. It argues that judicial review is not merely democratically legitimate, but is (at least in some circumstances) a reasonably good way to promote democratic flourishing.

Who Speaks for the People?

In a tiny city-state composed of public-spirited and compassionate citizens, there is an obvious way to implement "government by the people." All the citizens could assemble together to deliberate and vote upon questions of public policy. This model of government, which is sometimes referred to as "town hall democracy," has exercised a tremendous pull upon democratic theorists. Yet, "town hall democracy" has rarely (if ever) been realized in practice,[12] and, despite its attractions, democracy in a tiny country might prove less than ideal—for example, small communities may be intolerant toward minorities and eccentrics in their midst.[13] In any event, whatever its attractions, "town hall democracy" is an impractical model for the United States or any other large nation-state. The people of such states cannot assemble as a whole, and hence one job of constitutionalism is to construct institutions through which the people can govern themselves.

The most obvious such institutions are the legislature and the electorate. To some extent, these institutions resemble the town hall. In the legislature, representatives vote and deliberate, just like at a town meeting. In the electorate, almost all citizens vote, just as at a town meeting. But it bears emphasis that neither of these institutions is a "town hall." The legislature is an exclusive institution composed of professional office-seekers. Moreover, the forces influencing legislative action are complex. A full account would have to include, among other things, an analysis of interest groups, lobbyists, and the news media. Political scientists have described in detail how minority interests might successfully capture power in a legislature that uses majoritarian voting rules.[14] It is therefore possible that the legislature will not faithfully represent electoral majorities.

Suppose, though, that it does. Even a legislature that is scrupulously faithful to electoral majorities may nevertheless represent the people poorly, for electoral majorities are themselves unsatisfactory substitutes for the people as a whole. That is so for two reasons: first, the majority is not the same thing as the whole, and, second, the electorate is not the same thing as the people. We noticed the first of these points in the last chapter, in which we observed that a majority is by definition merely a fraction of the people. In order to speak on behalf of the people, a government must take into account the interests and opinions of all the people, rather than merely those of a majority or some other fraction of the people.

To be sure, majority rule is more democratic than minority rule. It is intolerable if countries are governed by a class of nobles or powerful army generals who rule for their own benefit or on the basis of their own idiosyncratic ideas about justice and morality. Minority rule is a distinct possibility in countries that permit officials to choose their own successors, or that select officials on the basis of their supposedly royal birth, or that watch powerful military factions fight for control of the government. A good way to guard against minority rule is to make sure that all public officials owe their offices, directly or indirectly, to a fair vote of the entire electorate. That is one reason why free elections are indispensable to democracy. But it does not follow that the best institution to represent the people will always be the one that is most thoroughly majoritarian.

The second point is equally fundamental. Both academic theorists and ordinary citizens tend to equate "the people" with "the electorate," and it is easy to see why. Nearly all of the people are eligible to vote, and, conversely, voting is virtually the only practical mechanism whereby masses of citizens can exercise formal political power. But equating the people with the electorate is a profound mistake. The electorate is made up of voters, and voters are not the same things as citizens or persons. "Voter" is a political office with specific powers and incentives attached to it. For example, voters act anonymously; they are neither required nor enabled to give reasons for their decision; and they must choose among a very limited set of options (for example, selecting one candidate from among a small set of competitors, or by voting "yes" or "no" on a ballot question). Moreover, each voter knows to a virtual certainty that her individual ballot will have no impact on the outcome of the election.[15] The office of "voter" thus gives people very little incentive to take their responsibilities seriously: each individual voter can be sure that her vote will affect neither her reputation nor the government's policy. As a result, people may behave very differently when they take on the office of "voter" than when they take on the office of "juror" or when they testify at a public hearing.[16]

We therefore should not presume that the best representatives of the people are the ones that are most responsive to electoral majorities. Indeed, when Aristotle listed the characteristics of democratic governments, he said that democracies use lotteries to choose public officials.[17] Under a lottery system, people take turns governing each other, and everybody has an equal chance at wielding government power. Aristotle argued that elections were less democratic than lotteries. When people vote on who should hold office, the government tends to become aristocratic: people choose among candidates on the basis of merit and, as a result, not all citizens have an equal chance to govern.

To modern sensibilities, it is shocking to think about choosing public officials by lot; it means that the woman seated next to you on the bus or the fellow behind you in the grocery store check-out line has as much chance as anybody of becoming your next senator.[18] On the other hand, Benjamin Barber, one of America's most uncompromising democratic theorists, has suggested that the United States ought to employ lotteries to fill some offices at the local level.[19] In any event, even if one thinks Aristotle's view whimsical or impractical, it, unlike majority vote, illustrates how one might go about creating a government that respects the right of all the people to participate in self-government. Aristotle's lottery is more impartial than majority rule, and it is arguably more inclusive than the American government. Under Aristotle's rule, for example, we would not have a Congress that is 81 percent male in a country that is more than half female—and almost 90 percent white in a country that is less than 75 percent white.[20]

Of course, Aristotle's particular concern—namely, that elections are meritocratic and hence elitist—cannot yield any reason to prefer Supreme Court justices or other appointed officials over elected ones; the appointments process is still more elitist than its electoral counterpart. Aristotle's lottery is important, however, because it illustrates a more general proposition: the authority of any institution to speak for the people must be justified on the basis of a pragmatic assessment of its ability to serve democratic values. In particular, those who believe that the legislature is entitled to speak for the people must defend that claim by analyzing the incentives that structure the behavior of legislators and voters; claims for legislative supremacy cannot be sustained on the basis of any intrinsic connection between direct elections and democracy.

Legislatures and electorates are imperfect institutions for the achievement of self-government. They will fail in predictable and systematic ways, and for that reason national governments routinely supplement them with other institutions, such as, for example, independent agencies, central banks, and constitutional courts. Nevertheless, it remains possible that elected legislatures, whatever their flaws, are the institutions best able to represent the American people with regard to the issues referred to in the Constitution. But it is equally possible that some other institution—such as the Supreme Court—can do the job better. To decide whether that is so, we must first consider in more detail what it means for an institution to speak on the people's behalf.

The Impartial Pursuit of Justice

Many, if not all, of the Constitution's abstract provisions share an important feature: they refer to, or directly implicate, moral issues. That characteristic is especially apparent in the constitutional amendments that protect individual rights. As we have already noticed, the Constitution's most significant rights-protecting provisions are drafted with explicit reference to freedom, equality, and other moral ideas; they speak, for example, of "the free exercise of religion," "the freedom of speech," and "the equal protection of the laws."

It is less obvious that the Constitution addresses moral issues in its abstract structural provisions, such as the ones that refer to "the executive power" or "the judicial power." Some people might suppose that these provisions articulate descriptive concepts of political science uninflected by moral concerns. There is something to be said for that position, but it strikes me as an exaggeration. First, political institutions are designed to serve various goals, including some that are moral in character. Interpretations of structural concepts will therefore have to be sensitive to moral concerns. A particular conception of, for example, the executive power will seem more plausible if it is useful to securing liberty and promoting justice. Second, we might regard the Constitution's structural provisions as expressing political principles even if

they do not state moral ones. They might embody prudential maxims that ensure the government does not yield to certain predictable
temptations—the political equivalent to individual rules of conduct like
"never put off until tomorrow what you can do today." Such political
principles function in a manner analogous to moral ones, since they
will sometimes require citizens to sacrifice short-term expediency in
order to uphold the long-term integrity of the political system.

Nevertheless, moral concerns do participate more prominently in
some constitutional issues than in others, and we will have to take such
differences into account in later chapters when we attempt to specify
the judicial role in greater detail. In this chapter, however, we can focus
on a more general point. In order to represent people adequately with
regard to issues of moral principle, a democratic government will have
to be sensitive to the complex ways in which its citizens think about and
confront moral matters. In general, people recognize that they have
both values and interests, and they believe that values and interests occasionally come into conflict. When such conflicts occur, people commonly believe that they ought to subordinate their interests to their
values, but they also recognize that it is not easy to do so. All of us know
that it is sometimes hard to do the right thing: our desires may lead us
in a different direction from our sense of moral duty, and we take actions that later make us ashamed.

To speak on behalf of the people, a democratic government must
respect the distinction (which the people themselves make) between
those issues that are matters of principle and those that are not. Of
course, the American people disagree radically with one another about
many issues of principle. In order to argue that judges can speak on behalf of the people about such issues, we must first explain what it means
for any institution—be it judicial, legislative, or something else—to
speak about moral principles on behalf of a morally divided people.

Many theorists suppose that if people in a democracy divide over
questions of value, then the majority's view ought to prevail.[21] Most of
the arguments offered in this chapter could fit within that majoritarian
paradigm. Voters elect the president and senators, who then nominate
and confirm appointees to the Supreme Court. Judicial review therefore channels, rather than destroys, the majority's power: the majority exercises influence by selecting Supreme Court justices and other
judges, but cannot alter or control their decisions after they are in of-

fice.[22] The crucial question would then be whether judicial review, by disciplining majority power in this way, improves the likelihood that the government will abide by the majority's moral and political principles. In the pages that follow, I offer reasons to suppose that it does.

As we saw in the last chapter, however, a democratic government should aspire to be impartial rather than merely majoritarian: it should respond to the interests and opinions of all the people, rather than merely serving the majority, or some other fraction of the people. It is not easy to say what it means for a government to speak impartially about contested values. With regard to issues involving the allocation of resources, impartiality might simply require that citizens share with one another. All other things being equal, a majority should command a majority of the nation's resources, but not all of the nation's resources. Yet, when people believe that a dispute raises questions of moral principle, sharing will not be an acceptable solution. The demands of impartiality become more complex. Consider a question such as whether abortion should be legal; what would it mean for a policy to share between the majority and minority positions on this issue? One can certainly imagine policies that might appeal to both sides and reduce the practical importance of the issue. Thus, for example, a society might implement and subsidize an effective system of child care, thereby diminishing some of the pressures that might lead women to choose abortion. But measures of this sort will never eliminate the abortion question entirely. As a conceptual matter, compromise is possible; the opposing sides could agree to "take turns"—if 75 percent of the people favored making abortion legal, it might be permitted in three out of four years, or in three out of four states. Yet, I suspect that most people on both sides of the abortion question would feel that it is wrong to "split the difference" on a moral question in this way.[23]

A successful democracy must strive for impartiality without erasing the distinction between questions of justice and questions of preference or collective self-interest. How is that possible? We have reached a crucial juncture in our argument. At first, it may seem impossible to make any headway: after all, we have assumed that people disagree and that compromise is an unsatisfactory solution. But there may be a bedrock of agreement beneath moral controversy, and that bedrock may provide a firm foundation for political institutions. Here is what I have in mind. Americans who disagree about (for example) abortion nevertheless often agree about the nature of their dispute: they agree that abortion is a moral issue, and that disagreements about morality are different from disagreements about mere preferences or interests. They may also share two additional beliefs. Americans on both sides of the abortion controversy, or any other moral dispute, might agree that they should have moral reasons to back up their moral positions. They might also believe that good faith moral discussion tends, over the long haul, to improve the quality of the moral reasons and moral positions which people adopt.

Of course, people might believe none of this. They might believe that moral positions are nothing more than tastes which people happen to have, and that moral argument is nothing more than a verbal dance, in which people move ideas about to no end. Or they might believe that moral truth is ascertainable only through silent communion with the One True God, and that reasoned discussion of morality is utterly impossible. But I think that most Americans do, in fact, believe that one should have moral reasons for taking moral positions, and that it is productive to discuss these reasons. Americans engage in moral argument, and they do so in a committed way—a way that suggests they think it matters.

Suppose, then, that we have this agreement-within-disagreement: beneath moral controversy is a shared sense (1) that morality is something different from mere preferences; (2) that moral positions should be backed up by moral reasons; and (3) that moral positions benefit from good faith discussion and argument. On the basis of these modest (though certainly contestable) propositions, we can construct two conditions that, if satisfied, might enable a government to rule impartially upon public moral disputes. First, the government must respect the people's belief that moral reasons are different from self-interested reasons. The government must therefore resolve moral issues on the basis of the right kind of reasons—reasons of moral principle rather than self-interest. The losing side must have some confidence that its views were rejected on the basis of an honest disagreement about the merits of the moral issue—not in order (for example) to pad the bank accounts or improve the position of the victors. Second, the government must respect the people's conviction that sustained public deliberation helps moral opinion to converge upon new and better positions. The government must therefore ensure that the vision of justice it articulates is one that has some popular appeal. It ought to reflect the benefits of public discussion, rather than the idiosyncratic whims or intuitions of a few privileged decision-makers.[24]

A government that honors these conditions will be engaged in a responsible effort to sift among competing moral claims made by its citizens.[25] It will be sensitive both to the character and the content of citizens' beliefs about political justice. Even a citizen who disagrees with a particular result can nevertheless believe that the decision resulted from her government's good-faith effort to pursue a project which should, in the very long run, lead to the adoption of principles that are valid according to her own criteria. There is thus a sense in which she can regard her loss as temporary. Since committed, rational discussion leads to moral improvement over the long haul, the disappointed citizen may hope that, eventually, either she will be persuaded that she was mistaken, or the government will change its position. Under these circumstances, a democratic government can plausibly claim to construct a conception of justice on behalf of a differing and disputatious people. Its citizens can reasonably believe that continuing engagement in the project of self-government will enable them, eventually, to construct a collective view which synthesizes and refines the best elements in each of their individual views.

In sum, if people have faith that institutionally structured political discussion is likely (over the long term) to produce moral progress, then their faith can enable them to regard choices among contested values as impartial, and hence democratic. This argument is fragile. It presupposes a faith in moral progress through reasoned argument, and people might lack that faith. If so, the democratic argument I am about to offer on behalf of judicial review becomes incomplete. We should be clear, though, about what such a lapse would mean. It would not rescue the authority of majority rule or legislative supremacy. Our case against majority rule would remain intact: majoritarian resolution of moral disputes is partial and therefore undemocratic. Moreover, the legislature's authority, like the judiciary's, would still have to be justified on the basis of a pragmatic argument about which institutions will best serve democratic values. Until we have some account of what it means for a government to decide moral issues impartially, or until we have some alternative account of what democracy requires, we cannot say anything about which institutions should decide constitutional questions.

Disinterestedness and Life Tenure

We have seen that a democratic government must respect the distinction between those issues that are matters of principle and those that
are not. We have also seen that a democratic government must rule impartially. To rule impartially on moral issues, the government must decide those issues on the basis of moral reasons that have some popular
appeal. With these conclusions in mind, we can return to the question
of whether the judiciary might be entitled to speak on behalf of the
American people about constitutional questions. The democratic legitimacy of judicial review turns upon whether there is any reason to
think that the judiciary is well constituted to resolve issues of principle
on the basis of moral reasons that have popular appeal.

It would, of course, be silly to think that judges are uniquely suited to
that task, or that they will do better than other officials with regard to
all questions about liberty, equality, or basic institutional structure. But
the practice of judicial review does not rest upon so sweeping a claim.
Even if the practice of judicial review is fully consistent with democratic principles, the Supreme Court will often have to work in partnership with other institutions.[26] Sometimes it should defer to those
institutions, and sometimes those institutions may have authority to resist interpretations announced by the Court.[27] The power of judicial
review presupposes only that judges can usefully speak on behalf of the
people with respect to some important issues of political principle, not
that judges alone can do so, or that judges can speak on behalf of the
people with regard to all such matters. Is there any reason to believe
that the judiciary is capable of contributing to democracy in that important but limited way?

Democratic principles impose some constraints upon the possible
answers to that question. Those principles preclude us, for example,
from saying that judges are especially good at identifying moral and
political principles because they are smarter than ordinary Americans.
We cannot say that we believe in "government by the people" if we
think the people are too dense to make their own judgments about fundamental issues of political justice. In effect, democracy requires us to
assume a parity of basic moral judgment: all mentally competent adults
are equally possessed of the capacity to tell right from wrong. That is
why we believe that they have the right to govern themselves, both in-
dividually (by making decisions about how their own lives will go) and

collectively (by sharing in decisions about how the community's life will go).

Justice Scalia has made this point in typically acerbic style. Scalia wrote a short concurring opinion in the Court's first "right-to-die" case, *Cruzan v. Director, Missouri Dept. of Health.*[28] In that case, the family of Nancy Beth Cruzan, a comatose woman, sought legal permission to disconnect the machinery that sustained her life. At the core of *Cruzan* were some of the most basic moral questions imaginable: for example, what is it that makes life worth living, and to what extent can incurable, chronic injury deprive life of its value? Scalia wrote that "the point at which life becomes 'worthless,' and the point at which the means necessary to preserve it become 'extraordinary' or 'inappropriate,' are neither set forth in the Constitution nor known to the nine justices of this Court any better than they are known to nine people picked at random from the Kansas City telephone directory."[29] At one level, Scalia was clearly correct: it would be undemocratic as well as implausible to suggest that judges know better than other Americans how to resolve profound moral questions about the termination of life-sustaining medical treatment.

Nevertheless, there is a simple reason why we should expect federal judges—and Supreme Court justices in particular—to handle matters of principle relatively well even if judges are no more virtuous or insightful than the average American. Federal judges enjoy a singular advantage: the independence that comes with life tenure. Unlike politicians, judges need not worry that they will lose their jobs if they take an unpopular position. The Constitution protects their jobs and guarantees that their salaries will not be reduced. Even if politicians and judges are equally moral and equally insightful, it is easier for judges to act on their moral convictions. Among judges, Supreme Court justices are especially free to exercise their judgment untainted by avarice or personal ambition. The justices have attained positions that are at the very apex of their profession. Rarely does any Supreme Court justice move on to hold, or even aspire to hold, any other job. For the most part, the justices' only remaining professional ambition is to have history remember them as having performed their jobs well.[30]

In the *Cruzan* case, for example, the Missouri attorney general may have been more interested in advancing his political agenda than in protecting Nancy Cruzan's interests. By taking the position that human life is always sacred, the attorney general scored points with Missouri's powerful anti-abortion lobby. Indeed, there is one piece of evidence which strongly suggests that Missouri's attorney general was using Nancy Cruzan as a political symbol: after winning the *Cruzan* case, the attorney general withdrew from later trial court proceedings. Missouri thereby enabled Cruzan's family to disconnect her from the machines that were prolonging her existence. If Missouri really cared about Nancy Cruzan's life, why would its attorney general permit her medical treatment to end after her legal battle left the public limelight?[31] Regardless of whether one thinks it moral or immoral to terminate life-sustaining medical treatment, one might well regard it as abominable for politicians to mess with the lives of severely ill patients for the benefit of their own careers or causes.[32]

Judges are, in a word, disinterested. Disinterestedness does not, of course, imply moral or political neutrality; on the contrary, once a controversial issue is in play, there is no way that judges can decide it "neutrally." They will have to deploy contested moral judgments. But at least judges will likely decide on the basis of a principled judgment—a judgment, in other words, about what is good from a moral perspective, rather than a judgment about what is good for their careers or their pocketbooks. What life tenure makes possible, public scrutiny makes obligatory. Through law journals, newspapers, political committees, and professional associations, Americans watch judges carefully to make sure that their decisions are untainted by personal interest. Nothing damages a judicial reputation like the suggestion that a judge has followed personal interest or political ambition rather than made an honest, principled judgment about right and wrong.

Moral Responsibility and Judicial Reputation

One might try to see politicians in a better light. After all, it is no accident that politicians lack the independence that judges enjoy; we compel most public officials to stand for election in order to render them accountable. Why should it disturb us if politicians care about the popularity of the choices they make? They will presumably be interested in conforming their decisions to the moral views of their constituents. And since we have no reason to think judges or politicians wiser or more virtuous than the average citizen, we have nothing to lose if politicians consult the moral judgment of the people they represent. So, we might conclude, the disinterestedness of judges has nothing to recommend it; it is merely another way of saying that judges are unaccountable to public opinion, which is why judicial review raises the specter of minority tyranny.

This defense of politicians fails for two reasons. First, judges are disinterested not only by comparison to other politicians, but also by comparison to ordinary citizens. We insist that judges should recuse themselves if they have a personal stake in the outcome of a case, but we permit, and often expect, ordinary people to "vote their pocketbooks" at election time. Moreover, life tenure again gives judges special advantages. Few people are fortunate enough to be able to act on their moral convictions without fearing loss of income, property, or prestige. Remedying the effects of race discrimination, for example, can be expensive, and voters who might otherwise be exquisitely sensitive to the demands of racial equality can be led astray by an understandable concern about the size of their tax bill. Moreover, hard circumstances can make even good people angry, spiteful, and intolerant. By guaranteeing judges prestige, a good salary, and life tenure, Americans insulate them from forces that often tempt reasonable people to mistake self-interest for moral principle.

Second, judges must take moral responsibility for their decisions. This feature of the judicial role has two components. First, federal judges act alone or in small groups (in the case of Supreme Court justices, a group of nine). As a result, they reasonably believe that their vote matters a great deal to the outcome of a case, and hence they have strong incentives to take full moral responsibility for the consequences of their actions. Voters, by contrast, exercise influence only as members of large groups. That fact diminishes the likelihood that voters will take responsibility for their choices. Second, federal judges are publicly accountable for their decisions. They are not required to stand for election, but they must quite literally *give a public account* of their reasoning. As a result, their reputation as a fair decision-maker is on the line when they rule. Again, voters stand in a very different position. People vote in secret and without explanation.

As an example of how these incentives work, consider again the political battle over Nancy Cruzan. Some Missouri voters apparently cared more deeply about moral issues than about their economic self-interest. They wanted to vote for a candidate dedicated to the proposition that all human life is sacred. Why not welcome electoral contests of this kind, which are waged around moral issues? Such elections might seem to be an ideal way for democratic government to satisfy its obligation to decide moral issues on the basis of moral reasons with popular appeal. The proposition that "all human life is sacred" supplies a moral reason for refusing to allow Nancy Cruzan's guardians to discontinue life-sustaining medical treatment. That reason obviously had popular appeal, else it could not provide a plausible basis for an electoral campaign.

There is, however, an ambiguity about why Missouri voters might find it attractive to vote for a candidate who stood for the proposition that "all human life is sacred." We may assume that some Missouri voters genuinely subscribed to this proposition and its application to the Cruzan family's plight. These voters were presumably dismayed when, after the decision in *Cruzan*, the state permitted the Cruzan family to discontinue Nancy's treatment. It would be naive, however, to think that reasons of this kind wholly explained the electoral battle over Nancy Cruzan. Cruzan's case excited a number of cultural oppositions—oppositions, for example, between competing religious perspectives and between differing views about abortion. As a result, Cruzan's predicament provided cultural groups with an opportunity to send a message about their power and prestige. "In Missouri," they were able to say, "pro-life forces enjoy enough power and prestige to do something that will strike many people as rather extreme: we can interfere with the capacity of devoted parents to make decisions on behalf of a daughter who has been in a persistent vegetative state for many years." Voters who felt this way might have cared little about what happened to Nancy Cruzan after Missouri won its Supreme Court case. They had made their point.

I do not mean to say that Missouri voters went to the polls with the conscious intent to "send a message" to opposing cultural groups. Perhaps they did, but it does not matter: concerns about cultural prestige may taint voters' judgment even if they recognize that it would be wrong to cast their vote on that basis. We too easily conflate what is in our interest and what is right. The circumstances of the voting booth exacerbate that tendency. Each voter acts anonymously and with the assurance that his or her individual ballot is unlikely to affect the outcome of the election. As a result, voters have little incentive to reflect carefully about where morality leaves off and self-interest begins.

Democracy, in sum, is not the same thing as "government by voters." From the standpoint of democratic theory, the first question we should ask is not how to make government accountable to voters, but under what circumstances "voters" (or "the electorate") can adequately represent the people. If we compare judges to voters as potential representatives for the people on moral issues, judges have two advantages. First, life tenure guarantees judges benefits (including social prestige and a comfortable salary) that voters may seek to win for themselves at the ballot box. Judges are therefore subject to fewer temptations that might lead them to disregard or distort their moral judgments. Second, because judges must account for their votes and their reasons, and because their votes will often be decisive, they have a greater incentive to reflect on the distinction between moral principle and self-interest. For these reasons, we may deny that voters are as *disinterested* as judges, even if we concede (as I think we should) that they are no less *insightful* than judges.

Judicial disinterestedness has limits, however, and these were starkly exposed by the Court's troubling performance in *Bush v. Gore*, which put a stop to the manual recount in the contested Florida presidential election of 2000.[33] *Bush* had four unusual features. First, the short-term political stakes were large and obvious. The Court was more or less picking a president: the decision in Bush's favor sealed his victory, and the opposite result might have tipped the election to his rival. Second, the justices' personal interest in the election was at least as great as ordinary voters'. Indeed, the justices' interest was almost certainly greater, since the presidential race was waged partly on the basis of the candidates' competing promises about what sort of judges they would appoint to the Supreme Court.[34] Third, the principles at issue in the case were exotic and their long-term importance was obscure.[35] No judge or scholar had a well-formulated position about the relative authority of state legislatures and state courts in disputes over electoral college slates, or about whether the Equal Protection Clause required manual recounts in presidential elections to proceed according to a uniform, statewide standard. Nothing like these issues had arisen within the last century, and it was conceivable that nothing comparable would arise again during the justices' lifetimes. Fourth, the justices had virtually no time to mull over the case. The journey from certiorari petition to final decision normally spans several months; in *Bush*, which presented issues of unusual novelty and delicacy, it lasted only a few days.

I am not saying, and I do not believe, that any of the justices in *Bush* knowingly cast his or her vote on the basis of a desire to elect a particular candidate.[36] What happened was less scandalous but still disturbing: the institutional incentives that normally encourage judicial disinterestedness were ineffective in *Bush*, and that fact vastly increased the risk that the justices' personal interests would taint their judgments about principle. Of course, even if the normal institutional protections were absent, the justices might have remained disinterested. Perhaps their conclusions were deeply rooted in moral conviction or ideological principle rather than partisan sympathy. If so, it is a stunning coincidence that the five most conservative justices voted to stop the recount, guaranteeing victory to the candidate most likely to provide them with allies, while the four most liberal justices voted to permit the recount and so preserve the chances of the candidate most likely to appoint more liberals.

In *Bush*, but in virtually no other Supreme Court case, it is easy to believe that the outcome would have been different if the roles of the parties had been reversed. *Bush* is thus an exceptional case. The decision will probably have a major impact upon the Court's reputation,[37] but, in my view, it has relatively few implications for how we *ought* to understand the general practice of judicial review. As we have seen, there is no reason to suppose that in *Bush* the justices were well suited to speak impartially about whatever moral issues were at stake. If the justices were right to grant certiorari and settle the election, their decision must be defended on some other ground—such as the need to have a final, orderly (if arbitrary) resolution of an election that was a statistical tie and that threatened (some people thought) to produce political chaos. Conversely, even if one believes that the Court stumbled badly in *Bush*,[38] that is not a good reason to deny that the Court is well situated to speak for the people about justice in other cases, in which institutional incentives work more effectively to produce disinterested decision-making.

Admittedly, those incentives can also misfire in ordinary circumstances. Judges may feel deep attachments to a political party, or to

their social class, or to the legal profession, or to some ideological platform.[39] Academics appointed to the Court may have a personal stake in
defending the theories that made them famous. Ideally, we should hope
that justices have a kind of "grand disinterestedness": they should be
contemplative and flexible rather than fanatical or dogmatic, and they
should have enough integrity to pursue moral intuitions even when
those intuitions lead them to question positions they have held and political affiliations they have cherished. These traits will help to distinguish good justices from bad ones. Although the institutional structure
of the Supreme Court insulates justices from certain forms of material
self-interest, it cannot produce this grander kind of disinterestedness.
If Americans appoint zealots to the Supreme Court, the Court's performance will suffer. Nevertheless, we should not predicate our assessment of judicial competence upon the assumption that presidents will
appoint especially bad justices, any more than we should assume that
they will appoint especially good ones. The kind of disinterestedness
that flows from life tenure and public accountability may be imperfect,
but it is still substantial enough to give Supreme Court justices a special
ability to represent the American people with respect to issues of moral
and political principle.

Democratic Pedigree

However great the benefits of life tenure and accountability, they do
not suffice to explain why a democratic people would permit judges to
speak on their behalf. Otherwise we would have fashioned an argument
in favor of constitutional monarchy—kings, after all, have life tenure,
but it would be patently undemocratic to submit constitutional questions to a hereditary monarch or a council of nobles. To make further
progress, we need some reason to believe that the American people will
be able to regard judicial conceptions of justice as in some sense their
own, rather than as impositions from a privileged or alien class.

The answer is not far to seek, although it is frequently overlooked by
democratic critics of judicial review. America's federal judges do not inherit their positions by virtue of their birth or class, nor do they win
them by superb performance on competitive examinations. They are
political appointees, nominated and confirmed by elected officials.[40]
Indeed, the American institution of judicial review does not really take

power away from electoral majorities. Instead, it constrains the manner in which that power is exercised. Majoritarian institutions can select Supreme Court justices but cannot control them after their appointment. In this regard, the Supreme Court is not so different from the Federal Reserve Board: the Board and its chair are selected by elected officials, but they are insulated from direct electoral pressures. This insulation does not make the Board an undemocratic or counter-majoritarian institution; on the contrary, the Board's independence is designed to increase the likelihood that the nation's economic policy will serve the majority's interests.

The familiar hand-wringing about the "counter-majoritarian" character of the federal judiciary obscures the respects in which judges owe their positions to electoral choices. One can, after all, imagine other ways to choose judges. Comparative constitutional analysis provides a rich variety of examples: some countries select judges partly through civil service examinations, and some (for example, Italy and Turkey) give sitting judges a role in the selection of new members of their constitutional court.[41] In principle, it would be possible to have a constitution that authorized the remaining members of the Supreme Court to choose a new justice each time one of their number retired. That is, in effect, what university faculties do: when vacancies on the faculty arise, the faculty itself selects a new professor. Likewise, the Vatican College of Cardinals chooses the Pope, and the Pope chooses new cardinals; there is never an election in which all Catholics may vote. I do not offer these contrasts in order to criticize universities or the Catholic Church; on the contrary, I do not believe that either universities or the Catholic Church should be democracies. The United States government, however, rightly aspires to be democratic. In light of the power exercised by American judges, it is crucial that the Constitution gives them a democratic pedigree.[42]

Judges' democratic pedigree affects the quality of their decisions. Judges are unlikely to be moral radicals. They are far more conventional and mainstream than other members of society whose position or profession frees them from materialist incentives that might obscure the demands of moral principle. Think, for example, of university professors (who have life tenure and comfortable jobs), students (who live off other people's money and have few responsibilities), wealthy philanthropists (who have so much money that they need not worry about material needs—even if they conceive of their needs very extravagantly) and clerics, artists, and intellectuals (whose vocation encourages them to foreswear material ambition in favor of moral and spiritual pursuits). Institutions like universities and churches help to form the moral conscience of a democratic society. These institutions can produce moral efforts more uncompromising and resolute than we should expect from judges. The civil rights movement of the 1960s, for example, benefitted from the leadership of religious ministers and the efforts of student volunteers.

Nevertheless, if we expect greater moral commitment from universities or churches than from the judiciary, judges are likely to represent the convictions of the American people better than would professors or students or clerics or artists. Even though federal judges are not elected, they are chosen by elected officials, and they are chosen on the basis of (among other things) conformity to mainstream conceptions of political justice. By contrast, artists and intellectuals (including professors) are notoriously non-conformist; it is hard to succeed in either realm without proving one's originality. Students' judgments are rendered suspect by their inexperience. Clerics speak from the perspective of particular faiths not shared by the people as a whole.

Defects in the Democratic Pedigree of American Judges

We can easily imagine institutional reforms that might enhance the democratic credentials of Supreme Court justices and other American judges. For example, although life tenure guarantees that federal judges need not worry about keeping their jobs, it also increases the risk that they will serve for long periods of time—some justices have stayed on the Supreme Court for thirty years or more—and thereby attenuate their democratic pedigree. In Germany, by contrast, members of the constitutional court are appointed for non-renewable twelve-year terms.[43] The German justices need not worry that unpopular rulings will cause them to be removed from office early, and since they are ineligible for re-appointment, they have no incentive to sacrifice moral principle in the hopes of retaining their seats. Moreover, since the justices' terms are limited, there is less risk that Germany will find itself subject to government by judges who once had a democratic pedigree, but who, after long service on the court, have lost touch with the nation's ongoing political and moral debate.[44]

Or, to take another example, because the Supreme Court is a court, it is almost inevitable that all the justices will be lawyers. One might worry that drawing every member of an important political institution from a single profession would produce an undemocratic bias. If the designers of a new political system wanted to avoid this problem while still retaining many of the advantages of judicial review, they might try vesting the power of constitutional interpretation in a non-judicial body whose members were insulated from direct electoral control but who had no power to rule upon law suits.[45] Indeed, the American founders considered creating a Council of Constitutional Revision, which would have passed upon the constitutionality of congressional legislation before it went into effect,[46] and today the French *Conseil Constitutionnel* functions in that way.[47] Since such a council has no responsibility for deciding non-constitutional legal issues or for overseeing the federal court system, and since constitutional issues would reach the council uncomplicated by technical questions of jurisdiction and procedure, arguably it would be easier to appoint non-lawyers to a council than to a court.[48]

On the other hand, identifying optimal structures of judicial review, like selecting optimal levels of constitutional inflexibility, is a tricky business, and we ought to beware the temptation to believe that the grass is greener on the other side of the fence. Judges who serve a single, non-renewable term have no reason to worry about retaining their jobs as judges, but they do have to worry about what they will do next. They might simply retire after serving on the court, but they might want high-paying jobs in the private sector, or they might want to run for political office, or they might covet another political appointment—as, say, attorney general or ambassador to Italy. Conversely, it is easy to exaggerate the risks associated with life tenure. It takes five justices, after all, to constitute a majority of the Court; superannuated judicial veterans are unlikely to be able to exercise much power unless they can forge coalitions with more recent appointees.

The concern about the fact that the Supreme Court consists entirely of lawyers strikes me as a more serious problem,[49] but it, too, is easily overstated. The mere fact that somebody is a lawyer tells us nothing about his or her views on federalism, affirmative action, the death penalty, abortion, school vouchers, pornography, or any of the other controversial issues on the Supreme Court's docket. Of course, it is possible that the legal profession as a whole has distinctive views upon one or more of these subjects. That fact would matter a great deal if lawyers had the authority to elect Supreme Court justices. But they don't. Supreme Court justices are appointed by presidents and confirmed by senators. And even if 70 percent of the legal profession favored affirmative action (to concoct a hypothetical and rather extreme example), a president opposed to affirmative action should have little trouble finding a suitable Supreme Court candidate from among the remaining 30 percent.

In any event, the relevant question is not whether the Supreme Court's democratic pedigree is as good as possible, but whether it is good enough to answer the charge that the Court is democratically illegitimate. If the charge were valid, it would give us a reason to abandon or curtail the practice of judicial review. In response to the charge, I have proposed that the Supreme Court can be regarded as a representative institution which is well constituted to speak on the people's behalf about matters of principle. One might reject my argument on the ground that the Court's democratic credentials are rendered unsatisfactory by the absence of any limit on the length of time that justices may serve or by the fact that all justices are lawyers. One cannot, however, answer my argument by suggesting that American democracy would flourish more fully if American justices, like their German counterparts, were subject to term limits. Judgments about the comparative merits of the German and American constitutional systems tell us nothing about whether democratic principles require American courts to defer to American elected officials.

Stare Decisis, Intellectual Brilliance, and Judicial Competence

Are there any further reasons why judges might be well positioned to speak on behalf of the people about matters of constitutional principle? Scholars have sometimes suggested that judicial review can be defended on the ground that judges have special intellectual virtues—as a result, perhaps, of superb education or rare experience or leisurely reflection.[50] At first, theories of this sort may seem to offend the democratic principles we noticed earlier. Democracy, we observed, presupposes a basic parity of moral judgment; we cannot endorse the idea of self-government unless we believe that ordinary people have sufficient moral insight to decide questions of justice for themselves. But democrats need not deny that reflection and learning can improve moral judgment. Nor need democrats believe that all people will be equally inclined to educate themselves. So one might believe that although all people have equal moral aptitude, American lawyers and judges have incentives to train themselves more assiduously than do ordinary Americans.

The proposition seems, however, empirically dubious. Indeed, popular culture often takes a dim view of lawyers' virtue: people never tire of jokes that compare lawyers to snakes and sharks. On the other hand, there are conflicting signals; for example, television shows and movies often treat lawyers as heroes.[51] Most people would probably agree that a life in the law can be both rewarding and uplifting. But it is not credible for lawyers and judges to assert that they are wiser or more virtuous than, say, doctors or farmers or schoolteachers or shopkeepers or scientists or ministers or those who pursue a whole range of other professions and vocations and roles.

Lawyers make another, more modest claim about judicial competence. They say that *stare decisis*—the obligation to respect legal precedents—disciplines judges in ways that improve their competence and restrain their power. Judges must explain why their resolution of a particular case is consistent with past rulings; in the process of developing these reasons, judges must both confront the opinions of past judges (who may have viewed justice in quite different ways) and assess the impact their own decision will have in later cases involving different facts and equities.[52] Moreover, because judges must usually follow precedent rather than overrule it, *stare decisis* constrains the number of opportunities that any given judge will have to act on the basis of his or her personal convictions.

I agree that *stare decisis* improves the quality of judicial reasoning; good judges should take care to reconcile their decisions with precedent. Yet, although *stare decisis* is an important component in good jurisprudence, its advantages are not sufficiently substantial to provide much support for the authority of judges to speak on the people's behalf. To begin with, *stare decisis* is least influential in the Supreme Court's most important cases, in which the Court must either approach a fresh issue not governed by precedent or else decide whether to overrule a controversial precedent.

Stare decisis, moreover, is a double-edged sword. When judges make bad decisions, their impact is magnified, since later judges may feel compelled to extend their reach. And *stare decisis* may corrupt judicial reasoning as well as enrich it. It may force judges to confront the judgments of their peers and predecessors, but it may also conceal from judges—or enable judges to conceal—the extent to which constitutional decisions must rest upon moral judgments: faced with a difficult case, a judge may find it easy to believe, or to pretend, that her very contestable conclusions are "dictated by precedent." Too often judges attempt to justify controversial rulings by citing ambiguous precedents, and too often judges veil their true reasons behind unilluminating formulae and quotations borrowed from previous cases.[53]

The claim that *stare decisis* improves judicial decision-making is merely an exaggeration, but the claim that *stare decisis* limits the freedom of judges to invoke their personal convictions about justice is a blunder. It is simply too easy, especially in the Supreme Court, for judges to duck or overrule a precedent they do not like.[54] "Five votes" is a sufficient if not excellent answer to any argument of *stare decisis*. And, once again, to the extent that precedent does constrain, that fact cuts both ways. When judges write bold opinions, *stare decisis* extends the impact of the principles they lay down. Surely conservative critics of the Court's abortion jurisprudence would wish to make this claim about *Roe v. Wade:* Justice Blackmun articulated a broad rule, and thereafter liberal and moderate justices insisted that it would be unduly "political" to revisit the questions Blackmun had decided.[55] For better or worse, *stare decisis* enhanced the impact of Justice Blackmun's political choices to exactly the extent it constrained later judges from making comparable choices.

Lest all of this seem harsh, I hasten to repeat: *stare decisis* is an important element of good jurisprudence. On balance, it improves the quality of judicial decision-making. And, regardless of how much *stare decisis* enhances judicial reasoning, it has other justifications. For example, it promotes fairness (like cases should be decided alike) and stability. But the effects of *stare decisis* are altogether too mixed and marginal to explain why judges should speak on behalf of the people about justice.

Indeed, there is an amusing irony about theories that defend judicial review by reference to the rigor, insight, or method of judicial reasoning. Such theories find the greatest favor with liberal law professors who use them to defend the Supreme Court's most ambitious campaigns on behalf of liberty and equality. Yet, if you ask these professors to name the justices from the last half-century whom they most admire, you will likely get a list of former politicians: perhaps Hugo Black, perhaps William O. Douglas, perhaps Robert Jackson, certainly Earl Warren, and especially William Brennan. None of these justices was notable because of his taste for jurisprudential nuance. Nor were they unusually consummate practitioners of *stare decisis.* They were distinguished by their moral conviction and their courage: they were willing to act on the basis of moral reasons even when political circumstances made it uncomfortable to do so. Conversely, conservative theorists champion the virtues of "common sense" over theoretical genius,[56] but their favorite judges include a collection of ivory-tower intellectuals: Felix Frankfurter (perhaps the most intellectual justice ever to serve on the Court), Antonin Scalia, and Robert Bork. That is no accident: it takes some pretty fancy theory to reach the improbable conclusion that a constitution chock-full of moral language should be interpreted in ways that willfully disregard contemporary moral sensibilities.[57]

Evaluating the Supreme Court as a Democratic Institution

Here, then, are the four crucial features of the judicial role in the United States. First, judges have life tenure and good jobs; hence they are insulated from the pull of interests that might distort the judgment of other decision-makers. Second, judges' votes often have a decisive impact; hence judges have an incentive to take personal responsibility for their choices. Third, judges must give a public account of their reasoning; hence they put their reputation for fairness on the line whenever they issue a decision. Fourth, judges are appointed on the basis of their political views and political connections; hence their views of justice are unlikely to be radically at odds with the American mainstream. The first three of these features increase the likelihood that judges will decide moral issues in disinterested fashion; the last feature makes it likely that judicial reasoning will be convergent with and embedded within a larger societal discussion about moral issues. In combination, these features make judicial review a reasonable device for deciding moral issues impartially—for deciding them, in other words, on the basis of moral reasons that enjoy popular appeal.

I have endeavored to link these features of judicial competence to a particular theory of democracy, one that emphasizes the ideal of impartiality. But you might agree with my account of judicial competence, and you might also agree that it justifies judicial review, even if you disagree with my argument about impartiality and democracy. For example, you might have a largely majoritarian view of democracy. You might nevertheless believe that judicial review involves a democratically legitimate delegation of power to a body that is not (wholly) democratic. And you might view this delegation as legitimate and beneficial precisely because judicial review has the four features summarized in the preceding paragraph.

Any defense of judicial review predicated upon those four features of the institution will have a distinctly pragmatic character. In that regard, this chapter follows the same method as the last one. In Chapter 1, we identified a connection between constitutional inflexibility and democratic government by calling attention to practical problems related to instability, inertia, and majoritarianism; here, we identified a connection between judicial review and self-government by calling attention to the inevitable imperfection of electorates, legislatures, and other institutions that might claim to speak for the people. In both cases, our argument has emphasized that, in order to understand the democratic role of American constitutional institutions, one must develop a practical understanding of what it would mean to adopt alternative arrangements.

By contrast, allegations that judicial review is undemocratic usually rest upon an unarticulated and unrealistic conception of democracy. They implicitly assume that, if freed from the influence of unelected judges, the American people could enjoy some pure, self-implementing form of popular sovereignty, unmediated by fallible institutions like the Supreme Court. That is nonsense. Any practical form of self-government will depend upon imperfect institutions, and people must choose among such institutions on pragmatic grounds. If constitution-makers refuse to trust judges to express or construct the judgment of the people, they will have to trust other imperfect representatives—and those representatives may turn out to do worse than judges would have done.

Of course, it is still possible for critics of judicial review to deny that the practice is democratically legitimate, provided that they do so on appropriately pragmatic grounds. Such theorists cannot make any progress by pointing to the fact that federal judges are unelected, but they may contend that judges do a poor job representing the people. They might, for example, assert that Supreme Court justices are not so disinterested as I have claimed them to be. Or, as already noted, critics of judicial review might maintain that the democratic pedigree of Supreme Court justices is inadequate, either because they can serve so long, or because all the justices are drawn from a single profession, or for some other reason. The democratic legitimacy of judicial review in the American constitutional system ultimately rests upon considerations that are fairly contestable and partly empirical, and reasonable scholars might conclude that the court is not a satisfactory representative for the people.

It is, however, becoming increasingly difficult to find evidence that the Supreme Court represents the people so badly as to raise questions about its legitimacy. The most egregious examples of judicial over-reaching—cases like *Scott v. Sandford*,[58] *The Civil Rights Cases of 1883*,[59] *Lochner v. New York*,[60] *Hammer v. Dagenhart*,[61] and *Adkins v. Children's Hospital*[62]—are now more than fifty years old, which is, by American standards, ancient history. During the last half-century, the Supreme Court's greatest moments have come when it intervened most boldly: *Brown v. Bd. of Education*,[63] where the Supreme Court had to assault the shameful injustice of segregation; *Reynolds v. Sims*,[64] where the Court began a successful battle against scandalous gerrymanders that excluded minorities from the political process; *New York Times v. United States*,[65] where the justices dared to protect publication of the Pentagon Papers against censorship during a war; and *United States v. Nixon*,[66] where the justices insisted that a sitting President answer a subpoena. The Court's greatest embarrassments have come when it refused to act: *Korematsu v. United States*,[67] where the Supreme Court permitted the military to confine loyal Japanese-Americans in concentration camps; *Dennis v. United States*,[68] where the justices acquiesced in McCarthyism; and *Naim v. Naim*,[69] where the justices shirked their responsibility to pass upon the constitutionality of anti-miscegenation laws.

Though virtually everybody is upset about one case or another, few observers look at the Court's track record and claim, with the benefit of hindsight, that the United States would have been better off during the last fifty years without judicial review.[70] Life tenure has enabled judges to stand up for values that Americans care about—such as racial equality and free speech and the rule of law—when voters and ordinary politicians lacked the will to do so.[71] Whatever doubts one might entertain about American judicial review in theory, it is hard for most Americans to maintain them (at least in a very thorough way) in practice.[72] The real controversy today is about *which* morally and politically contested issues judges should address, not about *whether* they should address such issues at all.[73]

To be sure, there are those—including Robert Bork and Antonin Scalia—who say that they regard *Roe v. Wade*,[74] the abortion case, as a disaster comparable to *Scott* and *Lochner.* But *Roe* is a controversial decision; it is not, like *Scott* or *Lochner* or *Korematsu* or *Dennis*, universally (or almost universally) reviled. Unlike *Scott* and *Lochner*, *Roe* cannot be associated with a Civil War or a Great Depression. Indeed, many people greatly admire *Roe*. Not all of those who disagree with it find it abominable, and, indeed, in *Casey v. Planned Parenthood*, three justices appointed by anti-abortion presidents said that *Roe*, if not correct, was at least reasonable enough to deserve continued respect.[75]

Moreover, even those who condemn *Roe* are willing to support bold judicial initiatives when the cause is more to their liking. Justice Scalia, for example, has provided the essential fifth vote for Supreme Court majorities that have stricken gun control laws on grounds of federalism and prevented state legislatures from re-drawing voting districts to enhance the power of racial minorities.[76] These decisions thrust the Court into raging political controversies, and they depended upon highly contestable interpretations of ambiguous constitutional text. No principled opponent of judicial activism could have joined either set of opinions.

Alternatives to the American Model of Judicial Review

In this chapter, I have tried to show how judicial review might be regarded not as a constraint upon democracy, but as a mechanism for implementing it. My focus has been upon the American constitutional system, and one of my chief purposes has been to argue that there are sound, pro-democratic reasons for American judges to make controversial value judgments when they interpret the United States Constitution. My claims, however, have implications that transcend the

American context. During the twentieth century, many nations created constitutional courts with the authority to revise or strike down legislative enactments. Argentina, Canada, France, Germany, Hungary, India, Ireland, Israel, Italy, South Africa, Spain, and the European Union (to name only a few important examples) have all embraced judicial review in one form or another.[77] The practices in these other jurisdictions differ from the American model in interesting ways. For example, the Canadian constitution provides a mechanism by which national and provincial legislatures can trump the judgment of the constitutional court.[78] The Indian Supreme Court, by contrast, has asserted the power to hold even constitutional amendments invalid.[79] Israel has developed a robust practice of judicial review without formally adopting a written constitution.[80] And, as one might expect, each country has its own distinctive process for selecting the judges who will serve on the constitutional court.[81]

Yet, despite these differences and many others, the world's constitutional courts share crucial features in common: in each country, judicial review provides a mechanism whereby political appointees with a more or less democratic pedigree are insulated against direct electoral control and authorized to limit legislative power on the basis of controversial interpretations of abstract moral and political principles. That fact should give pause to those critics of the American Supreme Court who maintain that it is plainly undemocratic for unelected judges to make and enforce their own independent judgments about controversial political issues. If that complaint were valid, it would indict as undemocratic not only the American government, but many (perhaps most, if one includes all the nations within the jurisdiction of the European Court of Justice) of the world governments that are commonly regarded as free and democratic.

By contrast, the theory advanced here justifies not only the American practice of judicial review, but also the many other versions of that institution that have been developed around the world. Some people may worry, however, that my argument has another, much less plausible implication for other constitutional systems. I have suggested that institutional incentives may induce legislators and voters to act on the basis of self-interest at the expense of moral principle, and that constitutional courts may therefore better represent the people when such principles are at stake. That argument might seem to prove too much. It might

seem to suggest not merely that judicial review is democratically legitimate, but that every country should have a constitutional court: if there
is a risk that legislatures will systematically misrepresent the people
with regard to matters of principle, then how can it be democratically
legitimate for any nation to reject judicial review in favor of legislative
supremacy?

It would indeed be odd to maintain that democratic governments
were obliged to create constitutional courts, but my theory does not
entail anything of the sort. There is a risk that legislatures and electorates will represent the people badly on matters of principle, but a country might reasonably decide that the risk is worth bearing. Although
legislators and voters have incentives to behave selfishly, they are not
compelled to do so. On the contrary, elected officials and voters can,
and sometimes do, treat moral principles seriously. Moreover, there is
reason to suppose that when voters and legislators muster the will to
act on behalf of moral objectives, they can do so much more effectively
than courts. Judges usually act only in response to lawsuits or some
other kind of referral; they have limited remedial powers; and they often lack the expertise and information needed to craft effective social
policy.[82] Finally, just as it is possible that legislators and voters will
overcome the incentive to behave selfishly, so too there is no guarantee
that judges will in fact behave disinterestedly: it is possible that they
will pursue partisan political agendas after appointment.

When it comes to the practical design of government institutions,
there are no certainties, only competing risks. Risks will vary from
country to country, and there will often be multiple ways to address
them. So, for example, judicial review might be more important in a
federal republic than in a unitary one. Healthy civic traditions may reduce the likelihood that voters and legislators will behave selfishly,
and such traditions will obviously vary from one country to the next.
A nation's size might matter: public deliberation may proceed quite
differently in a small country like New Zealand (which is roughly comparable to Colorado in size and population, and which has more or
less resisted the global trend toward judicial review) than in a mas-
sive country like the United States. Finally, judicial review is not the
only institution that might insulate political officials from direct electoral pressure. For example, in countries where political parties are
strong and ideologically coherent, politicians will have to please party
insiders as well as voters.[83] The incentives facing party leaders are dif-

ferent from those facing voters. In particular, they exercise much greater power than do individual voters; that power might tempt party officials to feather their own nests, but it might also inspire them to take personal responsibility for developing a principled political platform.

There are thus sound pragmatic reasons why democratic constitution-makers might reject judicial review in favor of legislative supremacy, just as there are sound pragmatic reasons for the opposite decision. Yet, although legislative supremacy is defensible in principle, pure exemplars of it are increasingly rare. Judicial review has been endorsed by a wide variety of democratic peoples, and the hold-outs are dwindling. Whereas American constitutional theorists once seemed rather parochial when they sang the praises of judicial review, it now seems provincial for political theorists to insist that British-style legislative supremacy is the archetype of democratic government.[84] Indeed, even Britain itself no longer conforms fully to "the British model." If one considers the devolution of parliamentary authority to Scotland, the ongoing reform process in Northern Ireland, and, most important, Britain's participation in the European Union and the European Convention on Human Rights, it seems overly simple if not plainly wrong to describe Britain as governed by an omnipotent Parliament in London.[85]

In light of the global trend toward judicial review, constitutional theorists should be prepared to consider the possibility that, as a practical matter, the best forms of democracy will always include some version of judicial review. So strong a claim could, however, be defended only on the basis of a detailed comparison between forms of government that include judicial review and those that lack it. My ambition here is more modest. I have aimed to destabilize the idea that there is any single institution—such as the legislature or the electorate—that is uniquely entitled to speak for the people. My goal is to highlight the wide variety of institutions that are not merely democratically legitimate but also are reasonable means by which to pursue democratic flourishing.

Conclusion

People often regard judicial review as an external constraint upon the democratic process. That is a mistake; judicial review is an ingredient in the process. Unelected judges, and especially the Supreme Court, form a representative institution with special characteristics. That institution combines a democratic pedigree with disinterestedness and moral responsibility. In a very simple procedural sense, judges are representatives of the people. Although most are not themselves elected,[86] they are political appointees, nominated and confirmed by elected officials. Life tenure, of course, renders judges more remote from the people than other public officials, but it also enables them to execute a task that other officials cannot. Life tenure enhances the possibility that judges will approach moral issues in a disinterested fashion, and so bring to bear upon those issues the right kinds of reasons—reasons that flow from a genuine effort to distinguish between right and wrong, rather than from self-interest. For a nation that treats some issues as a matter of justice—a nation that distinguishes, in short, between moral duty and self-interest—an institution of this kind is very useful. The people need an institution likely to reflect their judgments about justice, rather than their interests.

Of course, even if judicial review is democratically legitimate, it may be desirable for judges to defer to other political actors. It is wrong to indulge a presumption in favor of the authority of Congress or elected officials in general, but it would be equally wrong to presume that constitutional questions should be decided by the Supreme Court. The case for judicial review depends upon the competence of judges, and where that competence fails, so too does the argument. When considering some aspect of public policy, we must ask which democratically legitimate branch of government—Congress, the judiciary, or some other department—is best able to represent the people. The next chapter begins that project by asking whether judicial review diminishes opportunities for political participation, impairs the quality of public debate, or in some other way interferes with democratic flourishing.

3

Judicial Review and Democratic Flourishing

~

Does Judicial Review Impair Democratic Politics?

IN CHAPTER 2, we considered whether judicial review might be democratic even though judges are unelected. I now want to consider a second argument against judicial review from the standpoint of democracy. Many people suppose that even if judicial review is democratically legitimate, it is nevertheless democratically undesirable. People suggest, for example, that judicial review stifles popular political activity and reduces citizens to spectators. When legislatures decide issues, ordinary people can get involved: they can write letters, call their representatives, circulate petitions, arrange meetings, participate in campaigns, and cast votes. When the Court takes a controversial issue and decides it as a matter of constitutional law, many citizens will feel that they can no longer make themselves heard.[1] In theory, of course, they could publish articles criticizing the Court or bring new lawsuits designed to precipitate a change in the law. In practice, though, these avenues require technical legal ability and, often, elite credentials.

If indeed judicial review inhibits or impairs democratic political activity, that would be a reason for judges to defer to elected officials. We would, of course, have to weigh this reason against the considerations set out in the last chapter. If we gave up on judicial review in order to facilitate political participation, we would lose the benefits of judicial disinterestedness. That would be a real loss, but we might have to accept it in order to secure the kind of popular participation which, to many people, is the hallmark of a democratic political system.

The Deceptive Appeal of Direct Democracy

Our strategy in this chapter will parallel our approach in the last two. To assess the case against judicial review, we must compare the American system of government to real alternatives. We cannot content ourselves with comparisons to imagined utopias where altruistic citizens immerse themselves in high-quality political debates and effective social movements. We must instead consider the set of institutions that would exist in the absence of American-style judicial review. These institutions may themselves impede democratic flourishing in various ways, and, if so, we must take those impediments into account before passing judgment upon judicial review.

How should we conceive of a government in which the people actively control their government? Suppose someone proposes that democracy flourishes when the people have the right to vote upon any fundamental question of political justice. In such a system, everybody has an equal amount of power to control the government. Rather than concentrating responsibility in a small body like the Supreme Court, the system would disperse responsibility throughout the population.

Taken literally, this argument has implications that extend well beyond judicial review. As I have stated it, the argument calls for plebiscitary procedures: national votes in which the electorate as a whole passes judgment on policies. Some state constitutions provide for initiatives and referenda of this kind, but the United States Constitution does not. Matters not settled by the Supreme Court are still settled by relatively small bodies—for example, the 100-member Senate and the 435-member House of Representatives. At the national level, American democracy is representative rather than direct. We might therefore wish to soften the demand proposed in the last paragraph: we could propose that democracy flourishes when either the people or their elected representatives have the right to vote upon any fundamental question of political justice.

The distinction between direct and representative democracy need not much concern us, though. Under neither model is there any good reason to suppose that elections will provide opportunities or incentives for vigorous citizen activity in political communities with more than a few hundred thousand citizens. When numbers are that large, direct elections may guarantee every voter equal weight in determining the outcome, but the weight of each individual vote is nearly zero. As we noticed in Chapter 2, every voter can be confident that the election's outcome would be no different had she stayed home. Many political scientists consider it a mystery why people bother to vote under such circumstances[2]—and, indeed, many Americans don't.

But that is only the tip of the iceberg. If you want to influence an election in a large community, you need to get your views to hundreds of thousands of people—if we are talking about a nationwide election in the United States, you need to get your views to (at a minimum) tens of millions of people. How are you going to do that? You need, presumably, to get the attention of the national news media. That is not easy. It is, of course, extremely expensive to buy time on a television network.[3] You could send an op-ed piece or a letter to a national newspaper like the *New York Times*, but the *Times* is bombarded with submissions it does not take. Even people with elite credentials and professional publicists often find it hard to get their letters and columns published; for ordinary citizens the task may be virtually impossible. Moreover, capturing media attention does not win the battle. You may find that you can get publicity only if you compress your ideas into a "sound-bite"—which may not do your ideas justice. The people you seek to influence do not know anything about you aside from what they read and hear; they may misunderstand you badly, and they may even come to believe nasty things about you. You may become talk-show fodder for Howard Stern or Rush Limbaugh. Celebrities and powerful officials often complain about the way the press represents them; if they cannot retain control over their images, so much the worse for the ordinary citizen who suddenly finds herself in the public spotlight.

Elections—direct or representative—do indeed permit citizens to write letters, circulate petitions, arrange meetings, participate in campaigns, cast votes, and so on—but it is not clear that any of these activities give ordinary people control over their government. Their energy is just a drop in an ocean, carried along by demographic tides beyond their control. And they might reasonably worry that matters are even worse than this metaphor suggests: that, in fact, elections in large communities effectively delegate power to unaccountable institutions and persons who have the power to manipulate public opinion—such as, for example, the news media, well-financed lobbies, and the very rich.[4]

Indeed, the contrast with which we began this chapter—between distant Supreme Court justices and accessible legislators—is in many respects misleading. True, ordinary citizens will find it much easier to shake the hand of their representative, or even their president, than of a Supreme Court justice. True, if they write letters to their legislators, they are likely to get a response; Supreme Court justices rarely answer their mail. And, true, legislators routinely grant interviews about the issues pending before them, while Supreme Court justices almost never do. But so what? Handshakes may build solidarity but they offer little opportunity for policy discussion. The letter a constituent receives from a legislator may have been drafted by an intern and signed by a machine. For interviews, politicians have perfected notorious versions of double-speak and sound-bites.[5] At the national level in the United States, legislation and adjudication are both professionalized forms of policy-making; in neither arena will amateurs find it easy to participate effectively.

Practical Democracy

Making sense of democracy in modern nation-states is difficult. Citizens want different things and disagree vigorously. Admit the deficiencies of "majority rule," and it becomes hard to see how "the people as a whole" might govern themselves. One side must win while others lose. Sensitive to this predicament, constitutional theorists have developed increasingly abstract notions of democracy. These theories deflect attention from the institutional machinery of government—elections, offices, procedures, jurisdictions, and powers—and locate democracy elsewhere. Some theorists say, for example, that the essence of democracy lies in vigorous "public discourse" or "public dialogue." Some of these "dialogic democrats" add that democracy presupposes that individuals enjoy an attractive (even utopian) package of rights—rights that enable them to participate effectively in political life, or that guarantee them the benefits they would have enjoyed in some ideal, consensual, but practically unrealizable polity.[6]

These speech-centered theories have much to teach us. Indeed, I have already suggested that democratic politics is possible for a morally divided nation only if its citizens share a faith in the likelihood of moral progress through reasoned argument. In the pages that follow, I will argue that widespread discussion of fundamental issues is one essential element of democratic flourishing. Nevertheless, we cannot produce a satisfactory account of democracy unless we connect it to practical levers of power that determine who decides controversial issues and how. Without mechanisms to distribute power across the population, "dialogue" reduces to so much talk—perhaps ignored by whoever holds the reins of power, or perhaps dominated by a talented few. Indeed, although the idea of "public discourse" may seem inviting and inclusive to law professors and political theorists who fly around the country giving speeches, it may well appear quite exclusive to ordinary Americans, who know they will never be able to compete with these professional talkers.[7] Coupling "dialogue" to utopian theories of individual liberty only compounds the problem. The ordinary American would be flummoxed—and understandably so—by the suggestion that democracy entails not her right to participate in the decision of fundamental questions about political justice, but rather her obligation to respect some particular (usually quite liberal) theory of individual autonomy. Despite their defects, majoritarian elections have at least this much going for them: they explain how all Americans get a share of political power, even if they are not good talkers and even if their opinions do not coincide with some theorist's utopian vision of autonomy.

We need a practical conception of democracy that emphasizes processes and institutions without privileging majoritarianism. To make progress toward that end, we must first put aside the idea that free elections are constitutive of democracy. They are certainly useful to it, if not indispensable. As we noticed in Chapter 2, majoritarian elections are perhaps the best way to avoid minority rule, which is likely to come about if political power falls into the hands of self-selecting or self-perpetuating institutions (such as military juntas, hereditary monarchs, or, perhaps, powerful corporations and the news media). Moreover, elections help to measure preferences and interests, thereby providing information that everybody will think relevant to at least some questions. It would, for example, be silly to spend more money on sports facilities than on parks if 70 percent of the population preferred parks. But these connections between elections and democracy are instrumental ones: elections help to implement democracy because they achieve democratic goals, not because elections are themselves the goal of democracy. To understand when elections are useful, and when they should instead yield to other institutions (including judicial review), we must try to specify the goals they serve—the goals, in other words, that define what it means to be a flourishing democracy.

We have already identified one such goal. In Chapter 1, we observed that a democratic government must respond to the interests and opinions of all the people. We referred to this goal as *impartiality*. With regard to issues about the distribution of benefits and burdens, impartiality seems to require that government give all of its citizens a fair share. On issues of principle, however, the idea of sharing is not helpful: one cannot resolve the debate over the morality of capital punishment by urging opposing parties to share with one another. We addressed this complexity in Chapter 2, in which we elaborated two conditions that a democratic political system must meet in order to govern impartially on questions of moral and political principle. First, a democratic government must respect the distinction (which the people themselves make) between issues that are matters of principle and issues that are not. The government must therefore decide moral issues on the basis of moral reasons. Second, a democratic government must ensure that the moral reasons which it invokes are ones that have some popular appeal.

What other goals might we use to measure the success of democratic political systems? Our discussion of political stability and institutional inertia in Chapter 1 implicitly drew upon a second criterion for judging democracy, which we might call *effective choice*. A democratic government ought to be able to deliver what its citizens want. Despite their disagreements, for example, nearly all citizens will prefer a prosperous economy to a struggling one; they will prefer low unemployment rates to high ones. A democratic government ought to have the capacity to make and implement decisions about interest rates, market policy, and so on. More generally, even when citizens disagree about how to deal with some issue—for example, how to finance health care, or whether to permit abortion—they may agree that the issue is an important one. A democratic government must be able to make effective choices about these issues: it must be able to develop and implement policies that redress problems its citizens consider significant.

It might seem that, in fact, effective choice has nothing in particular to do with democracy; every government, after all, aspires to be effective. But effective at what? Some dictatorships, for example, might be quite effective at financing the hedonic whims of their leader even if they have no capacity whatsoever to cure unemployment or raise the standard of living. The criterion of effective choice is specially tailored to democracy: it requires that government be able to address the concerns of ordinary citizens. Of course, a government may be effective in this sense even if it is conspicuously undemocratic. Fascism may keep the trains running on time and reduce the crime rate, but that does not make it democratic. Effective choice is merely a necessary condition for democracy, not a sufficient one.

A system might score well on metrics of *impartiality* and *effective choice* even if its citizens had few opportunities to exercise power themselves. The system might install wise and beneficent rulers who would design effective policies, make principled decisions, and share the benefits among the citizens. For the *system* to be democratic, the selection of such leaders would have to be the product of institutional structure rather than fortunate accident—so, presumably, the government would feature free elections to measure citizen preferences and avoid the dangers of minority rule, and it would no doubt separate powers among different institutions so that they could check one another. Nevertheless, ordinary citizens might find themselves unlikely or even unable to maintain an active political life.

These observations suggest two more goals—*participation* and *public deliberation*—against which to measure the democratic character of political systems. The goal of *participation* recognizes that democratic political systems should provide citizens with opportunities to share in the active exercise of political power. More specifically, any citizen willing to commit time and effort should be able to make a meaningful difference in politics and feel that politics is a rewarding part of her own life.[8] Obviously, this goal will be unachievable if we understand "meaningful difference" or "rewarding part" to imply that any citizen can, with enough hard-nosed effort, tip the political scales to favor legislative proposals she desires. Politics will have losers as well as winners, and even those citizens who win will often have played no part in bringing about the outcome they favored.

I have in mind a more modest conception of what counts as participation. Even citizens who find themselves consistently on the losing side in political battles should feel that they can bring their views to the attention of public officials and their fellow citizens; that they can get an honest and thoughtful reply; and that they can sometimes engineer accommodations which, even if they do not count as a victory, will soften the impact of a loss. When these conditions obtain, it is reasonable to say that any citizen who puts in the time can alter both the public debate and, sometimes and to some degree, the ultimate outcome.

This modest view of political participation does not suppose that each and every citizen will have the chance to win a major political victory. It thus takes into account the fact of persistent political disagreement and the likelihood that some citizens will find themselves consistently on the losing side. The practical dynamics of a large nation-state are not so easily overcome, however; citizens cannot expect to make themselves heard or to work out accommodations if their voice competes with millions of others. There is, I submit, no way to secure participatory democracy at the national level in a country as large as the United States. In the sections that follow, I will argue that American democracy facilitates *participation* principally through institutions of local government. I will also argue that judicial review plays an important role in harnessing local institutions to serve this goal without compromising other components of democracy and political justice.

Public deliberation, the fourth and final democratic goal that I wish to identify, also insists on widespread political activity, but with a difference: it emphasizes intellectual engagement rather than the exercise of power. Democracies should encourage citizens to think and converse about basic questions of justice. Public discussion of this kind can take place even if most citizens lack the power to influence the outcome of the debate. Suppose, for example, that the fate of some controversial policy—dealing with, say, gun control—depends upon the position taken by Congress or the Supreme Court. Most Americans have little power to sway either of these institutions. Ordinary citizens may nevertheless find themselves stimulated and engrossed by the debate going on in Washington and across the nation. Joe and Brenda might, for example, read a syndicated newspaper column addressing the issue. They might discuss their reactions with one another, and their conversation may prompt them to do more reading, or to seek out opinions from other friends. The outcome of the discussion between Joe and Brenda will, of course, have little effect upon what happens in Congress or the Supreme Court. Even if Brenda comes up with a brilliant insight, she will find it hard to bring her ideas to the attention of national policymakers.

Of course, if millions of Joes and Brendas around the country have millions of conversations, ideas that emerge from these conversations may "trickle up" into institutions of power: the ideas may influence what famous columnists say, and they may determine who gets elected to Congress, who gets appointed to the Supreme Court, and so on. Public deliberation can change—and, we should hope, improve—what Americans as a whole think about justice. But that does not mean that Joe and Brenda themselves will feel they have had a chance to influence the course of the debate. The goal of *participation* demands that individuals have a chance to make an impact; the goal of *public deliberation*, by contrast, demands that individuals become engaged in argument, even though they will often lack the power to affect how the argument plays out.

These four desiderata—*impartiality, effective choice, participation,* and *public deliberation*—provide a set of criteria by which to assess how judicial review affects democratic flourishing. They do not, of course, provide a full-blown theory of democracy. I have emphasized these particular democratic aspirations because I think they are especially relevant to the study of American constitutional structure. There are a number of other criteria that any democracy should meet. For example: public officials should not choose their own successors; people should have equal status without regard to race, sex, or creed; political debate should be open and relatively unfettered; most public offices should be open to all citizens; public officials should have salaries that are not too lavish. We could spend a lot of time trying to figure out whether any or all of these desiderata might derive from the four goals I have already identified, or whether they instead amount to independent goals—and, if they are independent, whether they are internal to the idea of democracy, or whether they are better understood as aspects of some other idea, such as liberty or equality or fairness. I am not sure whether such exercises would teach us anything useful about democracy; I doubt that they would help us to understand or criticize American judicial institutions.

Democracy and Local Politics

We are now in a position to formulate more precisely the challenge with which this chapter began. One of our tasks is to figure out whether judicial review, despite its virtues, stifles popular political activity. People sometimes suppose that judicial review must have this effect because it removes some issues from the control of the national electorate, but, as we have seen, this assumption is mistaken: far from guaranteeing a vigorous citizenry, large-scale elections can render individual political action meaningless. We therefore cannot use such elections as the standard against which to evaluate judicial review's impact upon democratic activity. We must instead consider how judicial review affects the ability of a political system to achieve participation and public deliberation.

We may start with an uncomfortable fact: political philosophers from Aristotle to Montesquieu insisted that democracy could work only in small republics. If we believe that democracy turns upon participation, it is easy to see the advantages of small size. That is partly a matter of sheer mathematics. Having one vote among, say, 25,000 is much more important than having one vote among 50 million. But the differences between small jurisdictions and large ones are not simply mathematical; as political units become smaller, the dynamic of political participation changes.[9]

In a small city, for example, people who want to have a say in local politics will find it relatively easy to gain access to the public forum. You may find it hard to testify before Congress even if you are an expert, but you will likely be welcome to testify before your local city council or school board even if you have no special qualifications. Publishing a letter in the *New York Times* may be next to impossible, but getting a letter into a small town daily or weekly is often very easy. Indeed, one of the charms of local papers is that they publish nearly every letter they receive—even those from fourth-graders who want bigger parades and eccentric adults who complain incoherently about, say, raccoons.

Small political communities are also more intimate than large nations. In addition to formal political access, ordinary people will often enjoy informal access to their representatives. The fellow who chaired the city council meeting last night may sell you heating oil or fix your furnace this morning. You may run into your school board representative at a neighborhood block party. Politics is not so anonymous as it is when practiced on a national scale. If you do publish a letter in the local paper or speak up at a local meeting, people may recognize your name. Not everybody in town will know you, but many will, and some will know you well enough to "understand where you are coming from."

Moreover, in a small city one person's time, energy, and cooperation are likely to be a valuable commodity. Somebody who donates money or time—cleaning litter off the streets, participating in a neighborhood watch program, or helping out in the schools, for example—can make a perceptible difference in the quality of life in a small city. Contributions of this kind prevent local politics from becoming a zero-sum game in which one side must lose to the extent its competitors win. Individuals have the power, by commitment of their time or other resources, to increase substantially the pool of public resources. The intimacy of a small community magnifies the importance of such contributions: people are likely to learn about the efforts of their neighbors, and civic voluntarism can become a warrant for the good faith of citizens when they speak about controversial issues.[10]

For these advantages to apply, the locality in question must really be small. It is hard, of course, to say when a community is small enough: as a rough test, we might ask whether the local newspaper publishes every letter it receives (aside from those that are libelous), and whether people are likely to have met one or more of their city councillors at non-political social gatherings. Constitutional theorists sometimes praise federalism on the ground that the American states are cohesive communities in which intimate politics is possible, but that is nonsense: the states are much too large. Populations are huge, distances are great, and individuals will find it difficult to make themselves heard. Likewise, politics in mega-cities like New York is not local in the sense that I have described. Indeed, the local paper in New York City is also the national newspaper of record; good luck getting your letter published.

People who want the opportunity for real political participation in New York City may have to focus upon smaller units than the city as a whole—neighborhoods or boroughs, for example. Or they may have to move. Indeed, to the advantages we have thus far discussed we should add those that flow from mobility. If you feel for some reason unable to contribute to the politics of your own community, you may move to another. We should take care not to exaggerate this point, however. Moving is always costly. Moreover, mobility constrains the scope of local politics: try to tax the rich people in your community, for example, and you may find that they simply take their money and go elsewhere. Nevertheless, it is easier to change towns than to change countries, and if we value participation we should care that people are able to find communities in which they feel themselves valued.[11]

These considerations, though, begin to move us toward the obvious problems with local government. If we want to be truthful about local politics, we should tell a tale of two cities, one healthy and one withered. Cities are the best of democracies; they are the worst of democracies.[12] Small towns can be cruel to eccentrics and minorities living in their midst. They can also become dens of corruption. The fellow who chaired last night's council meeting may sell you heating oil the next morning; he may also sell heating oil to people who want city contracts—and he may integrate his two occupations into a single profitable enterprise. And, finally, towns have relatively little power to coerce cooperation from selfish people. Ask too much from them and they can simply go elsewhere. Unable or unwilling to raise money by taxing their own citizens, towns may be tempted to tap the resources of others who have no voice in local politics. The small-town speed trap is, unfortunately, an American cultural icon.[13]

The classic critique of small republics is Madison's *Federalist 10*.[14] Madison pointed out that if a polity is small, one portion of the population will often find itself with a clear, durable majority and so gain complete control of the government. If that happens, there will be little to stop the dominant faction from lining its own pockets or from persecuting people who do not share its ideology or traits. On the other hand, if the nation is large, the people are likely to divide into many different, overlapping groups. To build a majority, one will have to combine various groups, and no group will have any assurance that it will be part of tomorrow's majority. As a result, the risk of majority tyranny diminishes. Society's diverse groups check and moderate one another.

Ironically, a jurisdiction that is too big to facilitate democratic participation may still be too small to capture the benefits of Madisonian pluralism. Democratic participation requires a kind of intimacy: the jurisdiction must be small enough that anybody who really wants time on the public stage can get it. Madisonian pluralism, by contrast, is at risk whenever jurisdictions are homogenous: if a single, cohesive group comprises a majority of the population, it need not worry about accommodating the interests of others. It is possible for a community to be relatively homogenous without being intimate. This observation is particularly important for the assessment of state governments, all of which extend over populations and areas too great to permit the intimacy that sustains real participation. Some of the states—for example,

Florida, New York, Texas, and California—are clearly diverse enough to secure the advantages that Madison associated with large republics. That is not obviously true of all the states, however.

In any event, local autonomy is at once essential and dangerous to democracy. On the one hand, local governments are indispensable mechanisms for securing participation. On the other hand, they cannot by themselves provide people with the capacity to make effective choices. It is impossible to put together an effective economic or environmental policy, for example, without coordinating policies across large regions and multiple cities. In addition, the ease with which people can leave local jurisdictions hampers the ability of cities to implement policies: cities that try to redistribute wealth, for example, will see rich citizens flee. Moreover—and this is the lesson Madison taught—localities are risky vehicles through which to pursue impartiality or even participation. If a majority faction takes hold of the government and uses its power at the expense of minorities and outsiders, then the ideal of impartiality has been betrayed. Those outside the majority faction will not find the government responsive to their interests or opinions. Nor will they find that it provides them with any meaningful opportunity to be heard or to negotiate accommodations in local policy. Minorities might make a statement, only to find it dismissed and their interests suppressed.

Implementing democracy thus requires a delicate mix of local and national institutions. One needs local institutions, but one also needs a non-local mechanism to supervise and supplement them. Ideally, non-local (national and state) institutions should allow local institutions enough freedom to flourish but intervene when necessary to achieve impartiality. National institutions must also be strong enough to facilitate effective choice over issues—such as matters of economic or environmental policy—that require large-scale coordination. The challenge is to make national institutions powerful enough to do these jobs without making them so powerful that they suffocate local ones.

Judicial Review as a Mechanism for Regulating Local Government

Chapter 2, which considered whether judicial review was undemocratic, analyzed that practice by comparing the democratic credentials of courts and legislatures. It should by now be apparent that this simple contrast between courts and legislatures will not suffice for the present chapter, which aims to determine the overall impact of judicial review upon democratic flourishing. To execute that project, we must recognize that judicial review is, among other things, a device for regulating federalism.[15] It is an institution through which the national government supervises state and local institutions. Some people have suggested that this function is judicial review's most important task in American government.[16] Whether or not that is so, we can evaluate the impact of judicial review upon political participation only if we examine how judicial review regulates local politics.

That inquiry will inevitably require us to compare judicial review to other American political institutions and practices. American government uses a complex mix of institutions to regulate local politics. The states and the nation supervise localities through a combination of legislative, judicial, administrative, and other mechanisms—including, for example, ballot initiatives, which, in many states, permit a simple majority of the state-wide electorate to limit the discretion of local jurisdictions.[17] To assess whether judicial review diminishes democratic flourishing, we must ask to what extent the use of judicial review as a device for regulating local government threatens or protects opportunities for participation at the local level.

This question may at first seem miscast. It might seem that judicial review will tend only to reduce or eliminate (not protect) opportunities for participation that would be present in a system that lacked judicial review. After all, judicial solicitude for individual rights will inevitably take some questions away from local institutions: local school districts, for example will not be free to decide for themselves whether to sponsor prayers. We may think these restrictions entirely justifiable; indeed, we may think them (for reasons spelled out in the last chapter) to be fair representations of the American people's best judgment about justice, and hence democratically legitimate. But we cannot doubt that judicially enforced rights limit the scope of local autonomy—and so diminish the ability of local citizens to make a difference with regard to some fundamental political questions. Moreover, judicial rulings supplement legislative and other restrictions upon local autonomy. So, somebody might say, the right inquiry would be to ask *how* judicial review inhibits participation and whether this cost is worth bearing—

rather than to ask, as I have proposed, whether judicial review might actually protect local politics from incursions that would take place in the absence of that practice.

This line of thought is, however, mistaken in two ways, one simple and one subtle. The simple point is that judicial review (like other forms of supervision) can sometimes facilitate participation. As we have already noticed, if a single faction captures control of local government, participation as well as impartiality will suffer. Minorities will lose their chance to make a meaningful difference. Judicial regulation of local government can ensure that it remains open to all. In John Hart Ely's famous formulation, judicial review can be "representation-reinforcing."[18] That is so, for example, with regard to rulings that prohibit localities from disenfranchising minority voters.

Nevertheless, not all judicial interventions on behalf of liberty and equality are representation-reinforcing in this straightforward way. If, for example, the Supreme Court holds that local governments cannot prohibit abortions, that decision limits the set of issues that may become the subject of active local politics. Yet, the effect of such decisions is complex, for there is a second and more interesting way in which judicial review protects the vigor of local politics. If judicial review were eliminated, other institutions would evolve in response to that change. The nation must either put up with local abuses of power or else have some institution ready to correct them. If the judiciary were less well positioned to supervise localities, legislatures—either Congress or the state legislatures—might have to be made more capable of doing so. And if legislatures were more powerful, they might intrude upon local autonomy too much and thereby diminish the scope for participatory politics.

Of course, Congress and the states are already strong enough to overwhelm local communities. If Congress brings its awesome taxing and spending powers to bear on an issue, it can preempt state and local control over nearly any imaginable issue. The states have even fewer restraints on their power over local communities; indeed, at least as a matter of federal constitutional law, the states have almost complete freedom to restrict the power of local government bodies and to change their composition and size.[19] In principle, the judiciary could constrain Congress and the states in order to protect local autonomy; if the judiciary pursued a jurisprudence of this kind, its power would enhance local vigor in obvious ways. In practice, though, the federal judiciary's direct efforts on behalf of local autonomy have been marginal. So what sense does it make to suggest that American legislatures would have to be made more powerful in order to supervise localities effectively?

The key point is this: despite their great powers, American legislatures are designed for inaction. They are prone to gridlock. At the federal level, for example, any bill must overcome three separate hurdles: the House of Representatives, the Senate, and the presidential veto power. Because the president is elected independently from the Congress, American government is often divided—one party controls the White House, while another controls Congress (or at least one house in Congress). In the United Kingdom, by contrast, a party that holds a majority in the House of Commons can pass almost any legislation. The House of Commons controls the prime minister, and the House of Lords has relatively little power to constrain the Commons.[20]

Professor Frederick Schauer writes that the Constitution's tendency toward legislative gridlock is its "stupidest feature." In Schauer's view, the Constitution's barriers to legislative action may have made sense in the late eighteenth century, when activist government was more to be feared than desired; under present circumstances, he argues, the national legislature requires a greater capacity to formulate and implement policies on such matters as health care, the environment, and the economy.[21] In the vocabulary developed above, one might rephrase Schauer's point as a claim that Congress is too weak to enable Americans to make effective choices. Yet, stupid or not, the federal government's proclivity to gridlock has been replicated in all fifty states. Every state elects its governor independently from its legislature; every state except North Carolina permits the governor substantial veto powers; and every state except Nebraska has a bicameral legislature.[22] American government at all levels seems made to stop, not go.

Schauer's complaint is unusual only because it is so blunt; he is far from alone in thinking it unfortunate that the American system does so much to frustrate the creation of an effective governing coalition. From the standpoint of state and local government, however, Congressional inaction has a desirable side-effect: federal gridlock creates a space within which state and local bodies can act. And, likewise, state gridlock protects localities.[23] Oddly enough, scholars have largely ignored this consequence of constitutional barriers to legislative action. Indeed, in the same volume in which Schauer published his essay criticizing constitutional gridlock, Robert Nagel contributed an essay complaining that the Constitution contained no effective mechanism for protecting the states against federal incursion.[24] Nagel and Schauer answer one another: the Constitution protects federalism by making it hard for Congress to act, and the Constitution's barriers to congressional action make sense because they protect (among other things) federalism.[25]

As presently constituted, neither Congress nor the state legislatures could easily substitute for the judiciary as guardians against local instances of majority tyranny. A single complaint suffices to trigger judicial inquiry; by contrast, the barriers to legislative coordination could paralyze Congress even if a majority of legislators were willing to act.[26] On the other hand, if the legislature were reformed along the parliamentary model, so that it could intervene more vigorously, it might well resolve too many issues. The judiciary, after all, acts only when presented with an argument that liberty or equality have been impaired unjustly. State and national legislatures, by contrast, are inclined to act on behalf of the majority's preferences. A statewide or national majority may dislike a locality's choices for no good reason.

Of course, judicial review is not the only institutional device by which legislatures might be constrained.[27] Moreover, cultural traditions might protect local democracy even in a unicameral parliamentary system of government.[28] I do not mean to suggest that one can justify judicial review on the ground that it is uniquely suited to protect local, participatory institutions in a large nation. On the contrary, the principal democratic justification for judicial review is the one put forward in the last chapter, which pertains to impartiality: judicial review is a reasonable mechanism for ensuring that moral questions are decided on the basis of moral reasons rather than on the basis of collective self-interest. We began this chapter, however, by asking whether this virtue came at too heavy a price—whether, in particular, judicial review inhibited participatory democracy. Once we realize that thriving local institutions, not state or national legislatures, are the key loci for participatory democracy, it becomes entirely debatable whether robust judicial review inhibits or aids political participation. Indeed, it is at least possible that judicial review may be preferable to legislative supervision as a means for nurturing healthy local governments in American circumstances.[29]

This point is only one application of a larger insight about judicial review. Much of judicial review might be considered pro-democratic even by somebody who regarded legislative decision-making as inherently and substantially more democratic than judicial decision-making. As various theorists have emphasized,[30] relatively few instances of judicial review deal with legislative action. Even fewer deal with congressional action. From the standpoint of democratic rule, the most provocative controversies are those in which the Supreme Court confronts Congress head-on, but the most frequent and perhaps the most important pit trial courts against police officers, state and federal bureaucrats, school boards, city councils, and state legislatures. It would be infeasible for legislatures to review the conduct of police officers and bureaucrats on a case-by-case basis. One might therefore think that judicial supervision of such agents is pro-democratic even if one believes that legislative decision-making is always more democratic than judicial decision-making. Likewise, it would be impractical for Congress to review the conduct of state and local legislative bodies on a case-by-case basis. One might therefore think that federal judicial supervision of these bodies was pro-democratic even if one believes that congressional decision-making is always more democratic than judicial decision-making.

Judicial Review and Public Deliberation

Constitutional theorists occasionally say that Supreme Court decisions "foreclose . . . democratic debate" about the issues they address.[31] If this astonishing claim were true, it would certainly count against judicial review. The democratic ideal of public deliberation demands that citizens actively argue about fundamental questions of justice. If judicial review attenuated public argument, then judicial review would indeed render American democracy less robust.

In fact, though, Supreme Court decisions do not cut off public debate. They more frequently inspire arguments. The Court's controversial rulings about abortion and affirmative action, for example, did not prevent people from arguing about abortion and affirmative action. They prompted an outburst of commentary and criticism in every forum and from every source. Nor did these decisions prevent political candidates from announcing whether they favored abortion or affirmative action. Nor were voters precluded from choosing among candidates on the basis of their view about these issues.[32]

Of course, once elected, legislators had less power to select among policies than they would have had if the Court had not spoken. Yet, that observation pertains most directly not to *public deliberation* but rather to *participation:* it speaks to the ability of ordinary citizens to make a difference in their role as voters. Is there any reason to draw a connection between the power to vote and the quality of public deliberation? Some theorists contend that there is. They say that if voters cannot revise judicial decisions at the ballot box, then citizens will have no incentive to deliberate in serious and committed fashion. According to these theorists, public reaction to judicial rulings amounts to nothing more than an "impotent" "debating exercise" conducted by a "star-struck people speculat[ing] about what the Supreme Court will do next."[33] Such theorists argue that after the Supreme Court has spoken, "discussion is by hypothesis futile," and they emphasize that for "deliberative democrats, deliberation is best when accompanied by the power of decision."[34]

It is, however, a mistake to suppose that public debate is "impotent" and "futile" in the wake of judicial decision-making, but more practical when directed to legislative activity.[35] That view mischaracterizes the behavior of both judicial and legislative institutions. To begin with, it exaggerates the difficulty of revising judicial decisions. There are many ways in which public deliberation can alter the effects of a judicial decision—such as by persuading the Court to reverse its judgment, or by convincing the president to fill vacancies with nominees who disagree with the decision, or by convincing legislators to enact laws that work around the Court's ruling.[36]

Of course, most citizens will have no realistic shot at persuading the Supreme Court to change its position. But then again, most citizens will never have any realistic shot at getting Congress to change its position, either. All citizens will have the right to vote, but each individual's vote is little more than one drop in an ocean. To be sure, the electorate as a whole has tremendous power over Congress: it can take away the jobs of legislators who displease it. Yet, if citizens must feel that they have "the power of decision" in order to make deliberation meaningful, then the fact that power ultimately resides in the electorate is no more reassuring than the fact that it resides in Congress or in the Supreme Court: no citizen can reasonably expect that her deliberative behavior will have any significant influence upon the electorate as a whole.

We thus have no cause to suppose that Supreme Court decision-making eliminates or impairs public deliberation. On the contrary, there is a simple reason why we should expect judicial review to deepen public argument about political questions. Judges are supposed to respond to reasons, not preferences. The structure of federal judicial institutions, and especially of the Supreme Court, makes it likely that judges will be disinterested and hence capable of acting on the basis of reasons rather than interests. Legislators, by contrast, are supposed to respond to preferences as well as reasons.[37] The need to stand for re-election guarantees that they will be sensitive to preferences. As a result, analyzing Supreme Court decisions depends upon assessing the quality of reasons, whereas analyzing political decisions often amounts to counting heads.

National politics inevitably makes citizens into spectators: not everybody can be a congressman or a Supreme Court justice. It is natural to think of spectators as passive. Football fans, for example, may cheer passionately and argue vigorously about what their team did wrong, but they don't suit up and fight it out on the field. But watching judicial politics means watching an argument, and being a spectator to an argument is better than being a spectator to a game. Watching an argument requires you to think it through, and discussing the argument with other spectators means continuing the argument, now as an active participant rather than as a sideline observer. Watching an interest group deal is different. You can argue about how the players should have divided up the pie, or whether one side got a good deal, but you can't divide up the pie yourself.

Of course, I've exaggerated the contrast between judicial politics and legislative politics. To some extent, you can count heads on the Supreme Court—Thomas is a conservative, Breyer is a liberal, and so on. More important, politicians should and do consider the merits of the policies they enact. But the basic point holds. Legislators watch the polls much more closely than judges do. Newspaper coverage of congressional debate or presidential campaigns often focuses on opinion surveys and interest group deals. When an issue moves to the Supreme

Court, public argument does not die off; instead, it becomes more substantive, emphasizing the quality of reasons rather than their marketability.

Judicial Review and Legislative Vigor

Critics of judicial review sometimes argue that it harms democracy in a different way: not by suppressing popular political activity, but by damaging the character of legislative deliberation. An old version of this argument maintains that if judges concern themselves with liberty and equality, legislators will see no need to do so. Legislators will leave justice to judges; they will assume that the Constitution establishes a political division of labor, in which legislatures pursue self-interest while courts police the moral boundaries of political action.[38] A more recent version of this argument supposes not that legislators will cease to care about justice, but that they will care about it in unproductive ways. Judges, according to this argument, tend to conceptualize liberty and equality in terms of grand principles of right and wrong, and legislators too often follow their example. As a result, legislatures lose the ability to negotiate pragmatic solutions; they are instead consumed in symbolic battles about abstractions.[39]

Several commentators—including Supreme Court Justice Ruth Bader Ginsburg—have criticized *Roe v. Wade*[40] on grounds of this sort.[41] Justice Ginsburg is pro-choice, but she nevertheless believes that *Roe* went too far too fast: it laid down inflexible rules about when abortions were permissible, and by doing so it cut off a legislative process that might have produced a more satisfactory, less divisive resolution to the abortion controversy.[42] *Roe*, on this story, sparked a zero-sum controversy between "pro-life" and "pro-choice" factions. Legislators might have worked out policies that borrowed something from each side: they might, for example, have improved access to contraception, pre-natal care, and child-care services. They might have made the workplace more friendly to working mothers. And they might have decriminalized abortion slowly, in limited fashion, and without grand statements of principle. In short, legislatures could have settled the question more amicably, more reasonably, and more quietly. Instead, ever since *Roe*, legislators have crafted platforms designed to capture one or another side in an unending dispute. They have devoted their energy to marginal issues like "partial-birth abortions," which test the limits of grand principles and which seem impervious to compromise.[43] To be sure, nothing in *Roe* precludes legislatures from working to implement, say, enlightened and effective child-care policies. But, according to the argument we are considering, *Roe* has distorted the character of the debate, so that the nation is obsessed with rights and indifferent to ameliorative policies.

What should we make of this critique? We can begin by noticing an irony. The critique comes clothed in the rhetoric of judicial modesty. Its proponents caution against asking judges to do too much, and they emphasize the power of legislatures. On closer inspection, though, the critique makes an almost astonishing claim on behalf of judicial power. It suggests that the Supreme Court, by selective exercises of judicial review, can create or avert major social rifts. Without *Roe v. Wade*, some critics say, abortion might never have exploded into a raging and sometimes violent social controversy.[44] Judicial restraint, oddly enough, becomes the new "magic bullet" that confirms the crucial importance of what lawyers, judges, and law professors do: if only we get the judicial doctrine and rhetoric right, we will be on our way to achieving a harmonious, thriving, and happy society.[45]

These hopes seem highly implausible. Abortion policies raise questions about sex, religion, the family, and, less directly, women's role in the workplace. That is a volatile mix under any circumstances. In the 1970s, moreover, America was wrestling with the legacy of the sexual revolution and a surge in fundamentalist and evangelical religious belief.[46] Perhaps *Roe* sparked the fire, but it seems likely that the abortion issue was destined to ignite one way or another. Americans disagree about abortion, they feel passionately about it, and they would have disagreed passionately with or without *Roe*.

American democracy must contend with deep-seated, enduring disagreements on matters of principle. Often, these moral controversies will intersect with cultural divisions. In a country as diverse as the United States, issues like abortion, affirmative action, gun control, and capital punishment will become flash points for public controversy regardless of whether the Supreme Court exercises jurisdiction over them. Indeed, abortion has been much more prominent than gun control on the Supreme Court's docket, but the politics of gun control do not seem much different from the politics of abortion: in both cases, the debate is highly polarized and revolves around symbolic crusades (about, for example, "assault rifles" and "partial birth abortions") rather than practical policy strategies.[47]

There is another way to read the argument of those who think that judicial review comes at the expense of legislative vigor. One might construe them to say that, absent Court intervention, the legislature would be better able to negotiate a compromise among the bitterly divided factions that inevitably exist within American society. It certainly seems possible that constitutional adjudication will render society self-conscious about issues of principle that might otherwise be buried beneath some legislative deal. Indeed, that is partly what I had in mind when I suggested that Supreme Court decision-making might help public discussion to become more substantive. Intense public deliberation about the moral aspects of a conflict might diminish the legislature's ability to "cut a deal" between contending parties.

But what reason do we have to think that legislative log-rolling would be a good way to address moral divisions within society? Legislative action might represent nothing more than a victory by one dominant faction over less powerful ones. Indeed, if Americans regard an issue as a matter of moral principle (and if they do so, as we are now assuming, as a matter of ethical or religious conviction rather than because the Supreme Court has taught them to do so), then neither side is likely to be happy with a compromise. They will fight for what they believe is right. They will stop only when powerless to push further.

The task of a democratic government in a heterogenous society is to rule on disagreements impartially and in a way that respects the distinction between moral convictions and material interests.[48] Moral questions must be identified as such, and they must be debated and resolved on the basis of moral reasons. Those moral reasons will be controversial, of course. No matter how carefully we design political institutions, we can never be confident that they will decide moral questions correctly. Nor should we hope that they put an end to moral disagreement. The best we can hope is that American institutions will sponsor an articulate and thoughtful inquiry into the diverse opinions held by the American people, and that, over time, people will move in the right direction. As we have seen, the disinterestedness of Supreme Court justices enhances the likelihood both that they will engage in such an inquiry and that they will inspire American citizens to do likewise.

Judicial Review in Historical Perspective

Who knows what subtle effects judicial review might have on American legislative behavior? The question is, ultimately, both empirical and speculative; there is no way to say for sure whether legislatures would behave better if Supreme Court justices were more reticent about liberty and equality. The best we can do is to draw inferences from institutional structure, and to seek evidence from the ambiguous record of American history. In historical arguments about the relationship between judicial review and democratic flourishing, the words and deeds of Abraham Lincoln loom especially large.

Critics of the Supreme Court like to invoke Lincoln to buttress their claim that judicial review inhibits democratic flourishing. Four episodes from his career make him a promising ally for them. First, during his debates with Stephen Douglas, Lincoln excoriated the Supreme Court's *Scott v. Sandford* decision and promised to defy it. Second, in his First Inaugural Address, Lincoln declared, "if the policy of the government upon vital questions affecting the whole people is to be irrevocably fixed by decisions of the Supreme Court . . . the people will have ceased to be their own rulers, having to that extent practically resigned their government into the hands of that eminent tribunal."[49] Third, Lincoln may have refused to honor a writ of habeas corpus issued by Supreme Court Chief Justice Roger Taney.[50] Fourth, Lincoln and his Republican allies in Congress did what Franklin Roosevelt threatened to do: they packed the Court.[51]

It is always nice to have Lincoln on your side; he is the most awesome of American political icons. His example matters, though, for reasons that go beyond mere rhetorical impact. As we have seen, it is hard to say what it means for the people as a whole to govern themselves. To most Americans, any theory of self-government will be suspect, if not unacceptable, if it is inconsistent with Lincoln's political practice. Whatever government "of, by, and for the people" may mean, Lincoln is the most revered and unassailable of its American champions.

Lincoln's paradigmatic status within American political thought has complex consequences. If indeed Lincoln had democratic reasons for limiting the power of the Court, he did not do so simply to enhance the power of voters. Lincoln was never the electorate's servile agent. As we shall see, his argument against the Court's *Scott* decision was bound up with an argument against simple majority rule. Moreover, Lincoln eventually proved himself a ruthless exponent of executive power. He conducted, and may have precipitated, a bloody war that pitted the American people against one another. Democratic theorists who are gladdened by Lincoln's willingness to stand up to the Court should, at a minimum, be discomfited by his willingness to short-circuit Congressional authority.[52]

For the moment, though, we can focus upon Lincoln's attitude toward the Supreme Court; a careful examination of his position on that issue will eventually provide us with insights into democracy in general. Lincoln's most extensive discussion of the Supreme Court's role in American political society is contained within his attack upon the Court's ruling in *Scott*. Lincoln conceded the Supreme Court's authority over Scott's petition for freedom. He said that he had no intention to disregard the Court's ruling insofar as it applied to Scott himself. But, Lincoln continued, he did intend to fight the Court's ruling insofar as it purported to deprive Congress of the power to outlaw slavery in the federal territories. Lincoln said he would vote to enact laws identical to the one that the Supreme Court had declared unconstitutional.[53] Lincoln criticized Douglas for supposing that he was bound by general holdings or principles of the Court; to defer to the Court on matters of principle, Lincoln claimed, would surrender the people's right to govern themselves.

Modern commentary upon *Scott* often asserts that the Court's chief error was its decision to reach the constitutional questions posed by the case.[54] According to these commentators, the Court should have left the slavery issue to electorally accountable institutions. These claims sometimes travel together with the fantastic suggestion that, but for *Scott*, the United States might somehow have abolished slavery without suffering a civil war. Democratic theorists who use Lincoln to criticize judicial review often project these arguments onto him; they assume, in other words, that Lincoln promised to defy the Court's ruling in *Scott* because he believed that the Court had no business inserting itself into a controversial issue that should have been left to more "democratic" or "political" branches.

Lincoln's argument against *Scott* was different. He argued not that the Court was wrong to speak about the constitutional status of slavery, but that the Court was wrong on the merits. He took special issue with two points: the Court's claim that "slavery was expressly protected in the Constitution" and the Court's assertion that the Declaration of Independence, when it declared that "all men are created equal," meant to include only *white* men. Lincoln maintained that the Constitution carefully omitted using the word "slavery" because the framers deemed slavery immoral, and he said that the Declaration applied to *all* men, including black men.[55]

Lincoln's argument presupposes that other government institutions can—and should—take issue with the Court when it makes fundamental errors about constitutional principles. His argument does not, however, presuppose that issues like slavery are best left to legislative negotiation or majority will. On the contrary, Lincoln adamantly insisted that questions of moral principle—including, in particular, the slavery question—could not be compromised and had to be resolved differently from questions of mere expedience. That was one point of his famous House Divided Speech: the American "house" was "divided against itself" because slavery was an issue that permitted no compromise. The United States must "become all one thing or the other."[56] On matters of mere expedience, one can split the difference; Lincoln said he did not believe "in the right of Illinois to interfere with the cranberry laws of Indiana, the oyster laws of Virginia, or the liquor laws of Maine."[57] But moral questions, and especially the slavery question, had to be resolved one way or another on a national basis.[58] Douglas's blind obedience to the Court's ruling in *Scott* was odious precisely because it deadened the people to the underlying moral issue.[59] Lincoln maintained that people could accept Douglas's interpretation of *Scott* and judicial authority only if they suppressed concern about whether slavery was right or wrong.[60]

Lincoln was willing to insist on moral principle even if doing so meant bringing about a civil war. Douglas, not Lincoln, was the candidate identified with compromise and legislative conciliation. Lincoln, by contrast, was feared by the South as an extremist. Douglas maintained, and many Southerners agreed, that Lincoln's "House Divided" metaphor contained a thinly veiled threat to abolish slavery in the South. Lincoln denied the charge; he said that his speech made a prediction, not a threat.[61] Yet, one can see why such a prediction would unsettle the South. Indeed, it is possible to believe that Lincoln's combination of "predictions" and demurrers was a clever, and ultimately successful, rhetorical ploy to make sure that the South fired the first shot in a civil war that Lincoln, however reluctantly or ambivalently, believed necessary. Lincoln never admitted anything of the sort, and the possibility is thus sheer conjecture, but this much is clear: when the South eventually attacked Fort Sumter, Lincoln could take the high ground by treating the South as the aggressor against the Constitution and the Union.[62]

To summarize: Lincoln's version of democracy emphasized moral principle rather than electoral freedom, and he asserted that non-judicial institutions had a responsibility to enforce those principles. He did not say that judicial institutions lacked authority to do so. Lincoln is thus a poor witness against judicial review. There is also a more affirmative point to be had from Lincoln. Both his practice and his theory suggest that the Supreme Court can contribute to a thriving democratic politics even when the Court gets matters badly wrong. The lesson from Lincoln's practice is straightforward. The Court's decision in *Scott* did not cut off debate about slavery.[63] On the contrary, it became the centerpiece for the Lincoln-Douglas debates, which most commentators regard as one of the classic, and most edifying, political campaigns ever waged. It is at least possible that those debates would have been *less* substantive had the Court not spoken. Moreover, many historians believe that Lincoln's most devastating blow to Douglas's presidential aspirations came in a question that Lincoln first posed in the debate at Freeport: Lincoln asked Douglas whether the people of a territory were free to exclude slavery from it. This question neatly skewered Douglas. *Scott* said that the rights of slave-holders were "explicitly affirmed in the Constitution." If Douglas said that the Constitution permitted settlers to exclude slavery from new territories, he would have to qualify his unblinking support for *Scott*. He would thereby risk losing his Southern constituency. On the other hand, if he embraced this extension of *Scott*, he would alienate his Northern constituency. Douglas took the former course, and saw his star begin to fade among Southern voters.[64] The *Scott* Court helped Lincoln by the way it defined the options open to Douglas.[65] Perhaps Lincoln could have done equally well had the Court remained silent—but that is not obvious.[66]

Lincoln's theoretical contribution is more elusive. Lincoln made some tantalizing comments upon the connection between democratic opinion and government decision-making. He insisted that in a democracy, "public sentiment is everything."[67] If so, then (at least in the long run) public sentiment must control the Supreme Court. Lincoln thus apparently believed that the Court's moral judgments would eventually come to reflect the American people's judgment about justice. Indeed, that is probably the only way to explain Lincoln's audacious prediction about *Scott*'s longterm implications. Lincoln claimed that if *Scott* were accepted as legitimate, the Court would eventually render "a new *Dred Scott* decision" that would require all the states to accommodate slavery.[68] This extension of *Scott* is far from obvious; *Scott* itself insists only that Congress has no power to prohibit slavery in the territories, and it is not obvious what constitutional clause the Court might use to require free states to tolerate slavery. For Lincoln, though, the core of *Scott* was the claim that "the right of property in a slave is distinctly and expressly affirmed in the Constitution."[69] If the American public accepted that principle, then it could not permit states to stand in the way of the constitutional rights of slaveholders. Public opinion would eventually work itself into constitutional law.[70] Under these circumstances, the Court would have no trouble identifying ambiguous constitutional phrases upon which to build its argument.[71] After all, *Scott* itself fought an uphill battle against the constitutional text.[72]

Lincoln also had something to say about how public opinion evolves. This point is especially important to our study of democratic flourishing: we should prefer that public opinion changes deliberatively rather than unconsciously. Of course, neither we nor Lincoln could believe that opinion changes on the basis of deliberation alone—Lincoln himself led the North in a bloody war against other Americans who disagreed with his ideas about the Union and equality. Yet, Lincoln almost certainly believed that even military power depended upon public sentiment. You cannot inspire an army to fight (especially against blood relatives) unless the army has a cause it thinks worth killing for. On the other hand, although Lincoln believed that public sentiment was "everything," he did not think it immune to calculated influence. Indeed, his observations about the power of public opinion often formed the preface to another, more startling observation: some leaders—the most powerful of all leaders—could control public opinion.[73] A careless reading of Lincoln might suggest that he attributed this power to the Supreme Court. He worried, after all, that the American public might come to accept *Scott* and so turn its back upon the egalitarian ideal articulated in the Declaration of Independence. Closer scrutiny shows, however, that Lincoln was worried less by what Chief Justice Roger Taney had said in *Scott* and more by what his rival, Senator Douglas, was saying about *Scott*. Lincoln accused Douglas—*not* the Supreme Court—of "blowing out the moral lights around us" and "preparing the public mind" for a movement that would "mak[e] the institution of slavery national."[74]

By itself, *Scott* was merely an event that riveted public attention. Taney and his colleagues on the Court offered explanations for that event, but the American public was unlikely to read the justices' opinions; they were prolix and technical even by legal standards. Unlike the Court, Douglas had the ear of the people, and he reduced *Scott* to easily assimilated, plausible political principles.[75] Implicit in Lincoln's terse analysis is the following idea: what molds public opinion is (1) a riveting event (2) explained in graspable and memorable terms (3) by a popular (and perhaps charismatic) leader. Lincoln himself was a master of this art. He not only outmaneuvered Douglas on *Scott*, but also provided us with the most profound example of an American leader's ability to shape national opinion: Americans still recite Lincoln's speech explaining the horrible bloodshed at Gettysburg as the renewal of a national commitment to equality and liberty.[76]

To the extent that Lincoln worried about the autonomy of public reflection and the integrity of democratic self-government, he did not identify the Supreme Court or judicial review as problems. The Court must eventually yield to public opinion. The real threat to public control over self-government comes from the rare individuals who by consequence of their extraordinary rhetorical skill can manipulate public opinion. Supreme Court justices are unlikely candidates for this role (John Marshall and Oliver Wendell Holmes are the two exceptions). Indeed, it is fair to say that Lincoln worried at least as much about his own democratic credentials as the Court's. And reasonably so: it is not clear whether democracy can flourish when a single man exercises so much power.

Conclusion

Does judicial review suppress popular political activity, sap legislative vigor, or in some other way drain democracy of its energy? It is impossible to say for sure, but there is remarkably little evidence for any such view. The claim derives whatever plausibility it has from dissatisfaction with the state of American democracy. American politics is relentlessly competitive, and it is often coarse, divisive, and alienating. Democratic theorists long for a more sophisticated, inclusive politics. That is a noble dream. But it is a mistake to think that judicial action or judicial restraint can somehow make the United States into a modern-day Athens. Such proposals ask too much, not just from the judiciary but from democratic government. A country as large and diverse as the United States can never operate on the model of an amicable small town or a big, happy family. National politics cannot eliminate profound, angry disagreements, nor can it make Americans regard their compatriots as friends rather than merely as equals.

Bruising argument is healthy for a heterogenous democratic society. Roiling, contentious debate is evidence that people are asserting their opinions publicly and that they care about the merits.[77] The task of national institutions in such a society is to implement effective and impartial policies without suffocating discussion of the underlying disagreements and without eliminating opportunities for local participation. Judicial review is a reasonable mechanism for those tasks. It insists that moral issues should be decided on the basis of moral reasons, not on the basis of one group's interests. It supervises local institutions without displacing them. It improves public deliberation by encouraging people to discuss fundamental political issues in terms of reasons rather than influence.

None of which shows that judicial review is indispensable to democratic flourishing. It would be a mistake to condemn some other political system—for example, Great Britain's—because it lacked American-style judicial review. As we saw earlier, other institutions might achieve democratic goals equally well. One might expect that different institutions will work well in different political cultures. My arguments pursue a more modest claim: not that judicial review is essential to democracy, but that it reinforces self-government in the United States.

4

Text and History in Hard Cases

~

Judicial Method and Constitutional Cases

Supreme court justices often talk and write as though text and history should be the most important factors in reasoning about hard cases. Rarely do justices defend their decisions on the ground that they follow from the best understanding of some abstract political principle. They are anxious to show that their rulings were instead deduced from the constitutional text, or historical fact, or legal and social tradition, or past precedents. Turn from the United States Reports to American law journals, and you find a more elaborate consensus: not only are text and history important, but using them properly is a matter of enormous methodological subtlety.[1] Professors accordingly engage one another in erudite discussions about ideas such as hermeneutics and interpretation, translation, levels of intention, the difference between lawyers' history and historians' history, analogical reasoning, the common-law method, and the force of legal precedent.

Judges and scholars alike have assumed that using text and history properly is the essence of legal craftsmanship, and that legal craftsmanship is the key that unlocks the meaning of the Constitution's coded constraints upon American democracy. Chapters 1 and 2, however, took direct aim at the second half of this compound assumption. Chapter 1 argued that the Constitution's abstract phrases are not mysterious messages from past generations, but invitations that call upon Americans today to exercise their own, independent political judgment. And Chapter 2 maintained that the legitimacy of judicial review depends not upon distinctive features of legal reasoning, but on the disinterestedness of judges, especially Supreme Court justices. If so, it might seem that we should reject the conventional wisdom about constitutional interpretation. Why not admit that, contrary to common belief, text and history are unimportant in hard constitutional cases? Constitutional interpretation comes down to principled political argument. There is nothing distinctively legal about it. The text poses questions (e.g., "what is 'The Freedom of Speech?'") rather than resolving them, and history matters only to the extent that it would matter in ordinary, non-legal political arguments.

These blunt conclusions are not far from the truth. Political judgment will almost always be the most important ingredient in resolving any hard constitutional question. And, as others have rightly observed,[2] the constitutional text will almost never provide any useful reasons for deciding a hard case one way or another. That is not because judges are free to ignore the text. On the contrary, they must respect it. It says, for example, that presidential candidates must be at least thirty-five years old, and that each state must have exactly two senators. Judges must honor and enforce these rules, even if they think them silly. But hard constitutional cases almost never deal with these rigid, specific provisions. They emanate instead from clauses like the Equal Protection Clause, the Executive Power Clause, or the Free Speech Clause— clauses that invite, rather than suppress, the exercise of independent political judgment.

Historical argument, however, is a different matter. We have already seen one important role for history. In Chapter 1, we noticed that constitutional interpreters were bound to respect the framers' *linguistic* intentions—that is, their intentions about what statements they wanted to make. Sometimes, there will be serious questions about linguistic intentions, and, when that is so, historical argument about linguistic practices will play an important role.[3] In the concluding sections of this chapter, I suggest there is another reason why history should play a more prominent role in constitutional adjudication than in ordinary political argument. I will argue that history matters specially to constitutional adjudication not because (as originalists want us to believe) judges have an obligation to preserve the past, but because historical argument can sometimes help them to represent the people's convictions about justice. More specifically, a sensitive examination of the historical record may help judges to test the connection between their own intuitions about justice and those held by the American people more generally.

History's role in constitutional adjudication is thus nuanced in a way that justifies some of the attention which scholars have lavished on judicial methodology. We should, however, defer our consideration of history's claims on judges. It is more fitting to begin our investigation of judicial method where everybody agrees that judges should begin— with the constitutional text.

The Aesthetic Fallacy: Confusing Vices with Virtues

Lawyers, scholars, and judges frequently demand from the constitutional text more than it can deliver. Supreme Court opinions provide many amusing examples. My favorite is a 1969 case, *Stanley v. Georgia*.[4] In *Stanley*, the Court threw out the conviction of a Georgia man who had been prosecuted for possessing obscene films in his home. Georgia authorities might well have been surprised by this ruling, since the Court had ruled in *Roth v. United States* that "obscenity is not within the area of constitutionally protected speech or press."[5] The Court did not overrule that precedent, and it remains more or less valid today.[6] Nevertheless, the Court said that *Stanley* was different because it involved activities taking place within the defendant's home.

To justify this result, Justice Thurgood Marshall, writing for the Court, invoked the Free Speech Clause. He waxed eloquent about every person's "right to satisfy his intellectual and emotional needs in the privacy of his own home" and "to be free from state inquiry into the contents of his library."[7] Justice Marshall concluded, "If the First Amendment means anything, it means that the State has no business telling a man, sitting alone in his own house, what books he may read or what films he may watch."[8] In other words, the Free Speech Clause either means nothing at all, or it means that the state cannot prevent men from titillating themselves at home with filthy movies. Only an obsession with textual argument could make such a claim appealing. Perhaps the Constitution does protect the sanctity of the home—including people's freedom to watch crude pornography at home (or to engage in various other controversial sexual practices). But, contrary to Marshall's suggestion, it is easy to imagine other meanings for "the freedom of speech," and equally easy to imagine other sources for a powerful privacy right. And it is actually quite difficult to figure out why a clause protecting "the freedom of speech" should guarantee the right to *watch* obscene movies (but only at home) and not the right to produce them. After all, the amendment refers most explicitly to the rights of the *speaker,* not those of the *listener.*

How could Thurgood Marshall possibly have believed what he said in *Stanley?* Why didn't he admit that *Stanley* was a case about the state's power to invade people's homes for the purpose of regulating their sexual morality—not a case about the plain text of the Free Speech Clause? Occasionally, on days when I am especially exasperated with the Court's disingenuous jurisprudence, I wander into some unfortunate colleague's office and ask these questions aloud. Often my colleagues make excuses on Marshall's behalf. "Perhaps he had to say those things in order to get the fifth vote for his opinion," they suggest. Well, that's plausible; Marshall himself later voted to overrule *Roth.*[9] So maybe it's not Marshall's fault. But then some other justice in the majority must have refused to join unless Marshall said these implausible things about the Free Speech Clause. So why on earth did *he* (whoever he was) do that? Why not sign an opinion which said, on the basis of the Due Process Clause or the Ninth Amendment, that the state had meddled with private matters that were none of its business?

"Fetishism" describes a practice in which people invest ordinary objects with extraordinary powers. In *Stanley,* Justice Marshall engaged in what we might call "textual fetishism": he pretended that the language compelled him to reach a conclusion which in fact flowed from his own moral and political judgments.[10] This kind of fetishism is exceedingly common among lawyers, judges, and scholars. To be sure, law professors never produce anything quite so clunky as *Stanley*'s preposterous claims about the plain text of the Free Speech Clause. Unfortunately, though, they sometimes engage in more elaborate versions of the same practice—offering, for example, ingenious ways to derive abortion rights from the Establishment Clause, or equality rights from the Bill of Attainder Clause, or gay rights from the First Amendment's Speech and Assembly Clauses (to name only a few noteworthy examples from especially gifted professors).[11]

When law professors make arguments of this kind, they usually do so in a way that highlights a fundamental premise of much modern constitutional interpretation: the idea that the constitutional text possesses hidden harmonies that will reveal themselves to assiduous students and so diminish the need to make their own judgments about political morality. Thus Akhil Amar proclaims that the Constitution is like "[a] great play [which] may contain a richness of meaning beyond what was clearly in the playwright's mind when the muse came."[12] Others liken the Constitution to the "blueprint of a complex architectural edifice," replete with "numerous cross-references" that underscore the interdependent character of its discrete provisions.[13] They compare the Constitution to a sacred text, like the Bible.[14] Or they say that "the Constitution is an elegant and profound statement of a highly attractive conception of government,"[15] and that "[s]tudying the Constitution has some of the same intellectual delights as reading Aristotle: it opens the mind on a subject of the first importance."[16]

There is nothing wrong with such grand metaphors if they are not taken too seriously. Still, all of these accounts tend toward what I shall call the "aesthetic fallacy": they suppose that the Constitution has an underlying aesthetic integrity, so that we should be extremely reluctant ever to conclude that it is redundant, clumsy, ambiguous, or incomplete. This fallacy invites the conclusion that interpretive skill can enable judges to decode hidden textual meanings and thereby resolve constitutional disputes without relying upon contested judgments about morality or justice. For example, Amar suggests that we can conclude that federal conscription is unconstitutional on the basis of interrelationships among the Second Amendment (which protects the right to "keep and bear arms"), the Third Amendment (which prohibits the government from quartering soldiers in houses during peacetime) and the Militia Clauses of Article I, Section 9 (which provide Congress with a role in governing and using the militia).[17] And Laurence Tribe contends that by studying the fine points of constitutional clauses dealing with presidential appointments, gifts to public officials, duties of tonnage, and state import and export taxes, we can draw inferences about whether the Treaty Clause stipulates the sole means by which Congress may participate in the approval of international agreements.[18]

I count myself among those who have succumbed to the aesthetic fallacy. Not so long ago, I published two articles in which I suggested that the Constitution was an especially good guide to the American people's collective judgment about justice. I compared the Constitution to a political credo. By studying the Constitution, I claimed, justices could get special insight into what the American people believed about justice. To do this, I said, justices had to take into account the whole of the constitutional text—just as you have to take into account all of Locke in order to make sense of his philosophy.[19]

I had it backwards. I continue to believe that constitutional interpretation requires judges to make judgments about the American people's understanding of justice. But I erred in those earlier articles when I suggested that judges could somehow extract the necessary judgments from a sensitive reading of the constitutional text. The Constitution isn't a credo. Nor is it a work of political philosophy or a sacred text or an architectural blueprint or a great work of literature. It was created by human beings for practical purposes, and it has all the characteristics one would expect from a political document.[20] It was written by committees. It is occasionally vague, turgid, or redundant. It contains pedestrian provisions and unfortunate errors. It is full of compromises— some of them nasty, since it was written when this country was divided by slavery. And it is incomplete. It would be silly to interpret the Constitution in the way that we interpret poetry, philosophical texts, blueprints, or the Bible.

Of course, one might reasonably look for a coherent political philosophy in the thought of one or more constitutional framers. If, for example, one admires James Madison, one might use his philosophy to inform one's own conception of justice and hence to guide one's interpretation of the Constitution. But although Madison's influence upon the Constitution was immense, he was forced to make major concessions. Some of those compromises upset Madison profoundly; for example, after the Convention he told Jefferson that the Constitution was doomed to fail because it gave Congress too little power to counteract the injustices of state governments.[21] It is thus not credible to assert that the Constitution embodied Madison's philosophy or anybody else's. Madison's political theory is something that interpreters might bring to the Constitution, not something they find "encoded in the words of the document."[22]

More generally, we dishonor neither the Constitution nor the framers if we regard some of its provisions as clumsy, vague, regrettable, or redundant. On the contrary, when judges and scholars pretend that the

Constitution is perfect or wholly admirable, they inevitably distort its meaning and diminish its value as a practical political institution. To deal effectively with the Constitution's deficiencies, we must first recognize them.

The aesthetic fallacy has accordingly done considerable damage to American constitutional jurisprudence. Some of the damage has been cosmetic: the fallacy has encouraged textual fetishism and other misleading rhetorical practices, in which reasonable conclusions are defended on the basis of poor and disingenuous arguments. Unfortunately, the aesthetic fallacy has also encouraged more substantial errors. The Constitution has real vices: it contains some bad provisions, and it omits some desirable ones. The aesthetic fallacy has led judges and scholars to pretend that these vices are virtues. After all, if the Constitution is like a great work of art or a classic philosophical text, then there must be some good reason why apparently desirable provisions are missing, and why apparently repugnant ones are present. And so people begin constructing reasons where none exist.

Missing Provisions: Unenumerated Rights

Consider the famous debate over "unenumerated constitutional rights." Lawyers describe rights as "unenumerated" if they cannot be identified with any specific provision in the Bill of Rights. On this view, the right to be free from political censorship is "enumerated" because it can be attributed to the Free Speech Clause of the First Amendment; the right to choose whether to have an abortion is "unenumerated" because (at least in the view of most people) it cannot find a home in any comparably specific provision. Abortion rights, if they are constitutionally protected, must depend upon the Ninth Amendment or the Due Process Clauses or the Privileges and Immunities Clauses or the Equal Protection Clause, all of which are very abstract.

Lawyers disagree about whether judges should protect unenumerated rights, but, for the most part, they agree that unenumerated rights are somehow more dubious than enumerated rights. This view has two consequences. When judges protect unenumerated rights, they struggle to represent their decisions as interpretations of specific provisions in the Bill of Rights—as Thurgood Marshall did in *Stanley v. Georgia*, where (as we have seen) he defended a kind of privacy right by saying

that it followed ineluctably from the plain text of the Free Speech
Clause. Other judges refuse to enforce rights precisely because they are
unenumerated. The most notorious example is *Bowers v. Hardwick*.[23]
In *Bowers*, the Supreme Court reviewed the constitutionality of a Georgia statute criminalizing homosexual sodomy. Georgia had arrested
Bowers for having homosexual intercourse in his own home, and one
issue in the case was whether the privacy right in *Stanley* was broad
enough to encompass consensual homosexual acts as well as the view-
ing of obscene pornography. The Court upheld Georgia's law by a 5-4
vote. Justice Byron R. White wrote the majority opinion. He said that
the right claimed in *Bowers* should be treated with suspicion because it
depended entirely on the Due Process Clauses of the Fifth and Fourteenth Amendments. "There should be . . . great resistance to expand
the substantive reach of those Clauses, particularly if it requires rede-
fining the category of rights deemed to be fundamental," said White.[24]
White, who joined Marshall's opinion in *Stanley*, claimed that it had no
relevance to *Bowers*. The distinction was textual. According to White,
"*Stanley* . . . was firmly grounded in the First Amendment. The right
pressed upon us here has no similar support in the text of the Constitution."[25]

Why should judges treat unenumerated rights less respectfully than
enumerated ones? The Constitution itself seems to demand the opposite attitude. The Ninth Amendment insists that "the enumeration in
the Constitution, of certain rights, shall not be construed to deny or
disparage others retained by the people." White's opinion in *Bowers*
comes close to contradicting the Ninth Amendment. In White's view,
the omission of the "right of homosexuals to engage in . . . sodomy"[26]
from the Bill of Rights *does* disparage it by comparison to the "freedom
of speech," "the right to bear arms," and the other rights enumerated
in the first eight amendments. Marshall's opinion in *Stanley* does not
offend the Ninth Amendment quite so bluntly, but it nevertheless de-
parts from the spirit of the Ninth Amendment. The only way to make
sense of Marshall's fixation upon the Free Speech Clause is to suppose that he (or another member of the Court) preferred to invoke a
strained argument about enumerated rights rather than a straightforward argument about unenumerated ones.

There are two explanations for the widespread skepticism about unenumerated rights: one pertains to the constitutional text, the other

pertains to the judicial role, and neither stands up to sustained scrutiny. The textual argument illustrates the pernicious effects of the aesthetic fallacy; it goes roughly like this. If the Ninth Amendment or the grand phrases of the Fourteenth Amendment were construed expansively enough to embrace all the rights valued by free men and women, then the list of specific rights in the Bill of Rights would become almost superfluous. Rights like "the freedom of speech" would be protected under the Ninth and Fourteenth Amendments even had they not been mentioned explicitly in the First Amendment. According to the textual argument, we should avoid construing the Ninth and Fourteenth Amendments in a way that renders the Bill of Rights redundant; since the Constitution is a grand political composition, we should read it in a way that makes every phrase meaningful. We should respect whatever wisdom lurks behind the decision to enumerate some rights but not others.

Unfortunately, wisdom may not be what lies behind the Constitution's selection of rights. To some extent, the Bill of Rights may reflect a strategic misjudgment. As we saw in Chapter 1, it is not at all clear that a good Constitution would contain a specific list of rights; we might be better off if the Constitution contained *only* general guarantees like those articulated in the Ninth and Fourteenth Amendments.[27] But if we look carefully at the Bill of Rights, we may find something worse than arguable errors in judgment; we may find the taint of America's greatest evil, race slavery. Consider some of the rights that were missing from the original Bill of Rights: the right to travel, the right to vote, the right to marry, the right of parents to conduct the upbringing of their children, the right to choose a vocation and earn a living, and, most glaringly, any sort of equality right.[28] The founding generation declared independence by proclaiming that all men were created equal, yet equality is unmentioned in the original Constitution and the Bill of Rights. It is hard to believe that these omissions are unrelated to slavery. American race slavery imposed harsh and inhumane inequalities; it separated husbands from wives and parents from children; it prevented one race of people from moving about freely, participating in their government, and pursuing their fortune.[29] Rights that are fundamental to freedom—rights that would be strong candidates for inclusion in any modern bill of rights—might have been profoundly embarrassing to eighteenth-century Americans.

The omission of these rights is a real defect, and we should regard it as such. That does not mean that Americans should be ashamed of their Bill of Rights. On the contrary, Americans should continue to take pride in it: the Bill of Rights launched the project of protecting individual liberties through legal institutions. We should consider the Bill of Rights an awkward first step in a commendable direction. The framers themselves realized that their work was incomplete, and they pretty much said so in the Ninth Amendment. After slavery was abolished during the Civil War, the work begun by the Bill of Rights was pursued more adeptly by the general language of the Fourteenth Amendment.

Unfortunately, however, judges and scholars have not been content to treat the Bill of Rights in this way. They praise it as magnificent, not awkward. They view the Bill of Rights as limiting, not supplementing, the Constitution's more abstract provisions. They contend, as White did in *Bowers,* that the Fourteenth Amendment's Due Process Clause ought to be read narrowly with regard to rights not named in the Constitution's first eight amendments. They ignore the Ninth Amendment. Rather than admitting that the Bill of Rights is defective, lawyers and judges have manufactured an argument to make its omissions seem sensible. They say that the point of the Bill of Rights is to prevent judges from making political judgments. According to this popular theory, judges who confine their attention to enumerated liberties are merely enforcing the text, but judges who identify unenumerated liberties are making value judgments.

This argument, which emphasizes the judicial role rather than the aesthetic integrity of the constitutional text, is the second of the two explanations for skepticism about unenumerated liberties. I have already offered, in the preceding two chapters, a lengthy argument about why judges *ought* to make such judgments. Whether or not you found that argument convincing, and whatever you think about judicial review, it is preposterous to suppose that unenumerated rights require any sort of political judgment not equally necessary when dealing with enumerated rights.

If judges wish to avoid exercising political judgment, they will have to defer to the legislature whenever they are confronted with *any* ambiguous constitutional clause. Certainly judges would have no reason to treat the Equal Protection Clause differently from the Due Process Clause. Judges and commentators sometimes seem to regard the Equal Protection Clause as more constraining than the Due Process Clause, but the Equal Protection Clause by itself is sufficiently abstract to provide a plausible textual foundation for nearly any right you might imagine.[30] That is why Oliver Wendell Holmes ridiculed the Equal Protection Clause as the last resort of every unsuccessful constitutional argument.[31] But the point is more general. The judgments called for by the Free Speech Clause or the Free Exercise Clause or the Self-Incrimination Clause or the Takings Clause are just as contestable and just as controversial as the ones required by the Due Process Clause. The text by itself does not compel any decision about whether the Free Speech Clause limits the capacity of public figures to sue for libel;[32] or whether the Establishment Clause prohibits officially sanctioned prayer in the public schools;[33] or whether the Fifth Amendment's Self-Incrimination Clause requires police interrogators to inform suspects of their rights;[34] or whether the Takings Clause requires the government to compensate landholders when environmental regulations diminish the value of their property.[35] If you really believe that judges should abstain from deciding hard cases, then you should recommend judicial restraint across the board. You cannot tackle the problem by preferring specific ambiguous clauses over more abstract ones.

Although boilerplate constitutional rhetoric insists that textual specificity is valuable because of its power to constrain judges, cases like *Stanley* demonstrate that this power is marginal and perhaps non-existent. In fact, the obsession with textual specificity may actually increase the Court's power by obscuring the judgments it makes and so insulating them from effective public criticism. Lawyers have a knack for finding inventive ways to read rules. Trying to constrain a lawyer with ambiguous, complex language is a little like throwing Brer Rabbit into the brier patch: protected by a thicket impenetrable to pursuers, he moves about more freely than in an open field. The text of the First Amendment, for example, did not constrain the *Stanley* Court's discretion to limit state power in the area of sexual morality. The Court's emphasis on the speech clause did, however, make it harder for non-lawyers in the general public to understand what the Court had done and why it had acted.[36]

The conventional wisdom about unenumerated rights is thus dead wrong. They are no less legitimate and no more contestable than enumerated rights.[37] Judges should weigh claims about unenumerated rights on their moral merits: they should ask whether the claimed right is consistent with their own best judgment about the American people's view of justice, and they should ask whether judges are institutionally competent to describe and enforce the right. That prescription does not, of course, tell us anything about which way the cases should be decided. For example, White and his four colleagues in the *Bowers* majority might have voted the same way even if they had faced up to the judgments about liberty and equality demanded by the Constitution. It is possible to defend anti-sodomy statutes by making arguments that appeal to moral principle rather than the text of the Bill of Rights or conventional practices.[38] I do not find these arguments convincing, but some reasonable people do.

If White had put his opinion on moral grounds, he would at least have given the public an accurate account of the Court's responsibilities and its approach to them. And it is also possible that if the justices had worried more about liberty and less about clauses, one of them (for example, Justice Powell, who later said he had made a mistake in *Bowers*, and wished he had voted with the four dissenters[39]) might have reached a different conclusion.

Bad Provisions: Ghost Towns and Interpretive Quarantines

Because constitutions must leave people free to govern themselves, any constitution—no matter how good—must leave people free to enact bad provisions. Of course, constitutions can incorporate safeguards to discourage bad amendments. Indeed, I have suggested that the demanding procedures specified in Article V serve exactly this purpose: they are best regarded as efforts to ensure that Americans deliberate carefully about the long-term consequences of institutional reform. But no system is foolproof. A constitutional procedure that enables people to entrench good rules and institutions will also enable them to entrench bad rules and institutions. A people must have the freedom to make controversial political choices, and that freedom will necessarily entail the freedom to choose badly.

What should judges and other public officials do when they confront a constitutional provision that they consider unjust or undesirable? People sometimes assume that once a provision makes its way into the

Constitution, interpreters must treat it sympathetically. We should recognize here the blight of the aesthetic fallacy. People under the spell of that fallacy like to suppose that every constitutional provision is an admirable one, and that all provisions deserve equally robust application. Consider, for example, the Second Amendment, which provides that "A well regulated Militia, being necessary to the security of a free State, the right of the people to keep and bear Arms, shall not be infringed." Suppose you are a judge, and that you dislike the Second Amendment. To be more precise, suppose that you think that gun ownership has nothing to do with human liberty, and that the government should be free to regulate guns in almost any way that it likes. You think that the theories which motivated enactment of the Second Amendment are now outdated. Does that judgment provide you with any legitimate reason to give the Second Amendment a miserly reading? Some people say not. They insist that it is improper for judges to distinguish among constitutional provisions on the basis of whether or not they think them valuable. According to these commentators, judges must interpret the Second Amendment no less energetically than they would the Equal Protection Clause. They cannot treat the Second Amendment differently just because they think it to be silly, improvident, or anachronistic.[40]

At a very general level, of course, this conclusion is true. When judges approach *any* constitutional provision, they must proceed in two steps. They must first ask whether that provision is best understood as expressing an abstract moral or political principle. If not, the judges' moral views will have no role to play in the interpretation and enforcement of the provision. Conversely, if the provision does use abstract moral language, a judge's interpretation of the provision will inevitably vary with the theory of justice she constructs on the people's behalf. And that theory will, in turn, depend upon the judge's own convictions about justice.

Thus, a judge confronted with a Second Amendment issue must first ask whether that amendment expresses an abstract principle of governance. That turns out to be a tricky question. We might imagine versions of the Second Amendment that clearly fell on one side or the other of the line. Suppose, for example, that the Second Amendment guaranteed "the rights of gun ownership appropriate to all citizens of free republics." That language would reference a moral ideal, and the judge's own moral convictions would be relevant to its interpretation. Or, alternatively, suppose that the Second Amendment said, "The government shall not prohibit any citizen over the age of eighteen from possessing a musket." That language draws a bright line: if you're over eighteen and you want to have a musket, the government can't stop you. Of course, our hypothetical Musket Amendment may still raise some difficult questions—such as, "What counts as a 'musket'?" and "Is there an implicit exception for convicted felons?" and "Can the government demand that people license their muskets?"[41] And, of course, it is always possible that people will (because of these questions or for other reasons) interpret the Musket Amendment as stating some general, ambiguous principle—"the kind of fairness and liberty once exemplified by musket ownership." It is at least possible, though, that we might view the Musket Amendment as settling a controversy. If a judge regards the Musket Clause that way, her moral convictions should have no impact upon how vigorously she applies its rule.

The actual Second Amendment is much less specific than our hypothetical Musket Amendment. "Keep," "bear," and "arms" speak at a higher level of abstraction than do "possess" and "musket." What, for example, does it mean to "bear arms"? Is that a reference to participation in an organized military group (as the amendment's preamble, which refers to "a well-regulated militia," might suggest)? Or is the concept sufficiently expansive to embrace an individual, with no military affiliation, who wishes to carry a concealed weapon on the street? And what should count as "arms"? Muskets? Rifles? Machine guns? Swords? Bombs? Bazookas?

It is therefore tempting to suppose that the Second Amendment states an abstract principle of individual liberty. That would probably be the right way to construe "the right to keep and bear arms" if such language were to appear in an amendment drafted today. The modern usage of the phrase has been shaped by America's debate over gun control, where it is invoked almost exclusively by those who believe that private individuals should have a right to own guns for sport or self-defense.

Yet, nothing like today's debate about gun control existed when the Second Amendment was drafted.[42] It is therefore entirely possible that in the late eighteenth century "the right to keep and bear arms" signified a concept quite different from the modern one: the phrase might, for example, have been a term of art, or it might have been an abstract principle related to participation in the militia rather than to gun ownership. The Second Amendment may thus be one of the few constitutional provisions that raises serious questions about, in Ronald Dworkin's terminology, the framers' *linguistic* intentions, rather than their *legal* intentions.[43] Those questions are historical, rather than moral; a judge construing the Second Amendment will have to investigate how the phrase "the right to keep and bear arms" functioned in eighteenth-century political discussion.

Let's suppose that our judge concludes, after the appropriate historical research, that the Second Amendment does indeed express an abstract principle protecting the right of individuals to own guns—something like, "all the rights of gun ownership appropriate to citizens in a free republic." If that is her reading of the constitutional text, it will then be her job to construe it so as to express a judgment about justice on behalf of the American people. Obviously, the American people disagree vigorously about gun control and related issues. To construct a coherent judgment out of this controversy, the judge will have to rely heavily upon her own convictions about liberty and guns. We have been supposing that our judge is skeptical about gun rights. Suppose, then, that she concludes that the best judgment she can offer on behalf of the American people is as follows: any restraint on gun ownership is consistent with the demands of liberty and justice, so long as it is not manifestly irrational, arbitrary, or discriminatory.

How narrowly could this judge construe the Second Amendment? Suppose she says, "When the Second Amendment confers the 'right to keep and bear arms,' it means only that the government may not impose any *irrational* or *arbitrary* restraints upon gun ownership. So long as the government behaves rationally, the right is not infringed." This interpretation of the Second Amendment renders it toothless. Our hypothetical judge would never offer so mild a reading of the First Amendment or the Equal Protection Clause. But she has a sound reason for treating these amendments differently: they bear a different relationship to justice because they, unlike the Second Amendment, refer to important aspects of human liberty. The question is whether, by rendering the Second Amendment almost nugatory, she has somehow gone too far.

We can get some help from a whimsical passage in John Hart Ely's

Democracy and Distrust. Ely asked readers to imagine that the Constitution contained "one or more provisions providing for the protection of ghosts. Can there be any doubt, now that we no longer believe there is any such thing, that we would be behaving properly in ignoring the provisions?" Ely was hypothesizing an argument about the Ninth Amendment; his point was to ask whether we might ignore the Ninth Amendment if it presupposed the existence of something spooky, like "natural law." Ely rightly rejected this argument with respect to the Ninth Amendment—there is no reason, he said, to believe that it presupposes anything mystical. Curiously, though, his argument may tell us a great deal about the Second Amendment. Indeed, although this fact is by no means essential to the argument, the Second Amendment *explicitly* refers to something that no longer exists: namely, "well regulated militias."[44] I do not mean to suggest that militias are like ghosts: militias really did exist at one time. At the time of the founding, male citizens drilled regularly in public military corps under state and local leadership. People feared national armies, and these local, inclusive cadres were considered bulwarks against oppression. But local militias have gone the way of powdered wigs. They are no longer a part of American life. As a result, the "right to keep and bear arms" has ceased to have any sensible function. The Second Amendment is a constitutional ghost town.

Or so a judge might reasonably conclude. One could, of course, take other views. One might, for example, believe (with considerable strain, I think) that the National Guard is a "militia,"[45] in which case the Second Amendment might guarantee the right of people to join the Guard (to "bear arms") and to possess some weapon in their residence (to "keep arms") so long as they remained in the Guard. Or one might actually believe that gun ownership was a desirable element of human liberty. Some people hold this belief quite fervently. If you're one of them, I have no doubt that you should interpret the Second Amendment (or, for that matter, the Ninth Amendment) to protect the people's right to arm themselves to the teeth with horrible, dangerous weapons. All I can do is hope that you're never appointed to the Supreme Court!

In any event, my point here is not to argue for a particular construction of the Second Amendment. People with different views about justice will construe the Second Amendment differently, and these disagreements are entirely legitimate. My aim is only to underscore the

attitude judges should take *if* they think that a broad reading of a particular constitutional provision would produce injustice. Judges should
give such provisions the narrowest construction consistent with their
plain language. Sometimes, as with the Second Amendment, this task
might entail confining the sweep of abstract language. In other cases, it
will mean erecting an interpretive quarantine around a specific, unjust
rule, so that its premises do not infect the meaning of other, more ambiguous clauses. For example, Article II, Section 1 of the Constitution,
provides, "No person except a natural born Citizen, or a Citizen of the
United States, at the time of the adoption of this Constitution, shall be
eligible to the office of the President." Because of this provision, only
people who were American citizens at birth may become president.
Naturalized citizens are ineligible for the office. That is an odious discrimination. Indeed, if any state constitution prohibited naturalized
Americans from becoming governor, the Supreme Court would almost
certainly hold that exclusion unconstitutional under the Equal Protection Clause.

Supreme Court justices have tried to generalize from the Presidential Eligibility Clause in two very different ways. Justice Rehnquist
once invoked the clause in order to limit the reach of the Equal Protection Clause. He argued that since Article II discriminated against naturalized citizens, the Court should permit the states to discriminate
against people who were not citizens at all.[46] Rehnquist, however, made
this argument in dissent; other justices have drawn more affirmative inferences from the clause. They have suggested that because the Constitution explicitly imposes only one restriction upon naturalized citizens
(namely, they are ineligible to be president), those citizens must be
equal to their native-born counterparts in all other respects.[47]

I much prefer the second, optimistic construction of the Eligibility Clause to Rehnquist's, but both arguments illustrate the proclivity
of lawyers to try to get too much from the constitutional text. If a naturalized citizen ever sued for a place on the presidential ballot, there
would be no ducking the unpleasant but quite explicit commands of the
clause. Judges would have to deny relief. Fortunately, though, there is
no reason to apply the Eligibility Clause to any other problem. The
Constitution is not a poem, in which every line of verse must harmo-
nize with its surroundings. It is a practical political institution; more
specifically, it is an effort to facilitate the project of self-government in

America. Like any political creation, it contains errors and compromises—some of them quite ugly. Judges should resist the temptation to find a principle behind every compromise. There is no reason to give bad constitutional provisions any force whatsoever beyond what is necessary to make sense of their plain terms.[48]

History, Constitutional Interpretation, and the People's Judgment about Justice

When judges defend individual rights against legislative action, their decisions will frequently be unpopular. The legislature will often have a majority of the people on its side. That fact alone should not deter judges from sticking to their convictions. As we have already seen, the majority's reaction to a judicial decision is not the same thing as the people's judgment about justice. The majority's reaction may result more from self-interest than from moral judgment, and the majority is only one part of the American people.

Nevertheless, judges should not lightly disregard public disagreement with their rulings. The job of judges is to speak on behalf of the American people on (certain) matters of justice, and intense political opposition to a particular ruling may be a sign that the American people disagree with that ruling on principled grounds—that, in other words, the judge's convictions about justice, however disinterested they may be, are out of step with the people's.

Constructing the American people's conception of justice is not the same thing as expressing one's own conception of justice or as expressing the best conception of justice, whatever that may mean. In a democratic political system, judges engaged in judicial review cannot simply act on the basis of their own best judgment about justice; they must instead act on the basis of a conception of justice with which Americans in general could plausibly identify themselves. If judges make judgments about justice in order to apply abstract constitutional provisions like the Equal Protection Clause or the Executive Power Clause, they will have to show that those judgments are plausibly attributable to the American people as a whole. To do that, judges will have to produce an interpretation of American politics consistent with the values the judge seeks to enforce on the people's behalf.

When the judge's decision flies in the face of national electoral majorities, the task of reconciling justice and American public opinion will be especially challenging. Here historical argument may play a special role. By appealing to history, judges may attach a popular pedigree to unpopular decisions. Judges might, for example, interpret the significance of major events in American history in order to argue that Americans have come together on behalf of certain ideals—say, political equality—in times of crisis. Or they might collect together opinions of historical figures—like James Madison and Abraham Lincoln—whom Americans admire and who have spoken boldly on behalf of admirable values. Or judges might construe the meaning of American traditions and practices, which, the judges might argue, harbor within them values loftier or simply different from those that seem to have carried the day in recent legislative debates.

Judicial interpretation of the Constitution may accordingly draw upon history more heavily than would ordinary moral and political argument. That is because judges have an obligation to speak on behalf of the people, rather than merely for themselves. History may help judges to discharge the responsibility that goes with their role. History will, however, contribute to constitutional jurisprudence as servant, not rival, to justice. That is different from what originalists recommend. According to originalists, history imposes constraints that sometimes operate at cross-purposes with justice. The originalists say that judges must resolve cases on the basis of the framers' views, and that they must do so even when those views seem unjust. Originalists thus ask history to select among competing conceptions of justice; the approach recommended here, by contrast, uses conceptions of justice to select among competing interpretations of history. The American historical record is rich with contending factions and disparate opinions; it features eloquent slave-holders as well as passionate abolitionists, powerful bigots as well as dogged egalitarians. To pick out one or another as true representatives of the American people, judges must look beyond the brute facts of the historical record. All other things being equal, judges should assume that the institutions and actions which have best represented the people are those that have promoted justice rather than pursued some false vision of it.

When Supreme Court justices invoke historical argument, they often write as though history had compelled them to decide a case one way rather than another. Despite that rhetorical posture, however, most judicial uses of history are, I would submit, better understood as relying upon convictions about justice in order to sift among multiple, inconsistent historical representations of the American people. That is one reason why judicial uses of history fare so badly in the eyes of professional historians.[49] Historians complain that judges use facts selectively, and that they veil the complex, multivocal character of the historical record. Of course they do—they do so because their job as judges requires them, unlike historians, to use convictions about justice to construct a single, coherent narrative of American political identity.

Justice Brandeis and the Sedition Acts

As an example, consider the famous concurring opinion by Louis Brandeis in *Whitney v. California*.[50] *Whitney* was an early free speech case; in it, Anita Whitney challenged the constitutionality of California's criminal syndicalism statute, which made it a crime to join a group that advocated violence as a means to achieving political change. Brandeis, like the *Whitney* majority, voted to uphold Whitney's conviction, but he thought that the majority's rationale was insufficiently protective of political speech. The *Whitney* majority was willing to give legislatures great discretion to decide whether seditious speech was likely to incite criminal activity; Brandeis believed that judges should allow limitations on political speech only if there existed "a clear and present danger of serious evil"—otherwise, Brandeis said, the remedy for bad speech was "more speech, not enforced silence." Brandeis cast his argument in the form of a series of claims about "[t]hose who won our independence." Brandeis said, among other things, that "[t]hey believed that freedom to think as you will and to speak as you think are means indispensable to the discovery and spread of political truth; . . . that the greatest menace to freedom is an inert people; that public discussion is a political duty; and that this should be a fundamental principle of American government."[51]

The Brandeis concurrence in *Whitney* is stirring and Supreme Court justices have often quoted it to justify expansive readings of the Free Speech Clause. Yet, Brandeis's argument is easily challenged on historical grounds. Brandeis's portrait of the framers' attitudes toward free speech was, at a minimum, incomplete: some of "those who won our independence" passed and implemented the Alien and Sedition Acts of 1798, a set of statutes that were used to prosecute people who criticized the government.[52] David Brown, for example, received an eighteen-month prison sentence for offenses such as calling the Federalist-controlled government "a tyrannic association of five hundred out of five million" who reaped "all the benefits of public property and live upon the ruins of the rest of the community."[53] Perhaps it would be possible, after thorough examination of the evidence, to vindicate Brandeis's claim that "[t]hose who won our independence by revolution were . . . courageous, self-reliant men, with confidence in the power of free and fearless reasoning." The *Whitney* concurrence, however, features no such inquiry; Brandeis never even mentions the evidence against his conclusions.

If Brandeis were an originalist—if, in other words, he thought himself compelled to resolve constitutional questions on the basis of historical fact without regard to justice—then his failure to discuss historical evidence inconsistent with his conclusions would be inexcusable. If, on the other hand, Brandeis thought that his job was simply to decide cases on the basis of his own, best convictions about justice, then his resort to historical argument would be surplusage—or, at best, persuasive rhetoric that distracted attention from the real grounds upon which Brandeis rested his choice. But if Brandeis sensed that his job was to interpret the Constitution's references to moral ideals by calling upon his own best judgment about the American people's best judgment about justice, then his use of history is comprehensible and cogent. He puts his claims about justice in the form of a narrative about the founding generation in order to show that those claims are not whimsies of his personal conscience, but are plausibly attributed to the American people as a whole.

Most judicial accounts of American history resemble Brandeis's. They treat the framers with admiration, rather than contempt or even disinterest, and they treat American history selectively in order to construct from it a coherent vision of legal and political justice. They do not value historical facts as substitutes for or at the expense of justice. Instead, they endeavor to show that American history reveals the American people to be *more just* than contemporary public opinion might at first indicate. That is exactly as it should be. The legitimate point of historical argument is not to evade the judge's responsibility to do justice, but rather to validate the judge's claim to speak not simply about justice, but about justice *on behalf of the American people.*

Justice Roberts and the New Deal

Once we realize the rich complexity of the historical record and concede that judges must choose among possible representations of the American people on the basis of their own convictions about justice, we should quickly realize something else—namely, that judges will almost always conclude that the American people share their own, personal convictions about justice. The democratic pedigree of judges makes this result even more likely. Because they are political appointees, judges are unlikely to be moral radicals; they are therefore likely to find substantial support for their views in the American political record.

This result is no cause for alarm. Indeed, the opposite position—"we should hope that good judges must sometimes conclude that the American people are unjust"—is perverse. We have not required judges to study history out of some desire to "constrain judges" and increase the freedom of majoritarian institutions. We have instead recommended that judges turn to history only to discharge their obligation to speak about justice on behalf of the American people.

Nevertheless, on rare occasions a judge might conclude that, despite the ambiguities in American public opinion, she cannot honestly offer her own judgments about justice in the name of the American people. Under those circumstances, democratic principles require that she act on the basis of what she considers to be the people's best judgment about justice, rather than her own. Consider, in this connection, the famous change of mind that put an end to the *Lochner* era. In *West Coast Hotel v. Parrish*,[54] Justice Owen Roberts, who had sided with the "freedom of contract" doctrine in *Morehead v. New York ex rel. Tipaldo*,[55] changed allegiances. While *Parrish* was pending before the Court, Franklin Roosevelt proposed his notorious court-packing plan, which would have enabled him to appoint additional (and more sympathetic) justices to the Court. For that reason, lawyers often refer to Roberts's vote in *Parrish* as the "switch in time that saved nine": had Roberts not changed sides, Roosevelt might have implemented his court-packing plan, and the Court would no longer have consisted of nine justices.[56]

Today, *Lochner* is a symbol of Supreme Court jurisprudence run amok—when judges or lawyers want to insult their peers, they accuse them of "*Lochner*-izing."[57] Lawyers regard the "switch-in-time" as a turning point in Supreme Court history, and they think it important to explain why Roberts changed his vote.[58] Some people offer what we might call a "legal realist" explanation: they propose that Roberts was bullied into submission by his fear that the court-packing measure, or some similar attack upon the Court, might succeed.[59] On this theory, Roberts's history-making decision was unprincipled: he continued to think that *Lochner* was right on the merits, but he changed his vote to protect the Court's power (and, with it, his own). A second explanation proposes that Roberts reconsidered the merits of the *Lochner* doctrine and came to a different conclusion.[60] On this view, political pressure played little, if any, role in Roberts's deliberations; perhaps it spurred him to look again at issues he might otherwise have considered settled, but the new judgments he made were ones that he embraced as his own. Bruce Ackerman has offered a third, more radical explanation: Ackerman maintains that the Constitution was amended during the 1930s, so that Roberts's vote was a legitimate response to the amendment process. Of course, no formal amendment was actually passed during the New Deal era, so Ackerman's suggestion depends upon an elaborate theory about how amendment may occur outside the rules laid down in Article V of the Constitution.[61] Ackerman's theory is ingenious, but most people find it hard to believe that the Constitution was amended without the addition of any text—and, indeed, without anybody recognizing the amendment until Ackerman discovered it fifty years later.

There is a fourth possible explanation for the "switch-in-time," one that depends upon the distinction between a judge's own judgment about justice and that judge's judgment about the American people's judgment about justice. The extraordinary public support for the New Deal might have convinced Roberts to change his view about the people's judgment about justice, even if he did not change his own. He might have continued to believe, as a matter of personal conviction about justice, that government ought to respect the liberty of contract, and that, in particular, it ought to refrain from enacting minimum wage laws. But he might have concluded that his own judgment about political justice was at odds with the American people's view, and that, in light of this disagreement, it would be inappropriate for him to insist upon pursuing his own convictions. On the theory proposed here, such deference is entirely legitimate.

Roberts could, of course, have appealed to history in order to find some deep American commitment to liberty of contract that continued to exist beneath the political support for minimum wage laws and economic reform—just as in *Whitney* Brandeis appealed to history in order to find an American commitment to free speech beneath contemporary efforts to suppress the communist party. Roberts would not have wanted for evidence; American history is rife with encomiums and policies honoring the virtues of free labor markets. Roberts might plausibly have concluded that this history more accurately represented the judgment of the American people than did contemporary political events. But he might also have concluded that, in light of the intensity and duration of support for Roosevelt's policies, nineteenth-century support for freedom of contract was no longer an accurate guide to the judgments of the American people in the 1930s.[62]

I do not know whether this proposal accurately describes Roberts's thinking. For our purposes, what matters is not the biographical accuracy of the example but rather its structure. Roberts might legitimately have changed his vote because he changed his view about the state of public opinion. More generally, a judge may legitimately conclude that the best way to speak on behalf of the people is to offer a view about justice which is more popular than her own and which seems reasonable (though incorrect) to her. In a democracy, it cannot be a matter of indifference if a vast number of your fellow citizens think differently than you do—they are your equals, after all, and the fact that they hold a position different from yours is some evidence that you are mistaken. A conscientious judge will want to give some weight to the fact that public debate is leading more and more people to reject her own position. Exactly how much weight she gives to such developments will depend upon her views about democratic deliberation. Apparent shifts in public understanding can always be explained away as transient blips or as the product of misinformation or mass hysteria or a thousand other factors. Here again, no judge will be able to escape the need to make independent political judgments. But every judge should be able to identify some series of events (they might be rare or improbable) which would lead her to defer to popular opinion rather than offer her own convictions on the people's behalf.

Constitutional Failure

I have assumed that Roberts considered Franklin Roosevelt's view about the liberty of contract to be reasonable, albeit incorrect. What should justices do if they conclude that the American people's judgment about justice is not only different from their own, but unreasonable? Suppose, for example, that Justice Roberts had been deciding *Brown v. Board of Education* rather than *West Coast Hotel v. Parrish*; suppose he had been considering whether to defer to popularly held convictions that were, in his view, racist and evil. Could we, under those circumstances, allow—much less recommend—that he defer to "the best judgment of the American people," rather than act on the basis of his own best judgment about justice?

The assumptions we have stipulated describe a crisis of democracy: we are supposing that, in the eyes of our hypothetical Roberts, the American people are palpably unjust. If it is rare for judges to experience, at the end of the day, a tension between their own judgments about justice and their judgments about the American people's best judgments about justice, it should be even more uncommon for them to experience that tension with regard to a principle that is, in their view, essential to any reasonable view about justice. But it is certainly possible for a conscientious judge to conclude that her nation's people are unjust; one might think that was true for some judges in Nazi Germany, or South Africa, or the antebellum United States (when American law accommodated slavery)[63]—or perhaps even in the United States today, although anybody radical enough to hold such a view is unlikely to find himself or herself appointed to the bench. Under such circumstances, a fundamental assumption of American constitutionalism fails: it is no longer obvious that the American people are entitled to govern themselves on the basis of their own judgments about justice. The people would be too corrupt to deserve the privilege of self-government.

This crisis is not unique to the constitutional theory advanced here. Other theories might leave our hypothetical Justice Roberts free to dis-

regard the racist judgments of the people, but to what end? At a minimum, Justice Roberts's ruling would come at the expense of democracy, which should be a cause for regret, even if we think the ruling
justifiable. But Justice Roberts might find his ruling entirely futile: people might disregard his ruling, or attack the Court—by packing it or
by taking other steps to diminish its authority. After all, if the people
are indeed unjust, what reason would Justice Roberts have for thinking that they would abide by a just decision? And if the people might
be willing to honor his ruling despite their inclination to do otherwise, wouldn't that provide Roberts with some reason to revise his
unflattering estimate of their character?

The United States Constitution is a practical device that organizes
political behavior in order to facilitate self-government. Like any practical device, constitutions can fail.[64] People who are free to govern
themselves can do so badly. They can come to endorse a degenerate
understanding of justice. Or they can amend their constitution in horrible ways. They could, for example, ratify amendments that explicitly
approve of race slavery, or that call for the persecution of political dissi-
dents.

When a people misuses its freedom severely, a judge may find herself
fundamentally alienated from the people and the government that appointed her to office. One hopes that this sort of radical alienation
would be rare. A judge who feels this alienation should test herself
carefully. She should ask herself, in particular, whether she is so confident in the rectitude and importance of her own convictions that she
must conclude that democracy or the constitution has failed in some
way. A democracy will not long survive unless its citizens are able to retain their faith in one another even when their disagreements are passionate, intense, and durable.

Still, there is no denying that democracy and justice might pull apart
from one another. A judge who confronts such a predicament will face
awful choices. My instinct is to say that she should do everything in her
power to promote justice, and, at the same time, to restore a situation
in which justice and democracy co-exist harmoniously. I do not see why
she should be obliged to assist a people bent upon doing injustice, nor
do I think that she would have any obligation to resign her office. But I
have not investigated those questions thoroughly, and a judge faced
with such dire circumstances will get little aid from the theory set out

in this book. My effort is to understand how the United States Constitution helps to implement self-government—not how judges should respond when a democratic people turns evil.

Conclusion

Neither textual exegesis nor historical research can save judges from the need to make independent judgments in hard constitutional cases. In cases that are genuinely difficult, the constitutional text inevitably raises questions rather than answers them. History can provide more help than the constitutional text; historical study can, for example, enrich a judge's representation of the relationship between her moral judgments and the people's. No judge, however, can produce a useful interpretation of American history without invoking her own, independent moral intuitions. A judge who uses history as a substitute for moral and political judgment is either misusing history or misrepresenting it or both.

Unfortunately, judges (and scholars, too) often indulge in a kind of fetishism. They pretend that they are not making political judgments themselves, and that their decisions were forced upon them by textual details or historical facts. This fetishism has two unfortunate consequences. At a minimum, it harms self-government by obfuscating the public's understanding of what the Supreme Court is actually doing. At worst, it misleads the judges themselves. In an effort to live up to extravagant and indefensible claims about the power of text and history, they let irrelevant facts about America's constitutional text (such as the omission of any specific references to parental autonomy and education) or history (such as the bigoted persecution of homosexuals) affect their interpretation of provisions like the Ninth Amendment and the Equal Protection Clause. By doing so, they needlessly empower the "dead hand of the past," and they diminish the Constitution's capacity to facilitate self-government. Judges would do a better job interpreting the Constitution if they were more honest with us, and with themselves, about the political judgments it demands. The next two chapters offer more in-depth analyses of how the Court might do better.

5

Liberty, Strategy, and Tradition

∽

Strategic Judgment in Constitutional Law

IN CHAPTERS 2 AND 3, I argued that so long as judges act within the limits of their competence, judicial review can be pro-democratic rather than anti-democratic. But what does it mean for judges to act within the limits of their competence? One might suppose, as an initial hypothesis, that judges should stick to what they do best. In Chapter 2, I argued that by comparison to other political actors, judges are well-situated to recognize and respect moral principles. So perhaps judges should do no more than announce and enforce such principles, and leave everything else to others.

Yet, if judges restrict themselves to matters of pure principle, they will do virtually nothing. In order to formulate legal rules with bite, judges will inevitably have to resolve questions of strategy—questions about what sort of institutions and devices are likely to do a good job implementing the principles that judges announce. To borrow the pithy language of Lawrence Sager, there is a "strategic space" between constitutional norms and constitutional rules.[1] As an example, consider the Supreme Court's landmark decision in *New York Times v. Sullivan*.[2] *Sullivan* is one of the Court's most important decisions about the freedom of speech; it dealt with a politically charged libel action that arose in the 1960s. Civil rights activists had purchased an advertisement in the *New York Times*. The advertisement described recent events in Alabama and appealed for donations. L. B. Sullivan, a police commissioner in Montgomery, Alabama, sued the *Times*, claiming that the advertisement defamed him. Although the advertisement contained only minor inaccuracies, and although it neither mentioned Sullivan's name nor referred to his office, an Alabama jury returned a $500,000 verdict against the *Times*. The Supreme Court reversed and announced a highly protective First Amendment doctrine. The Court said that speakers who criticize public officials for the performance of their duties cannot be made to pay damages unless the statements were made with "actual malice"—that is, with knowledge of their falsity or with reckless disregard for the truth.[3]

It is easy to formulate moral principles consistent with the Court's decision in *Times v. Sullivan*. One might say, for example, that no person should be subjected to an adverse civil or criminal judgment merely because she has expressed ideas critical of the government. The Alabama verdict in *Sullivan* may have contradicted that principle quite directly: the size of the verdict and the triviality of the misstatements both suggest that the Alabama jury was motivated in substantial part by hostility to the political position espoused in the *Times* advertisement. But the rule announced by the Court in *Sullivan* went further. It did not merely protect speakers against politically motivated reprisals; instead, it created a broad immunity for false statements about political officials. *Sullivan* prevented officials from recovering damages for injuries done to their reputation by criticism that was false but merely negligent, rather than reckless. Perhaps the *Sullivan* Court thought there was no way to avoid politically biased verdicts except through the creation of a broad safe harbor for political speech. But if so, that judgment is obviously strategic, not moral.

Can we eliminate this strategic element from *Sullivan?* Suppose we defend *Sullivan* on the basis of a different principle—such as, "the government must not adopt any policy that denies people a reasonable opportunity to express their own ideas about what is true or good, or that fails to respect people's freedom to make their own judgments about which opinions and ideas are valuable ones."[4] We might say that Alabama's libel law discouraged people from expressing their opinions, and that it thereby prevented Alabama citizens from hearing (and making up their own minds about) allegations against their public officials. These conclusions again reflect a heavy dose of strategic judgment, however. Alabama did not, after all, make it unlawful to criticize police commissioners. Instead, Alabama provided a legal forum in which people could dispute the truth of statements and hold speakers responsible for damage caused by their errors. And, of course, at the end of the libel trial in *Sullivan*, Alabama citizens were free to draw their own conclusions about what had happened. They might have concluded that the trial verdict was unfair, and that L. B. Sullivan was a scoundrel.

In theory, strict libel laws might improve the ability of speakers to articulate their views. Speakers will be forced to research their positions carefully, since if they say something false they may have to pay damages. When they do speak, however, they may find their ideas taken more seriously, precisely because everybody knows that false statements subject speakers to a stiff penalty. Moreover, libel trials, if fairly conducted, may give speakers a prominent public forum in which to prove the truth of their claims.[5]

Of course, libel laws do presuppose that auditors will sometimes misjudge the truth of a speaker's statements—otherwise, falsehoods could never damage anybody's reputation. Does it follow that libel laws fail to respect the people's ability to distinguish truth from falsehood? Not at all. The premise underlying libel laws is obviously true. We all know that unfounded rumors can damage reputations. It is one thing for government to respect people's freedom to make judgments about which opinions are valuable or correct, and quite another for government to assume people's judgments are infallible.

If we think that restrictive libel laws are inconsistent with the state's obligation to respect the people's ability to evaluate ideas, that conclusion must rest upon a pragmatic judgment—such as a concern that juries will reach the wrong outcome, or that responsible speakers will be silenced because it is expensive to defend against meritless suits. *Sullivan* thus has an ineliminable strategic component. I do not intend that observation as a complaint. Harry Kalven said soon after the *Sullivan* decision that it was an occasion for "dancing in the streets."[6] I agree; *Sullivan* marked a turning point in the Court's treatment of free speech claims. Instead of merely articulating principles of free speech, the *Sullivan* Court created effective protection for political dissent and debate. The Court continued that project in subsequent cases.[7] But efficacy sounds in the domain of strategy. To praise *Sullivan* because it put in place effective protections for free speech is to say that *Sullivan* was a cause for celebration not because it was an especially pure or precise statement of moral principle, but because it combined moral principle with wise strategy.

Sullivan is not unusual in this regard. On the contrary, as others have pointed out before me, strategic judgments are ubiquitous in constitutional law.[8] To be sure, the exact boundary between the moral and strategic domains will be dependent upon the content of one's moral principles, and it may be possible to justify some important rulings without reference to strategic considerations. Consider, for example, the Court's famous conclusion in *Brown v. Bd. of Education* that "[s]eparate educational facilities are inherently unequal."[9] Some people subscribe to the view that equality principles forbid the government from segregating people along lines of social caste; others believe that equality principles make it immoral to classify people on the basis of race. If you hold either of those views, then you might regard *Brown*'s holding as a pure statement of moral principle. On the other hand, some people believe that racial segregation is impermissible only insofar as it is designed to disadvantage minorities. If that is your view, you may find it attractive to view *Brown*'s holding as dependent partly upon a strategic judgment—namely, that segregated educational institutions will, in practice, tend to make racial minorities worse off. Moreover, even if you conceive of *Brown*'s holding as a pure statement of principle, its implementation will eventually require a host of strategic choices—about, for example, what litigants must show in order to prove that the relevant principle has been violated, or about what remedies should be available to litigants who meet that burden.[10]

In sum, converting principles into legal doctrine will inevitably require strategic choices. If we are attracted to the institution of judicial review as a practical mechanism for enforcing moral principles, we cannot recommend that judges resolve only moral questions and leave strategic judgments to others. That recommendation would assign judges very little authority; the courts would have to pull back from decisions, including *Sullivan* and *Brown*, that enjoy widespread approval. If judges in fact have a comparative advantage over other American political officials when it comes to the identification of moral principle, and if we want judges to give practical effect to that comparative advantage, then we must permit judges to make some strategic judgments as well—even if we believe that judges have *no* comparative advantage over other political institutions with regard to matters of strategy.

Of course, it does not follow that judges have license to resolve every strategic question that affects any constitutional principle. If judges make incompetent strategic choices, they may impair the principles they seek to defend. The road to maladministration and misgovernance is paved with good intentions. Indeed, in my view the strongest arguments for judicial restraint derive not (as people commonly suppose) from judicial review's counter-majoritarian features, but from the inability of judges to claim expertise with regard to the practicalities that predominate when moral principle is translated into legal policy.

This chapter and the next address some of the issues that arise from the interplay of strategy and moral principle in constitutional adjudication. This chapter examines whether the strategic element of constitutional adjudication requires any refinement to the methodological conclusions reached in Chapter 4. Chapter 6 will attempt to identify which strategic issues are most suitable for judicial resolution.

The Mysterious Authority of Tradition

When Supreme Court justices confront novel constitutional claims, they often appeal to tradition for guidance. The justices say, for example, that the Fourteenth Amendment to the Constitution protects those rights that are "deeply rooted in this nation's history and tradition,"[11] or which are "so rooted in the traditions and conscience of our people so as to be ranked as fundamental."[12] These formulae are frequently incanted but rarely explained. Why should it matter whether a claimed constitutional right has solid foundations in tradition? Why not demand instead that judges enforce those rights (and only those rights) that the government is morally obliged to respect, regardless of whether the American government has traditionally respected them? Traditional practices may, after all, be exquisitely unjust. Moreover, judicial solicitude for individual liberty is likely to be most valuable precisely when the individual's interests are *not* protected by extant legal and social traditions; if Americans have traditionally respected some right, judicial action on its behalf will be largely superfluous.

Some justices defend tradition's authority by reference to its ability to constrain judges from making moral choices. Justices White and Scalia, for example, have used that sort of argument to explain why judges should use tradition to limit the substantive rights protected by the Due Process Clause.[13] This justification for privileging tradition obviously depends upon the idea that it is troubling or illegitimate for judges to decide cases on moral grounds. Even were we to embrace that basic premise, the resulting argument is highly dubious. Tradition is itself an opaque text; judges must make controversial interpretive claims in order to ascertain what counts as "American tradition" and what it means for contested rights and liberties. Judges will have no morally neutral way to make the necessary interpretive judgments.[14] Even if they did, it would remain difficult to explain why judges should endow traditional rights with constitutionally protected status. Judicial solicitude for tradition seems both arbitrary (since traditions may be unjust) and superfluous (since a traditional right enjoys, by hypothesis, widespread recognition and respect). If judicial review were in fact problematic from the standpoint of democracy, the most plausible response would be to urge judges to intervene as rarely possible—not to counsel them to intervene whenever legislatures make novel intrusions upon traditional practices.

I will not, however, pursue the internal inconsistencies of the position adopted by Justices White and Scalia. In the preceding chapters, I have argued that constitutional adjudication in the United States *requires* judges to make moral judgments. The forthright consideration of moral arguments by unelected judges is an asset to democracy, not an embarrassment. For those who accept the basic argument of this book, the explanation that Justices White and Scalia offer for tradition's authority is utterly impotent. If their rationale were the only way to justify the Court's use of tradition, we should advise judges to follow adjudicative protocols that are less historical and more openly normative.[15] Fourteenth Amendment jurisprudence in fact contains interpretive maxims well-suited to that assignment. Though judges often allude to tradition, they quote with equal reverence formulae holding that the Constitution protects those rights which are "implicit in the concept of ordered liberty"[16] or which "are . . . *fundamental;* which belong to the citizens of all free governments [and] for 'the purposes [of securing] which men enter into society.'"[17]

Yet, we cannot dismiss appeals to tradition so abruptly. The most intriguing uses of tradition have come not from justices who are hostile to judicial exercises of moral judgment, but from moderates, like Justices O'Connor, Powell, and the second Harlan. These justices claim that tradition is valuable as a guide to the exercise of moral judgment.

For example, when Justice Harlan called upon his colleagues to recognize a constitutional right on the part of married couples to use contraceptives, he wrote that the task of identifying fundamental rights was "of necessity a rational process, [but] not . . . one where judges have felt free to roam where unguided speculation might take them." According to Harlan, judges are appropriately guided by "the traditions from which [this country] developed as well as those from which it broke." He added, "[t]hat tradition is a living thing."[18] Harlan's words have echoed through the Court's subsequent decisions about privacy and personal autonomy. They have attracted moderates like Powell and O'Connor, who have often cast the swing vote on a divided Court. Harlan's statements about tradition and judgment played a key role, for example, in the plurality opinion co-authored by Justices O'Connor, Kennedy, and Souter in *Casey v. Planned Parenthood of Southeast Pennsylvania*,[19] the case that saved the abortion right from being overruled by a group of justices that included White and Scalia.

How can tradition sensibly guide the exercise of moral judgment?[20] Harlan's rhetoric is sonorous, but his view borders on mystical. He specifies no method by which to identify tradition or distill its meaning. In light of this obscurity, one might dismiss references to tradition as nothing more than obfuscatory boilerplate, inserted by justices who want to have it both ways. These justices, we might hypothesize, recognize that it is desirable for the Supreme Court to stand up for moral principle, but they are reluctant to admit the role that contested principles are playing in their decisions.[21] Or, alternatively, one might suppose that the references to tradition are serving precisely the same function as did Justice Brandeis's references to the framers in *Whitney*.[22] That is, the justices appeal to tradition to show that their moral principles are sufficiently widely shared that they can be offered on the people's behalf. If that is tradition's best use, then it will rarely, if ever, be used to select among competing moral principles; instead, moral principles will be used to select among competing interpretations of American tradition.

There is something to both of these hypotheses. Tradition cannot possibly bear the weight that some justices have placed upon it. The Court should acknowledge more forthrightly the extent to which its decisions turn upon contested moral principles. On the other hand, the two skeptical hypotheses do not tell the whole story. Tradition has, I shall argue, an additional role to play in constitutional cases: tradition may in some cases be a useful guide to the best *means* by which the judiciary can pursue constitutionally desirable *ends*. The validity of moral principles may be largely independent of existing societal practices, but it is hard to believe that suitable strategies for implementing those principles will be equally independent of historical and social context.

Tradition and Strategy

The impact of any particular procedural device, political institution, or legal doctrine is an empirical question, and history provides a reservoir of relevant data. Moreover, many principles will reflect an implicit balance among competing obligations; when that is so, traditional practice may embody a reasonable accommodation of the government's multiple obligations. Suppose, for example, that we accept the following principle: "parents should be free to direct the upbringing of their children, except insofar as parental freedom is inconsistent with the best interests of the child." The principle references two distinct values, parental autonomy and children's well-being. Government must maintain rules and institutions that protect both values. How much freedom should government give to parents? There is widespread agreement about some conclusions: parents may not beat their children, nor may parents prohibit their children from learning how to read. But do parents have a right to teach their daughters that females have no chance for happiness or success in the field of scientific research? More specifically, do parents have a right to insist that their daughters attend private schools in which girls are discouraged from pursuing scientific careers (or, perhaps, any profession at all)? A judge confronted with this question in a constitutional case might consider the freedoms traditionally accorded to parents by American law and society. The judge might conclude that those freedoms reflected a workable balance between the government's obligation to respect parental autonomy and its obligation to ensure that children flourish. And the judge might therefore worry that departures from that tradition would engender a host of unintended and perverse consequences—so that, for example, recognizing new "children's rights" would unleash a torrent of meritless lawsuits and bureaucratic regulations that would punish or paralyze parents who were in fact treating their children decently.

A judge "might consider, might conclude, and might therefore worry"—all those "mights" are essential, because history and tradition are rich turf for fallacious reasoning. States traditionally refused, for example, to prosecute husbands who raped their wives.[23] It does not follow that this tradition represented a reasonable balance between the government's obligation to respect marital privacy and its obligation to protect people against physical assault. Traditions may reflect moral errors: for example, the view that women are morally inferior to men. Traditions may also reflect unjust power relationships: for example, the political, legal, and financial advantage that men long enjoyed as a result of unfair discrimination against women. So if there is some societal tradition that allows parents to discourage the scientific and professional aspirations of their daughters, that tradition might be terribly unjust—it might reflect a failure to appreciate or respect the equality of women. Absent critical examination, it is impossible to say whether any tradition represents a "workable balance" achieved through long-term commitment to a principle that deserves our respect, or whether it is the embodiment of an enduring injustice that cries out for constitutional remedy.

History and tradition thus are not magical formulae that can make complex strategic issues disappear. They are sources of data that require analysis and interpretation. Nor are history and tradition the only, or obviously the best, sources of data: judges faced with strategic, empirical questions can seek help from social science, comparative studies, personal experience, or common sense. But these alternatives have their own problems. Tradition need not be a perfect resource in order to be useful when consulted with appropriate caution. Citation to extant practices is no substitute for moral analysis, but tradition (if carefully interpreted) may provide useful clues about how to apply moral principles to practical problems.

This role for tradition is consistent with the argument advanced in the last chapter. If judges examine tradition because it is a useful guide to doctrinal strategy, they are not setting history up as a rival to justice. They are instead making tradition the servant of justice. Indeed, they are doing so in a way that is not at all special to adjudication or constitutional interpretation; legislators, too, might seek useful guidance from tradition. In theory, then, tradition's utility for strategic decision-making might legitimate the conspicuous homage that some Supreme Court justices have paid to tradition. To determine whether this explanation is sound, we need to develop a more precise account of the rights and liberties at stake in the cases in which tradition figures prominently.

Novel Intrusions on Valuable Liberties

The Supreme Court's most acute invocations of tradition have occurred in a series of cases about bodily integrity, reproduction, the family, and sexuality. Justice Harlan's oft-quoted reflections upon "the traditions from which [this country] developed as well as those from which it broke" were provoked by a Connecticut law banning the use of contraceptives. More recently, interpretations of tradition have played a pivotal role in cases about abortion, homosexual sodomy, extended family households, euthanasia, the paternity rights of adulterous fathers, and parental autonomy.[24] Judges and commentators usually trace this line of cases back to *Meyer v. Nebraska*[25] and *Pierce v. Society of Sisters*,[26] *Lochner*-era precedents in which the Supreme Court held that the Fourteenth Amendment's Due Process Clause protected parents' right to control the education and upbringing of their children. The *Meyer* Court struck down a Nebraska law that prohibited schoolteachers from instructing children in a foreign language, and the *Pierce* Court held unconstitutional an Oregon law that required parents to send their children to public schools.

The opinions in *Meyer* and *Pierce* are refreshingly brief. They contain no extended discussion of tradition's role in constitutional interpretation, but *Meyer*, which is the earlier of the two, does contain significant references to tradition. *Meyer* affirmed that the Fourteenth Amendment protects the right of people "to enjoy those privileges long recognized at common law as essential to the orderly pursuit of happiness by free men." And the Court declared that "[t]he American people have always regarded education and acquisition of knowledge as matters of supreme importance which should be diligently promoted." The Court also said that "[k]nowledge of the German language . . . [h]eretofore . . . has been commonly looked upon as helpful and desirable."[27]

One must be cautious about pushing these references too far; *Meyer's* allusions to common-law precedent and American practice are intermingled with observations about the "natural duty" of parents to educate their children and about whether learning German can "reasonably be regarded as harmful."[28] Nevertheless, it is possible to understand *Meyer*'s invocation of traditional American practices and beliefs as a response to a strategic question. Unless one is mired in the textual fetishism discussed in Chapter 4, it will seem plausible that the Constitution recognizes some principle protecting the freedom of parents to control the upbringing of their own children. Let's suppose, so that we can be more precise, that the principle takes the form we considered earlier in this chapter: "parents should be free to direct the upbringing of their children, except insofar as parental freedom is inconsistent with the best interests of the child." The crucial question is how far this freedom should extend. As Justice Holmes—who dissented from the *Meyer* decision—observed, "No one would doubt that a teacher might be forbidden to teach many things."[29] So, for example, states could prohibit teachers from providing young children with sexually explicit materials. Moreover, the state is presumably free to require that children receive instruction in English—because learning English is in the best interests of any child growing up in the United States, an English-speaking country. If we put Nebraska's claim in its best possible light, it would go something like this: the only reliable way to ensure that children will learn English is to prohibit them from being taught in any other language.[30] In the view of Holmes, this question was one "upon which men reasonably might differ" and he therefore concluded that he was "unable to say that the Constitution prevents the experiment being tried."[31]

So viewed, *Meyer* comes down to an empirical disagreement about whether Nebraska's law was necessary to implement an agreed-upon principle. The majority had various ways to answer Holmes. One was simply to say that Nebraska's judgment was, despite Holmes's assertion to the contrary, unreasonable—and *Meyer* can be read to take that path. But one can also read *Meyer* to say something more complex: namely, that never before had Americans thought that the best interests of children depended upon denying them knowledge of foreign languages. The Nebraska law was, in other words, a novel intrusion upon a traditional practice that had, in American experience, worked reasonably well to protect two competing interests. And because the law made a novel intrusion upon a well-established, healthy tradition, it ought to be regarded with skepticism. The state had the obligation to show that the tradition was defective, or that the world had changed in some way that rendered it unreasonable to continue to respect traditional practices. The state came forward with no argument sufficient to justify that burden; hence the Court intervened to protect parental freedom against the state's unprecedented infringement.

Here, then, is one way to defend the Court's use of tradition: where a law makes novel intrusions upon choices, practices, or commitments that government and society have traditionally respected as private, courts might reasonably demand that the government demonstrate a need for its new imposition on liberty. A surprising number of the Court's privacy and autonomy cases can be interpreted as challenges to unusual or unprecedented forms of regulation. The Connecticut birth control cases, *Poe v. Ullman*[32] and *Griswold v. Connecticut*,[33] fit that pattern. The Connecticut laws had been on the books for a long time, but they were unusual. Although various states had restricted the *sale* of contraceptives, only Connecticut criminalized their *use*, and Connecticut's ban encompassed even the use of contraceptives by married couples.[34]

A similar point may apply in *Moore v. City of East Cleveland*,[35] another case in which the Court invoked American tradition to justify upholding an unenumerated constitutional right. In *Moore*, the Court struck down a zoning ordinance that prohibited certain extended families from living together in a single residence. East Cleveland had used the ordinance to prosecute Inez Moore, a grandmother who had violated the law by housing two of her grandsons; the arrangement would have been permitted by East Cleveland's ordinance had the grandsons been brothers, but they were cousins. At least one justice thought that the zoning ordinance in *Moore*, like the Connecticut law in *Griswold*, was aberrational. In a concurring opinion, Justice Stevens wrote that "[t]here seems to be no precedent for an ordinance which excludes any of an owner's relatives from the group of persons who may occupy his residence on a permanent basis."[36]

Comparable arguments were available in other privacy and autonomy cases, including some in which justices sympathetic to the claimed right did not rely upon tradition. For example, *Eisenstadt v. Baird*[37] generalized *Griswold* to protect the use of contraceptives by single persons as well as married ones; *Carey v. Population Services*[38] further extended

Griswold to encompass the sale of contraceptives as well as their use. The regulations challenged in *Eisenstadt* and *Carey* might at first seem traditional rather than novel: laws criminalizing the sale and distribution of contraceptives to unmarried persons were relatively common. Yet, as the opinions in *Eisenstadt* and *Carey* noted, these laws were riddled with exceptions and rarely enforced.[39] As a result, contraceptives were widely available. Prosecutors chose targets selectively. *Eisenstadt*, for example, was a Massachusetts case in which the state brought criminal charges against a man who had delivered a lecture on contraception at Boston University. The state seemed to suppress the distribution of contraceptives only in order to suppress public discussion about the use of contraceptives—a policy that raises concerns related to the freedom of speech as well as privacy. Although the laws stricken in *Eisenstadt* and *Carey* may have been ordinary, their enforcement was extraordinary and could be characterized as a departure from traditional practice.

Tradition and the Abortion Cases

Traditional practice thus provides one baseline against which judges can make a *prima facie* assessment of the strength of a state interest. When a state makes an exceptional intrusion upon some liberty that American governments have traditionally respected, the Court should not simply defer to the state's claim that the intrusion is essential to safeguard public well-being. That doesn't explain, however, what the majority in *Casey v. Planned Parenthood* meant to accomplish when it quoted Justice Harlan's homage to tradition.[40] *Casey* dealt with abortion laws, and neither the enactment nor the enforcement of such laws could reasonably be regarded as a social novelty. "Back-alley abortions" took place in back alleys because the state was prepared to prosecute physicians who performed abortions. Indeed, even after *Roe*, societal traditions have made abortions hard to obtain. Most physicians are reluctant to provide them. In a few states, abortion services are virtually unavailable.[41] So how can reflection upon "'the traditions from which [this country] developed as well as those from which it broke'" help to justify the result in *Casey* and *Roe?*

It can't. To be sure, the Texas law challenged in *Roe* was non-traditional. Texas had the nation's most absolute anti-abortion statute. The statute made no exception even for pregnancies that resulted from rape, as was alleged to be the case in *Roe*.[42] Had the Court in *Roe* merely stricken the Texas statute, it might have pointed out that Texas denied a liberty (namely, the liberty of women to terminate pregnancies that had been imposed upon them by violent crimes) which American states traditionally respected. But the Court's ruling in *Roe* went far beyond the peculiarities of the Texas statute. *Roe* held, and *Casey* reaffirmed, that a "woman has the [constitutional] right to terminate her pregnancy" until the fetus becomes viable.[43] That right secures liberties broader than those that women had traditionally enjoyed. *Roe* and *Casey* did not restrict their focus to regulations that were exceptional, unprecedented, or abnormal; on the contrary, they proscribed regulations that multiple states had regularly and vigorously enforced.

That does not mean that *Roe* and *Casey* were wrongly decided. Tradition's legitimate role in constitutional adjudication is merely instrumental. The judiciary's most basic responsibility under the Ninth Amendment, the Due Process Clauses, and the Equal Protection Clause is to identify and implement principles of justice. Sometimes the judiciary will be able to accomplish that task by defending traditional practices, but sometimes the judiciary will have to reform or undermine such practices. The right recognized in *Times v. Sullivan*, for example, curtailed traditional state-law protections for the personal reputation of public figures. The crucial questions in *Roe* and *Casey* were questions about justice, not tradition: first, what moral principle (if any) protects the right of a woman to abort a pregnancy, and second, in what way and to what extent can the judiciary implement that principle?

Hidden Puzzles about Missing Principles

Unfortunately, the Court has routinely given tradition more authority than it deserves and thereby ducked the questions that matter most. The pattern is nicely illustrated by Justice Powell's opinion for the Court in *Moore v. City of East Cleveland*. As we have seen, the ordinance stricken in *Moore* was arguably a departure from tradition, and so tradition might legitimately have aided the justices to decide whether a particular regulatory device was a justifiable imposition upon people's freedom to associate with and care for their relatives. But Justice Powell characterized tradition's relevance differently: he wrote, "[o]ur decisions establish that the Constitution protects the sanctity of the family precisely because the institution of the family is deeply rooted in this Nation's history and tradition."[44] In Powell's view, tradition determined not only how best to implement basic principles of liberty, but also which liberties deserved constitutional status. That was an error. It would have been better to say that both the Constitution and American tradition protect familial relationships because people have a profound interest in controlling what happens to their bodies; in choosing whether or not to have children; and in deciding with whom to share their lives. Perhaps tradition has something useful to tell us about how best to implement principles that protect these liberties. But the value of the liberties does not itself turn upon the existence of a protective tradition. On the contrary, if these liberties were denied in some society, we should brand it unjust.

By using tradition to identify constitutionally protected liberty interests, justices sympathetic to unenumerated rights have caused two kinds of mischief. They have invited the argument that practices disfavored by tradition enjoy no constitutional protection. More important, they have also obscured the principles at stake in privacy and autonomy cases. Justices have used tradition not only to question the importance of state interests, but also to identify practices that are important to liberty. Justices have thereby evaded the need to specify precisely the principles they are enforcing. They have been content to point out that the practice they are protecting has traditionally been part of the liberty Americans have enjoyed. But the fact that a practice has gone unregulated does not mean that it is important to any principle of constitutional justice.

In some of the Court's unenumerated liberties cases, this problem is superficial: if one is sympathetic to the constitutional claim, one can easily supply a principle of justice to back it up. So, for example, *Pierce* and *Meyer* dealt with the freedom of parents to educate their children; *Moore* upheld the freedom of family members to nurture bonds of care and companionship; and cases such as *Stanley v. Illinois*[45] and *Michael H. v. Gerald D.*[46] addressed a father's freedom to participate in the upbringing of his child. All of these cases involve relationships that are widely acknowledged to be constitutive of human flourishing and closely connected with people's highest and most noble aspirations. Although we will undoubtedly disagree about particular cases, most of us will endorse some principles that guarantee us the freedom to be parents, to keep our families together, and to guide the education of our children.

Much more puzzling are cases like *Griswold* and its progeny: the contraception cases, the abortion cases, and *Bowers*. Conventional analysis lumps these decisions together with *Pierce, Moore,* and *Michael H.* as "substantive due process" cases about privacy and autonomy.[47] In fact, the cases involve significantly different claims. In *Pierce, Moore,* and *Michael H.,* the constitutional claimants are asking for the right to take on responsibilities: they want to participate in familial relationships that no doubt will bring them important benefits and great joys, but that also demand considerable sacrifices and impose weighty obligations. In *Griswold, Eisenstadt, Carey,* and *Bowers,* individuals wanted the freedom to engage in non-procreative sexual intercourse without the risk of pregnancy (in *Griswold, Eisenstadt,* and *Carey*) or criminal prosecution (in all of those cases, plus *Bowers*). Non-procreative sex is arguably a hedonistic indulgence, and it is far from obvious that the Constitution should treat it with the same respect as a parent's desire to care for her child.

In *Eisenstadt,* the Court described its contraception cases as about "the right of the individual, married or single, to be free from unwarranted governmental intrusion into matters so fundamentally affecting a person as the decision whether to bear or beget a child."[48] If that characterization were apt, *Griswold* and *Carey* would be like *Pierce* and *Moore:* cases about the right to decide whether to participate in certain noble and weighty relationships. But the characterization is a bit of a dodge unless, perhaps, the Court is tacitly assuming that contraception is important to prevent pregnancies resulting from rape. After all, even if the state denies you access to contraception, you can still decide whether or not to bear or beget a child, provided that you are free to decide whether or not to engage in heterosexual intercourse. Problems arise only if you're forced to have unwanted sex, or if you want to have sex without becoming a parent.

Roe, Casey, and the other abortion cases are more complex: they stand at the intersection of the *Pierce* line of cases and the *Griswold* line. Jane Roe and her successors were not asking for the freedom to engage in non-procreative sex. These women were already pregnant; they wanted the right to terminate their pregnancies so that they could control their health, so that they could decide not to become mothers (or decide when to become mothers), and so that they could govern their own capacity to hold jobs, participate in public affairs, and form new relationships. These are interests comparable to those at stake in *Pierce* and *Moore*. But the right recognized in *Roe* and *Casey* is broad enough to encompass even pregnancies that resulted from voluntary, consensual sexual intercourse—indeed, it extends to pregnancies that resulted because a woman who desired not to become pregnant nevertheless elected, for whatever reason, to have sex without using birth control. That is what gives rhetorical bite to Justice White's acid dissent in a companion case to *Roe*, in which he declared that *Roe* presupposed that "the Constitution of the United States values the convenience, whim, or caprice of the mother more than the . . . potential life of the fetus."[49] Decisions about whether to bear a child cannot fairly be categorized as matters of "convenience, whim, or caprice," but one might fairly use such terms to describe the failure to use contraceptives—or, more controversially, to describe the pursuit of sexual pleasure.

Of course, moral principles may require that the government allow you some freedom to escape the consequences of your own choices. For example, an unhappy marriage is a foreseeable risk of marriage— just as pregnancy is a foreseeable consequence of heterosexual intercourse. It does not follow that the government is free to prohibit divorce. Likewise, a pregnant woman has a profound liberty interest in deciding whether to carry her pregnancy to term, even if that pregnancy resulted from her own mistakes or imprudence. Still, one might attempt to justify anti-abortion laws as, in part, a regulation of sexual intercourse. If non-procreative sex is merely a species of hedonistic behavior, then perhaps the state has the power to attach a heavy legal price to it. If so, the state might concede that women have a right to decide whether to terminate a pregnancy, but insist that women lose that right when they voluntarily have heterosexual intercourse. This argument renders *Roe* and *Casey* analogous to the Court's other cases about sexual freedom. In *Griswold*, *Eisenstadt*, and *Bowers*, the state tried to claim that when people engaged in a certain kind of sexual relationship, they forfeited their general right to be free from incarceration. Likewise, on the argument we are now considering, women have a right to decide whether or not to continue a pregnancy, but they cannot insist upon that right if the pregnancy is the consequence of their own hedonistic behavior. Is that position untenable? If so, why? Is there a constitutional principle that protects the right to engage in non-procreative sexual intercourse? If such a principle exists, the justification for it must lie outside "the right of an individual, married or single, to be free from unwarranted governmental intrusion into . . . the decision whether to bear or beget a child."

The justices who wrote for the Court in *Griswold, Eisenstadt, Carey, Roe,* and *Casey* never acknowledged that these cases were in any way about sexual freedom—the Court's rhetoric is all about tradition, marriage, and reproductive autonomy. Indeed, there is great irony in the way that tradition has threaded through the Supreme Court's cases about sex. In *Griswold,* the justices avoided discussing the constitutional status of sexual conduct by emphasizing that the case dealt with marriage. "We deal here with a right of privacy older than the Bill of Rights," wrote Justice Douglas for the Court. "Marriage is a coming together for better or for worse, hopefully enduring, and intimate to the degree of being sacred."[50] In *Eisenstadt,* which dealt with sexual relations between unmarried persons, the Court avoided talking about sex and instead cited *Griswold.* Yet, insofar as *Griswold* relied on the traditional respect accorded the marriage relationship, it is not clear that *Griswold* supports the right claimed in *Eisenstadt.* Indeed, one might think that American culture had valued marriage as a means to regulate and discipline sexuality: the state's traditional respect for marriage may, in other words, have reflected a judgment or belief that other forms of sexual relationship were harmful or immoral.[51] If that were so, and if the state's traditional attitude toward marriage was in any way crucial to the outcome in *Griswold,* then *Griswold* seems quite consistent with the state law challenged in *Eisenstadt.* Far from dishonoring marriage, the Massachusetts law in *Eisenstadt* presupposed that it was desirable for people to marry before having sex.[52] Nevertheless, viewed through the lens of *Eisenstadt* and *Carey,* *Griswold*'s celebration of the marriage tradition became precedential support for the decidedly non-traditional rights embraced by the *Casey* majority and the *Bowers* dissent.[53] The Court's reliance on a combination of legal tradition (its own precedent) and social tradition (respect for marriage) has enabled justices to give constitutional protection to sexual conduct without naming any principle to justify that result.

Sexual Freedom and the Protection of Vulnerable Groups

Some commentators have suggested that *Roe* and *Bowers* are better viewed as raising concerns about discrimination and the mistreat-

ment of politically vulnerable groups—in particular, *Roe* and *Casey* are
about discrimination against women, and *Bowers* is about discrimination against homosexuals.[54] As I shall later explain, I think that these
theorists are correct to emphasize the possibility of illegitimate government animus. But understanding *Griswold* and its progeny through that
lens is by no means easy, and it turns out to be a serious mistake to try
to reconceptualize them in terms of vulnerable *groups*. Indeed, that
move leaves us without any apparent way to explain *Griswold*,
Eisenstadt, or *Carey*, none of which seem to involve vulnerable groups.
But let's put those examples aside: what is more interesting is that the
explanation proves unsatisfactory even with regard to *Roe*, and perhaps
with regard to *Bowers*. Take abortion first. In one respect, abortion laws
look like a classic instance of discriminatory legislation: these laws impose burdens on women that men do not share equally, since only
women get pregnant, and therefore only women will ever be forced to
carry a child to term. Yet, if indeed "there is a substantial state interest
in potential life throughout pregnancy,"[55] it is hard to see how the state
could protect that interest without imposing disparate burdens on men
and women. The state could (and no doubt would) prohibit men from
assisting women to have abortions, or from pressuring women to have
abortions that they don't want. But precisely because women, and only
women, get pregnant, the state's regulation will have a different impact
on women than on men. The connection between a person's sex and
the regulatory purpose of the law is too tight: women's unique capacity
to sustain fetal life is biological, not the consequence of stereotype or
accident or legal generalization. As a result, the discriminatory character of abortion regulations does not raise the same presumption of in-
validity that would attach to most instances of discrimination.

I don't mean to deny that laws prohibiting abortion impose an unfair burden on women—I think they do. I just don't think the fact
that the burden falls on women tells us why the burden is unfair. Indeed, it would be entirely possible for abortion rights to be more popular with men than with women. Polls have sometimes suggested precisely that.[56] One can easily devise cynical explanations for this result.
For example: perhaps some men like casual sex, dislike contraceptives,
and want the freedom to coax their girlfriends to abort their pregnancies. Insofar as abortion laws restrict sexual freedom, they restrict the
sexual freedom of men as well as women, and men may resent that imposition more keenly than do women.[57]

The anti-discrimination argument works better in *Bowers*. Homosexuals have been subject to grotesque and outrageous discrimination,[58] and, although it is easy to see why many women oppose abortion rights, it is hard to imagine why any significant number of homosexuals would favor the criminalization of sodomy. In fact, the Georgia policy at issue in *Bowers* smacked of bias. To defend its law in the Supreme Court, Georgia decided, somewhat disingenuously, to declare that the law prohibited only homosexual sodomy, and not heterosexual sodomy. It is reasonable to think that the state's only reason for outlawing one form of sodomy, but not the other, is bias against homosexuals.

Yet, while the anti-discrimination theory surely captures part of what is at stake in *Bowers*, it does not provide a fully satisfactory account of the constitutional claims asserted there. If one believes that *Bowers* was wrongly decided, it is implausible to think that Georgia could have saved its law by construing it to prohibit all sodomy, homosexual or heterosexual. Moreover, in *Bowers*, as in *Roe*, the connection between the state's asserted purpose and its classification is so tight as to raise problems for ordinary arguments about discriminatory classifications. Georgia was punishing homosexual *conduct*, not the *status* of being homosexual.[59] The law challenged in *Bowers* does not prohibit gay and lesbian persons from publicly declaring their love and their sexual desire for one another, or from cohabiting with one another, or from kissing in public. If the state has any legitimate reason to object to homosexual sodomy, then obviously its efforts to act upon that reason will have a disparate impact upon homosexuals. The illegitimacy of the classification must ultimately depend in part upon the idea that the state has no good reason to prohibit homosexual sodomy—or no constitutional power to do so. Describing the law in *Bowers* as a discrimination against homosexuals seems to assume that premise, rather than explain it.

One can try to fix these stories about vulnerable groups by adding ptolemaic epicycles of varying kinds. But if the point of that effort is to avoid addressing the awkward possibility that the Court's decisions presuppose a constitutional right to sexual freedom, then I think the project is doomed to fail. Here's why: I suspect that almost everybody who is sympathetic to *Griswold*, *Eisenstadt*, *Carey*, *Casey*, and the *Bowers* dissent (or even four out of the five) would likewise be sympathetic to other claims that more obviously presuppose constitutional solicitude for non-procreative sexual activity in general—even when that sexual activity is not distinctive to some recognizable, politically vulnerable group. For example, suppose that a state prohibits heterosexual fellatio, consensual or not. The state argues that men sometimes pressure or coerce reluctant women to perform fellatio. The state would like to prosecute these men for rape, but the men always assert that the woman consented, and it is hard for the state to prove beyond a reasonable doubt that she did not. The state accordingly decides to simplify prosecution by banning fellatio altogether, whether consensual or not.[60]

Is the law that I have described unconstitutional? I think that it is, and I think that most other people who are sympathetic to *Griswold* or *Roe* would agree. But why? Because the decision to engage in fellatio is related to the decision whether or not to bear or beget children? Because heterosexual couples who engage in oral sex constitute a politically vulnerable class? Neither of these suggestions seem sensible. Perhaps we could come up with some theory that would dispose of my hypothetical anti-fellatio law without recognizing any constitutional principle pertaining to sexual conduct in general. But it is easy to generate more such hypotheticals, and, as the examples accumulate, it becomes hard for those of us who endorse *Griswold* and its progeny to deny that there must be some constitutional principle which requires the state to respect people's sexual freedom. So, for example, suppose that a state prohibits consensual anal intercourse; the state supports its law with evidence that anal sex is associated with greater health risks than other forms of sexual contact. Or suppose that another state criminalizes promiscuity, defined as having sexual relations with more than six persons in a single, twelve-month period; the state defends its law on the ground that promiscuity spreads sexually transmitted diseases. Imagine that still another state requires the use of condoms in any non-procreative sexual encounter that might expose a person to the semen of his or her sexual partner; the state defends its measure as a means to prevent the spread of sexually transmitted diseases, especially AIDS. Are there people who would defend *Griswold, Eisenstadt, Carey,* and *Casey,* and who would join the dissent in *Bowers,* but who nevertheless would uphold the constitutionality of *any* of the laws described in the last paragraph? No doubt there are some—but I suspect they are few.[61] Is there any way to explain the unconstitutionality of all these laws without recognizing a constitutionally protected liberty interest in non-procreative sex? I suppose there must be; constitutional lawyers are clever people.[62] But the most likely explanation is this: those of us who are sympathetically inclined toward *Griswold* and its progeny do in fact believe that the Court should closely scrutinize *any* law that restricts consensual sexual conduct of adults.[63] The crucial question is why.

The Constitutional Significance of Sexual Conduct

To fully defend *Griswold* and its progeny (including the *Bowers* dissent), one must acknowledge that these cases are partly about sexual freedom and explain why sexual conduct deserves constitutional solicitude, which the Court has been reluctant to do. In his *Bowers* dissent, Justice Blackmun tried to do that. He lauded sexual behavior as constitutive of meaningful relationships. Blackmun said that "sexual intimacy is 'a sensitive key relationship of human existence, central to family life, community welfare, and the development of human personality.'"[64] He said that *Bowers* was not about "a fundamental right to engage in homosexual sodomy" but rather about "the fundamental interest all individuals have in controlling the nature of their intimate associations with others."[65] "Intimate association" is an ambiguous term; it might refer either to a deep but platonic friendship or to an anonymous sexual encounter. Friendship, like reproductive autonomy, is manifestly important to individual flourishing. It is therefore easy to explain why people should enjoy a constitutional right to cultivate friendships. But do references to "friendship" or "love" provide a convincing explanation for the right recognized by the dissenters in *Bowers?* It is far from obvious that sexual contact is an essential constituent of loving relationships.[66] Moreover, Blackmun's argument would presumably allow the government to target a few sexual practices for prosecution, provided that it left available a sufficiently wide range of substitutes. For example, even if sex is constitutive of loving relationships, it is implausible to suggest that any one specific sexual practice—such as, for example, heterosexual sodomy—is "central to family life, community welfare, and the development of human personality." And, in any event, a loving relationship is certainly not a pre-requisite to sex. *Eisenstadt, Carey, Casey,* and the *Bowers* dissent all recognize rights not in any way confined to durable relationships. They protect casual encounters along with committed unions.

There is another way to explain why sexual conduct might have special constitutional value. Non-procreative sex might be important to human flourishing even if it were nothing more than a way of pursuing corporeal pleasures. Such pleasures may not be as noble or uplifting as love or friendship, but it does not follow that people can live well without them. We might therefore insist that the government should allow everybody some space for the private pursuit of pleasure, and we might recommend that the Constitution safeguard sexual freedom as part of what Brandeis called "the right to be let alone—the most comprehensive of rights and the right most valued by civilized man."[67] That slogan captures the common intuition that sexual practices should be considered "private," and that the government has no business sticking its nose (or its police officers) into the bedrooms of citizens.

But this argument, like the others we have thus far considered, quickly runs into trouble. Most people assume that the government has considerable power to regulate the private pursuit of pleasure. For example, states prohibit the possession or consumption of small amounts of marijuana; some jurisdictions prohibit the possession or consumption of small amounts of alcohol. These laws apply even to conduct that occurs within the home: the government may send police officers into your bedroom to search for marijuana or other contraband. It is possible that drugs are exceptional for some reason—perhaps, for example, because they may be chemically addictive. We should therefore consider whether the government is otherwise limited in its ability to regulate the pursuit of pleasure by citizens within their homes. Suppose that some town, worried by recent outbreaks of food poisoning due to the presence of *E. coli* bacteria in undercooked meat, makes it a crime to serve or consume rare hamburgers, even at home.[68] The town's law restrains the private pursuit of pleasure by carnivores. It deprives them of the right to decide how to use their bodies, and it takes a paternalistic attitude toward the health of its citizens. The law is decidedly untraditional, since the state does not generally regulate how people cook their own food. But does its enactment contravene any principle of justice? Is there a constitutional principle that allows you to "have it your way" when you grill burgers at home?

People need some freedom to satisfy their physical appetites, and prosecuting those who eat undercooked beef seems intrusive and silly. Perhaps the Constitution ought to prohibit such meddlesome laws. Still, it seems unlikely that the outcome in cases like *Griswold* and *Carey* should depend on whether there exists some general privacy principle that also extends to other pleasures of the home, such as wolfing down undercooked burgers. On the contrary, I suspect most people who are sympathetic to *Griswold*, *Roe*, or the *Bowers* dissent will believe that the constitutional case for sexual freedom is stronger than the constitutional case for any right of culinary freedom. The government's constitutional obligation to stay out of citizens' bedrooms seems clearer and more unyielding than its obligation to stay out of their dining rooms and kitchens. Why would that be so? Not, surely, because consensual sex is harmless. Lust motivates many crimes; sexual relationships that begin consensually may end violently. Consensual sex can transmit deadly diseases. Consensual heterosexual intercourse can *create* third parties, babies whose well-being may eventually depend upon the state's intervention.

If sex is not less harmful than other private pleasures, perhaps it is more important. Sexual desire is powerful, and its object is sometimes unique. If the state prohibits you from eating hamburger, you should be able to find something else to satisfy your cravings; if the state prohibits you from having sex with your desired (and willing) partner, that's another matter. But this argument begins to become implausible if the state has banned only some limited set of sexual practices—such as heterosexual sodomy—and allowed people to engage in others. Nor, for that matter, is it obvious that sexual acts are the most important or irreplaceable pleasures of the home life. For example, if your idea of a romantic evening involves a good bottle of wine and a candle-lit dinner, the Constitution may offer you no comfort: the state can ban alcohol entirely, limit the use of candles (they might cause fires), and perhaps regulate your menu. On the other hand, if your idea of a romantic evening involves watching an obscene movie and then coupling with two or three complete strangers, the Constitution may immunize you against prosecution. Does that make any sense?

Maybe, but not because kinky sex is indispensable to human flourishing. The idea that all sexual conduct deserves special constitutional attention is best justified if we emphasize the reasons why government tends to criminalize sexual behavior, rather than the reasons why sexual behavior is important.[69] Government often regulates sex for the wrong kinds of reasons. It is that fact, rather than the value of sexual pleasure, that makes sex a matter of special constitutional concern. Sexual desire commingles intense pleasures, dark power relationships, and the mysteries of human creation. It rivets attention and frustrates understanding. As a result, people have a tendency to define their own identity and status by demonizing the sexual practices of others. One way to do that is through verbal condemnation of other people's sexuality. A more dramatic way is to criminalize other people's behavior. A still more awesome measure is to prosecute and punish that behavior.

In other words, Justice Blackmun had it half right in his *Bowers* dissent. There is a constitutionally significant link between sexual freedom and personal identity, but the link takes a form different from the one he suggested: for constitutional purposes, what matters is not that people define their identities by having sex, but that they sometimes do so by condemning other people's sexual behavior. As an example, consider the Connecticut birth control law stricken in *Griswold*. My point is not that the law's proponents defined their identities by engaging in sex only for purposes of procreation, nor that the law's opponents defined their identities by having non-procreative sex. My suggestion is rather that Connecticut's law remained on the books because some people wanted to define their identities by condemning non-procreative sex (undoubtedly, many of the people who defined their public identities in this way were hypocrites who practiced in private what they condemned by law). Or consider *Bowers*. My suggestion is that some heterosexuals define their identity by condemning and punishing homosexual conduct. That condemnation may effectively constitute one version of heterosexual identity even if the person who issues it never engages in heterosexual intercourse. Indeed, a "closet homosexual" could constitute his social identity as heterosexual by condemning and persecuting homosexual behavior.

If this argument is correct, then consensual sexual conduct deserves solicitude from the constitutional judiciary because sexual behavior provokes a form of democratic dysfunction. In particular, sexual mores inspire cultural divisions that distort judgment and render regulations of sexual behavior suspect. This political tendency generates a special kind of concern with government animus, a concern that focuses not upon the vulnerability of any particular group or social class, but instead upon the politically provocative character of sexual activity. The relevant constitutional principle would attach to the Due Process Clauses and the Ninth Amendment, and it would run something like this: the state may not condition fundamental benefits of citizenship (such as freedom from criminal prosecution, or the right to decide whether to terminate a pregnancy) upon whether a person conforms to the state's judgments about how to pursue sexual pleasure in a way that is proper rather than debasing.

Perhaps you agree with me that constitutional principles of justice should protect sexual conduct against regulations motivated by a desire for social prestige or domination. Or perhaps you think that it is possible to justify *Griswold* and its progeny by reference to some different principle—such as a broad right of privacy, or a principle related to sexual equality. Or perhaps my extensive critique of these cases has convinced you that no principle, including the one I propose, can justify judicial solicitude for consensual sexual activity. Obviously, I would prefer that you agree with the argument I have made, but the argument is principally intended to serve two purposes that are independent of its substantive conclusions about the Court's jurisprudence of sexual and reproductive freedom. The first of those purposes is to identify a way in which the Court has misused tradition: the Court's homages to "tradition" have obscured the question of principle that has to be answered in cases like *Carey* and *Eisenstadt* and *Bowers* and *Casey*. Whatever legitimate uses tradition may have, that is not one of them. The second purpose is to illustrate the range of moral arguments that the Court might make with regard to this issue (and other issues) once it recognizes that appeals to tradition provide no escape from the need for moral judgment.

Lochner

This chapter has dealt with the doctrine conventionally (if somewhat deceptively) known as "substantive due process." Thus far, however, I have avoided the most notorious application of that doctrine, *Lochner v. New York*,[70] in which the Supreme Court struck down a New York law limiting the number of hours that bakers could work. The Supreme Court found that the law was inconsistent with the "freedom of contract" protected by the Due Process Clause of the Fourteenth Amendment. *Lochner* has become a great anti-precedent. For more than fifty years, constitutional scholars and lawyers have struggled to prove that, if their theories were embraced, no *Lochner* could happen again.[71] They assume that the decision in *Lochner* was not merely wrong but illegitimate. In other words, they suppose that the justices who decided *Lochner* failed to respect certain basic limits upon the judicial role, and that they decided the case on grounds which were political rather than constitutional, judicial, or legal. Most people consider it a great weakness if a constitutional theory fails to impose some sort of methodological barrier to prevent judges from repeating the sins of the *Lochner* Court—from, as lawyers say, "*Lochner*-izing."[72]

Since I explicitly call upon judges to make judgments of moral principle when deciding hard cases, I am a prime target for accusations of "*Lochner*-izing." A calm version of that indictment (far milder than what I expect to hear) might sound like this: "Look, Eisgruber, you say that judges should articulate moral judgments on behalf of the American people, and you ask judges to consult their own principles in order to make such judgments. But suppose a libertarian is appointed to the court. She might believe that there is a moral principle which says people should have the freedom to work long hours in order to improve their lives. If that's what the judge believes, you've not given her any reason to refrain from reaching the same result as the *Lochner* Court." My hypothetical critic might gather still more ammunition from this chapter's treatment of tradition: "When the *Lochner* Court issued its ruling, maximum hour regulations were relatively novel. The Court was therefore protecting against a novel intrusion upon a principle of individual liberty—just as you suggest the *Griswold* Court did. So your theory not only permits *Lochner*, but invites it."

What can I say to this charge? I should first confess some sympathy with the hypothetical libertarian judge. For many people, the freedom to work hard is among the most important aspects of liberty. Some vocations—such as farming—are virtually impossible to pursue without putting in long hours of physical labor. Some people—including most Wall Street lawyers—choose to work long days in order to pull down high salaries; apparently, they enjoy the challenge of the work, or the increase in their marginal spending power, more than they would value leisure time. Many talented people (including, for example, social activists and public officials) work staggering hours for little pay; for them, their dreams and their vocation are intimately tied together— work is what makes life worth living. For some poor Americans (including many recent immigrants), the chance to work long hours in order to make a better life for their children is the most valuable part of liberty. In many ways, it is easy to explain why the Constitution would include a right to pursue a vocation or improve one's standard of living—much easier than to explain why the Constitution protects sexual freedom. The freedom to work matters enormously to most people, and hard work is usually viewed as a virtue.[73]

So I cannot repudiate *Lochner* on the basis of some blunt claim that moral principle has nothing to do with issues about work and economic well-being. Cass Sunstein agrees with that point, and he has supplied a different diagnosis of how the *Lochner* Court went wrong. According to Sunstein, the *Lochner* Court's crucial methodological mistake was to privilege some traditional forms of social organization (including "freedom of contract") as "natural" or "pre-political" baselines against which to measure the constitutionality of government regulation.[74] Can I avoid the charge of *Lochner*-izing by embracing Sunstein's position? Sunstein is no doubt partly right: to the extent that the *Lochner* Court based its decision on the idea that "freedom of contract" was somehow "natural" or "pre-political," it surely erred. Capitalist markets do not pre-date political regulation—they are the product of it. In any event, we cannot conclude that some practice (such as physical violence) is in any way immune to regulation simply because it existed in the "state of nature." The fact that a particular practice is traditional, or that it has pre-political foundations, does not tell us anything about its moral status.

But it does not follow that tradition is or should be a constitutionally irrelevant baseline. As we have seen, tradition can matter in a softer, strategic way: not as a source of moral principles, but as evidence about what sorts of institutions and practices might successfully implement complex moral principles. If there is a moral principle that protects the right of people to work hard in order to make a better life for themselves, then a constitutional judge in 1905 might reasonably have supposed that "freedom of contract" was a time-tested, practical institution that gave effect to that principle. And a constitutional judge in 1905 might accordingly have decided that government regulations which departed from that longstanding tradition should receive special judicial scrutiny. If that is the way the *Lochner* Court used tradition as a baseline, then it was not behaving illegitimately.

The problem with the *Lochner* Court's arguments in favor of "freedom of contract" was not that they respected vocational freedom or historical tradition, but rather that they did so in the wrong way. I have contended that traditional practices can sometimes supply useful evidence about how to close strategic gaps between moral principle and judicially enforceable doctrine. But tradition's authority is only evidentiary; it is defeasible, not dispositive. Some traditions are founded upon injustice, and some traditions that have successfully nurtured liberty may be rendered obsolete by changing conditions. It would be absurd to think that departures from tradition were *per se* unconstitutional— legislatures would thereby be rendered incapable of responding to new problems or entrenched injustices. At most, the fact that the legislature has engaged in some novel regulatory endeavor will give judges a reason to demand that the state come up with a persuasive reason for its innovation. As the first Justice Harlan pointed out in his *Lochner* dissent, New York supplied the Court with plenty of evidence that "freedom of contract" was no longer (if it had ever been) an effective institution by which to accommodate both vocational freedom and the community's legitimate interest in the health of its members.[75]

The fact that New York's maximum hours law seemed novel and untraditional therefore did little or nothing to resolve the strategic issues relevant to the "freedom of contract." Those issues are tremendously complex and important, as becomes clear if we try to make precise the moral principle necessary to justify *Lochner* or any hypothetical modern counterpart to it. The crucial point is this: the bakers in *Lochner* wanted not only the right to work, but the right to receive the "market rate" for their work. They claimed, after all, the "freedom to contract," rather than merely "the freedom to bake," which would do them no good. Yet the rates that one can charge for goods or services, and the contracts into which one can enter, will depend upon the rules and conventions that constitute the marketplace. These rules and conventions may be quite unfair, and it is implausible to think that there is any moral principle requiring government to tolerate such unfairness, much less allow anybody to reap benefits from it. It would therefore be unsatisfactory for the *Lochner* Court, or a modern libertarian, to suggest a moral principle entitling all people to charge or receive the "market rate"—no matter how unfair that rate might be—for their labor. If there is some moral principle that might justify a doctrine like freedom of contract, it would have to be more complex: such as, "In a fair and well-functioning marketplace, people should be free to enter into contracts that enable them to improve their life by working harder and longer."

Suppose we find that principle attractive (as I in fact do). Can we reasonably call upon judges to enforce it? To do so, judges would have to be able to say what counts as a "fair and well-functioning marketplace," and they would have to be able to figure out which rights help to create such a condition and which ones impair it. It is obviously difficult to say what counts as a "fair and well-functioning marketplace," but it is also hard to say, for example, what constitutes "freedom of speech." That does not mean judges should shrink from the question. But there is something special about the difficulties that attend implementation of the marketplace principle. That principle is radically expansive in scope: it amounts to the right to participate in a good economic system. It is not a discrete side-constraint upon government decision-making; instead, it is so general as to comprehend almost all of economic policy and most issues of social welfare. In order to decide whether or not the marketplace is "fair and well-functioning," judges would presumably have to take into account (at a minimum) all of labor law, property law, and tax law.

It is the inevitable generality of claims related to social welfare that renders economic rights an inhospitable domain for judicial intervention. Issues pertaining to income and economic well-being are not about any particular human or political end, but rather about power: they are about one's ability to purchase what one wants from others on one's own terms. Power is a matter of relationship. Laws and transactions make a web of economic relationships, and it is that web as a whole, rather than particular nodes within it, that seems the appropriate target of moral scrutiny.[76] That appears less true of other aspects of human liberty. When, earlier in this chapter, we discussed cases about free speech and personal autonomy, we formulated principles that spoke to discrete parts of government practice. So we hypothesized, for example, that "the government must not adopt any policy which denies people a reasonable opportunity to express their own ideas about what is true or good," and that "the state may not condition fundamental benefits of citizenship (such as freedom from criminal prosecution, or the right to decide whether to terminate a pregnancy) upon whether a person conforms to the state's judgments about how to pursue sexual pleasure in a way that is proper rather than debasing." It might perhaps be possible to formulate some comparable principles relevant to vocational liberty—so we might think, for example, that there are constitutional principles which limit the government's power to exclude people from the vocation of their choice. But the freedom to contract in a fair market is not discrete; on the contrary, it demands a comprehensive assessment of the fairness of the economic system.

The difference between comprehensive and discrete moral principles is not a distinction particular to *Lochner*. It applies not only to conservative constitutional claims about "freedom of contract," but also to liberal constitutional claims about a minimum standard of welfare. The distinction will occupy us through most of the next chapter, where we will apply it to a host of other controversies in fields as diverse as voting rights, the separation of powers, and federalism.

But is the distinction between comprehensive and discrete moral principles sufficient to save me from the charge of *Lochner*-izing? Suppose that we imagine some judge who believes that moral principles protect "the freedom of contract" even if markets are not "fair and well-functioning." That judge could, under my recommended approach to constitutional adjudication, legitimately side with the *Lochner* Court. In that regard, though, my constitutional theory is no different from any other. The hubbub that constitutional lawyers make about *Lochner*-izing is ultimately a bit silly—like a summit meeting of naked emperors, each preening and boasting that his clothes are the most fashionable of all. It is time to admit the obvious: no plausible constitutional theory can rule out *Lochner* on purely methodological grounds. Certainly one cannot avoid *Lochner* by demanding that judges pay attention to text, history, or tradition. The constitutional text explicitly prohibits states from "impairing the obligations of contracts."[77] No less an authority than John Marshall, perhaps the greatest constitutional judge in American history, claimed that this clause was intended to protect the "freedom of contract."[78] Whether Marshall was right or wrong, there is surely plenty of evidence to suggest that the framers were intensely concerned with contractual freedom and property rights.[79]

We are all vulnerable to the errors of the *Lochner* Court. Indeed, if *Lochner* was illegitimate, rather than merely wrong, it was illegitimate in a modest way. The *Lochner* Court acted on the basis of a plausible principle that had plenty of support in the text, in American history, in traditional practice, and in legal precedent.[80] In the end, there are only two ways to avoid decisions like *Lochner*. One path is to insist, as Oliver Wendell Holmes did in his *Lochner* dissent, that judges should never enforce the Constitution in controversial cases.[81] Virtually nobody (Holmes included) has been able to adopt that position consistently. The other alternative is to hope that judges act on the basis of sound moral judgment and prudent strategic calculation—a hope which is reasonable, but which will undoubtedly be disappointed on some occasions.

Conclusion

Tradition, which figures prominently in several landmark Supreme Court decisions, has at least two legitimate jurisprudential applications. Like other forms of history, it can help a judge to argue that her conception of moral principle is not idiosyncratic, but can plausibly be offered on behalf of the American people as a whole. Tradition can also help judges bridge the gap between moral principle and judicial doctrine. In particular, a long-standing tradition may embody a workable balance among various goals and values that government and society may legitimately pursue. By examining tradition, judges may be able to identify institutions and practices that can successfully implement moral constraints upon government action.

But if judges use tradition to address the strategic choices confronting them, they must examine it critically. Some traditions may be founded upon injustice, and other traditions may have outgrown the conditions that once made them useful. Judges must, moreover, avoid the temptation to use tradition as a *source* of moral principle, rather than as a *means* for implementing it. The Supreme Court has not, unfortunately, respected that distinction. The Court has conflated cases dealing with familial responsibility and cases dealing with sexual freedom. As a result, it has made the former set of decisions more vulnerable than they should be, and it has failed to provide a candid account of the principles that underlie the latter set.

6

Judicial Maintenance of Political Institutions

❦

Democratic Integrity and Constitutional Strategy

To IMPLEMENT democratic principles, a nation must make many pragmatic choices. It must decide, for example, how to share power among national, regional, and local government bodies; how to allocate responsibilities among the branches of the national government; and how to structure its electoral processes. Some of these issues may be settled by explicit constitutional rules (indeed, we noticed in Chapter 1 that the most fundamental purpose of a constitution is to design institutions through which people can govern themselves). Others may be addressed through abstract constitutional standards or simply left to ordinary legislation.

Several of the American Constitution's abstract clauses—including the Executive Power Clause, the Commerce Clause, and the Necessary and Proper Clause—speak to questions of institutional design. Not surprisingly, many of the Supreme Court's most controversial cases have dealt with political structure rather than individual liberties. It is easy to see reasons why judges might play a beneficial role in such controversies. Legislators and voters sometimes betray democratic principles when they reform political institutions. For example, powerful parties may seek to reform political institutions in ways that consolidate majority power at the expense of minorities. Moreover, legislators and other public officials may be unfaithful agents: they may serve their own institutional or personal self-interest at the expense of their constituents. Thus Congress may try to increase its own power over the executive branch or state governments even if that change makes American government less fair or democratic. More insidiously, elected officials may seek to protect their jobs from voter control. Legislators may, for example, try to design "safe seats" so that they are never in danger of losing an election, even when they perform poorly.

Unfortunately, judges may be poorly equipped to correct these problems. This chapter will suggest that constitutional claims about the integrity of democratic institutions frequently turn upon comprehensive assessments of the American political system, and that such claims rarely provide a sound basis for judicial action. It does not follow that the Supreme Court should avoid entirely cases about the structure of democratic institutions and processes—some of the Court's most celebrated and beneficial rulings have come in the field of voting rights. But if the Court is to contribute effectively to the maintenance of American political institutions, the justices must define the occasions for intervention more carefully than they have done.

Discrete and Comprehensive Moral Principles

As we saw in the last chapter, strategic issues are ubiquitous in constitutional adjudication. Ideally, judges should tackle such questions only if judicial intervention is likely to leave the country better off than judicial deference. It might seem to follow that judges should address strategic questions only if they can handle them as well as any other branch of the government: if legislatures are better strategists than courts, wouldn't the country benefit if legislatures handled all strategic questions? Not necessarily. If the legislature is unfaithful to constitutional ends, it does not matter whether the legislature is adept at crafting effective means. The crucial question is not whether the judiciary's strategic judgment is better than that of other political actors, but whether the judiciary's judgment is good enough in light of its superior commitment to moral principles.

How good is "good enough"? Here things get mushy. We are weighing two kinds of institutional competence ("fidelity to moral principle" and "strategic acumen"), and it is impossible to come up with a rigorous measure for either. There are consequently a wide range of reasonable positions available. Although we cannot hope to produce a precise assessment of the judiciary's strategic skill, and although the ultimate disposition of any particular issue will turn upon intuitive assessments that vary from one person to the next, we can nevertheless refine the relevant options. "Strategic competence" is not a monolithic attribute; judges might be good at some strategic decisions and poor at others. People may be able to agree that judges can handle some strategic tasks skillfully even if they disagree sharply about how to view the judiciary's strategic competence in general.

For example, one might think that judges are especially able to handle strategic issues pertaining to the litigation process. Some constitutional provisions address courtroom procedure directly. Thus the Sixth Amendment guarantees a series of rights relevant to "criminal prosecutions," including the right to trial by "an impartial jury." To implement this right, one must decide both what it means for a jury to be "impartial" and what rules or practices are likely to secure the relevant version of impartiality. Moreover, even rights that have little to do with the courtroom may ultimately depend upon judgments about legal procedure. We saw in the last chapter, for example, that *New York Times v. Sullivan*[1] involved judgments about what rules would effectively prevent juries from punishing unpopular speakers.

The claim that judges are relatively adept with issues about courtroom behavior is useful but modest. In the remainder of this chapter, I want to pursue a more ambitious suggestion about the judiciary's strategic competence. The idea is one we encountered at the close of the last chapter, when we examined economic liberties. It distinguishes between two kinds of moral principle. Some principles are comprehensive: they demand that some system, considered as a whole, should treat people fairly. Comprehensive principles might provide, for example, that the nation's economic system should be fair and well-functioning, or that its political process ought to be democratic, or simply that the government should pursue justice in the best possible way. Other moral principles are discrete: they announce particularized side-constraints upon governance. For example, a side-constraint might declare that "persons should not be penalized for engaging in vigorous criticism of popular public officials," or that "the government should never mandate segregation along lines of race or religion."

As the last example should make clear, the distinction between comprehensive and discrete moral principles is different from the more familiar distinction between questions of institutional structure and questions of individual right. Some side constraints secure individual liberties, but others describe structural restrictions upon government action.[2] What matters is whether the principle calls for assessment of an entire system of social interaction or whether it instead proscribes specific forms of government action. Principles in the former category are comprehensive even if they express individual rights; principles in the latter category are discrete even if they relate to institutions.

Constitutional cases about democratic institutions often involve claims that must be framed in terms of comprehensive principles in order to be persuasive. For example, in *Timmons v. Twin Cities Area New Party*,[3] the Court dealt with a Minnesota law prohibiting "fusion candidacies," in which a single candidate for office appears on the election ballot as the nominee of two different parties. Third parties can benefit from the option of nominating a "fusion" candidate: by endorsing a major party's candidate, a third party may be able to tip the balance in a close election. That gives the two established parties an incentive to cooperate with the smaller one.

The Court analyzed Minnesota's anti-fusion law under the rubric of free speech doctrine: the justices asked whether the law suppressed the speech rights of political candidates or political parties. Six justices answered that question in the negative, and the Court upheld the Minnesota law. Whether or not that result was correct, the Court almost certainly erred by characterizing *Timmons* as a case about free speech. As Samuel Issacharoff and Richard Pildes point out, the case is more plausibly regarded as raising issues about the integrity of legislative elections.[4] The *Timmons* majority said that Minnesota's prohibition on fusion ballots reinforced the two-party system—which implies that Minnesota's laws protected the state's two most powerful parties against challenges from smaller parties. Issacharoff and Pildes accordingly contend that Minnesota's anti-fusion rule manipulated the electoral system to entrench or "lock up" the power of incumbents. They believe that courts should hold such "lockups" unconstitutional, and they think that *Timmons* was therefore wrongly decided.[5]

Yet, Minnesota's law might have been pro-democratic even if it entrenched the two-party system. Protecting the two-party system is not the same thing as protecting your own seat or eliminating electoral competition. If you're a Democrat, protecting the two-party system may mean, among other things, ensuring that you'll always have a strong Republican challenger. Multiple parties might produce *more* choices for voters than would a two-party system; it is not at all clear, however, that they would produce *better* candidates, or more hotly contested races, or better and more accountable representatives. Indeed, some political scientists believe both that strong political parties are essential to effective governance in the United States and that the American party system is in jeopardy; encouraging the proliferation of minor parties might make it difficult for the major parties to revive their strength.[6]

So was Minnesota's anti-fusion statute a partisan "lockup" or a benign policy that might promote electoral competition? There was no way for the Court to resolve that issue without making a comprehensive judgment about the fairness of the political system as a whole. It would be odd to think that a society was more or less just simply because it had fusion candidacies or thriving third parties. The value of third parties and fusion candidacies depends upon whether they will facilitate various goals of the electoral process—such as attracting good candidates, making voters feel satisfied, and selecting competent and accountable representatives. The case for fusion candidacies is thus wholly instrumental and contingent upon the political system's other institutions and arrangements.

This feature of the right claimed in *Timmons* marks it as dependent upon comprehensive moral principles. Other rights, by contrast, can be defended in terms of more discrete principles. For example, the Court's *Sullivan* decision might be justified on the basis of a principle stipulating that "the government must not penalize persons for criticizing its officials or policies."[7] This principle is a side-constraint on the government's behavior: the government is prohibited from stifling criticism even when doing so would enhance the overall quality of public debate. Because of this side-constraint, even critics of *Sullivan's* holding can feel a sense of injustice about how the Alabama courts treated the *New York Times*.[8] The remedy provided in *Sullivan* may (in some people's view) have gone too far; it may have damaged other constitutional values and overprotected the freedom to criticize the government. Nevertheless, whatever one thinks of *Sullivan's* overall impact, it seems almost inarguable that it advanced one important element of democratic morality: namely, the principle that people should be free to criticize the government without fearing that it will penalize them for doing so.

Judges will usually be better equipped to make the strategic judgments called for by discrete principles than those required by comprehensive ones. Judges take up constitutional issues in the course of deciding controversies between particular parties. As a result, those issues come to them in a way that is incomplete in two respects. First, not all interested persons will have standing to appear before the court. Judges receive evidence and hear arguments from only a limited number of parties. To be sure, modern rules of civil procedure help to accommodate the need for multiple-party suits, and non-parties may be able to express their views in an *amicus* brief.[9] Still, most constitutional cases are structured around an argument between two opposing parties. As a result, judges may not have the information necessary to gain a comprehensive perspective on the fairness of an entire social, political, or economic system. Second, the judiciary has limited options when it fashions relief. A court must issue an order that resolves the particular dispute in front of it, and it can only pass upon the questions that have been litigated in that case. So, for example, in *Timmons*, the justices might have concluded that Minnesota's election scheme did indeed frustrate electoral competition. They might also have believed, however, that the prohibition on fusion candidacies is at most a marginal disincentive to competition.[10] They might even have believed that the prohibition would be utterly irrelevant if various other changes were made to (for example) the campaign finance system. It does not matter: the Court's options were limited to striking or upholding that prohibition.[11]

The judicial perspective on strategic issues is thus incomplete both in terms of the interests represented before the court and the solutions available to it. This feature of adjudication may actually be beneficial when the judiciary is called upon to enforce discrete principles. In *Sullivan*, for example, the newspaper's predicament highlighted the value of a side-constraint requiring government not to penalize dissent. Because adjudication spotlights harms that result from particular misuses of government power, it reduces the risk that discrete moral principles will be traded off against generalized benefits. On the other hand, where the moral principle at stake is itself comprehensive, so that the crucial questions are about complex trade-offs over an entire system of relationships, it is hard to see how the case-specific structure of adjudication can be anything except a handicap.

Areas of Special Judicial Capacity and Concern

Even if it is generally inadvisable for courts to make judgments about the fairness of entire social or political systems, there will be exceptions to that rule. For example, we have already noticed that judges are especially knowledgeable about litigation procedure. In addition to having that expertise, judges can assume that they (or their colleagues) will eventually have the opportunity to address aspects of the litigation process not before them in a particular case: because the process as a whole is under judicial supervision, it is reasonable to think that subjects excluded from the ambit of one case will be presented in a later one. So we might think that courts have a special capacity to implement principles pertaining to the overall fairness of the legal system.

We might also think that the judiciary should implement comprehensive principles relevant to its own position in the separation of powers. An exception of this kind seems necessary to justify *Marbury v. Madison*,[12] since it is not possible to defend judicial review without reference to the benefits it confers upon the political system as a whole. One might try to justify *Marbury* on the ground that justices have special expertise regarding their own role in the political system, but that line of reasoning seems rickety. There is no reason to think that judges are uniquely trustworthy arbiters of their own competence. After all, many people have an exaggerated faith in themselves, and judges are no exception. The justification for *Marbury* must take a different form. We might hypothesize that the judiciary must look out for itself because no other institution has the incentive to do so. Or we might simply observe that it is impossible to ask judges to refrain from making any judgments about the extent of their own competence. There is no way for a judge to decide a case without deciding how far to trust her own judgment and (conversely) when to defer to somebody else.

We might accordingly recommend that judges impose constitutional limits upon the design and reform of democratic institutions only if they can do so on the basis of either a discrete moral principle or some exceptional claim about judicial competencies and responsibilities. But that recommendation requires an important qualification. My argument about discrete and comprehensive principles speaks only to the *relative* strategic competence of judges: I have suggested that judges are better at the calculations necessary to enforce discrete principles than they are at the calculations necessary to enforce comprehensive ones. Somebody who accepts that proposition might nevertheless believe that judges are *good enough* at strategic calculation to tackle the problems posed by comprehensive moral principles. For example, Issacharoff and Pildes contend that the German Constitutional Court has competently reformed Germany's system of proportional representation.[13] They suggest we should have more confidence about the abilities of the American Supreme Court to do comparable work. I am not so optimistic about the American Court's abilities, but I have offered no argument to back up that skeptical intuition. Alternatively, somebody might believe that judges usually botch even the strategic judgments called for by cases like *Sullivan*.

The argument offered here will be most useful to those who want to escape a particular dilemma, one that would compel us to conclude that the judiciary should either abstain from deciding the strategic issues that arise in run-of-the-mill individual liberties cases (such as *Sullivan*), or else plunge into the context-specific problems posed in cases about the maintenance of democratic institutions (such as *Timmons*). I am offering a third choice—but it will be of little interest to readers who think the strategic judgments in *Sullivan* too adventuresome, or who are confident that the Court can make the judgments necessary to dispose of *Timmons*.

With that qualification in place, the remainder of this chapter will use the distinction between discrete and comprehensive principles to examine the Supreme Court's role in building and repairing the institutional structures of American democracy. We will address the separation of powers, voting rights, and federalism. These topics are often thought to compose separate constitutional domains, but that is a mistake: all three doctrines require the Court to refine the rules that specify which institutions and officials can claim authority to represent the American people. As a result, the three doctrines confront closely related problems and implicate a common set of principles.

Separation of Powers: The Legislative Veto

Much of the Constitution deals with the allocation of power among the branches of the national government. The separation of powers is a means for promoting democratic accountability and securing individual liberty. One might accordingly believe that the Constitution's references to "legislative powers," "executive power," and "judicial power" raise issues of moral principle. If so, one might conclude that judges should play a prominent role in the interpretation of these provisions. The Supreme Court has in fact adjudicated many important controversies about the separation of powers, but the Court's readiness to intervene is unfortunate. Separation of powers cases illustrate a basic point of this chapter: there are many different ways to design democratic institutions, and selecting among the possible designs requires a level of strategic competence that the Supreme Court lacks.

As an example, consider the legislative veto case, *INS v. Chadha*.[14] Congress invented the legislative veto to enhance its power to oversee administrative agencies.[15] Statutes containing legislative vetoes delegated agencies broad power to fashion rules, but stipulated that the rules would not take effect if Congress (or, in some cases, a single house of Congress, or even a single congressional committee) voted to disapprove them. Of course, even in the absence of a legislative veto, Congress could reverse an agency's judgment by passing a new statute. But that would require not only action by both houses of Congress, but also either the president's assent or the super-majority necessary to override a presidential veto. The prospect of a presidential veto is especially important since an agency that promulgates a controversial regulation might well be expressing the president's own policy preferences. By putting legislative vetoes into statutes, Congress created a new, more flexible mechanism by which it could supervise agency behavior. The legislative veto thus shifted the balance of power between Congress and the president in the struggle to control administrative agencies.

Presidents consistently claimed that legislative vetoes were an unconstitutional expansion of the powers granted Congress by Article I. In *Chadha*, the Supreme Court agreed. The Court said that Congress could make law only by following the steps laid out in Article I, Section Seven, which required, among other things, bicameral approval and presentment to the President. Because legislative vetoes allowed Congress to circumvent the presentment requirement (and, in some cases, the bicameralism requirement), they were inconsistent with Section Seven and hence unconstitutional.

This argument was at best incomplete. Obviously, legislative vetoes did not comply with Section Seven's presentment requirement—that was the whole point of the device! But why should we think that Congress was "making law" when it exercised a legislative veto? A great deal of policy-making occurs outside the process described in Section Seven. Indeed, agencies make policy whenever they promulgate regulations. If Congress can use its Section Seven powers to endow agencies with rule-making power, then why can't Congress endow itself with oversight devices that likewise do not conform to the procedures spelled out in Section Seven? The answer must be that while Congress is free to create novel rule-making institutions, it cannot establish for itself rule-making procedures beyond those specified in Article I. Perhaps so, but that conclusion cannot be deduced from the sheer language of Section Seven. Section Seven lays out one way in which Congress can make rules, but does not indicate whether that mechanism (in addition to other explicitly designated devices, such as the Senate's power to advise and consent with regard to treaties) is the exclusive means by which Congress can influence the content of legal rules.

Abner Greene has proposed a principle to fill the gap in the *Chadha* Court's argument. Greene suggests that in *Chadha* and several other cases, the Court was intuitively guided by a prohibition upon congressional self-aggrandizement.[16] If Congress fiddled with the separation of powers in some way that diminished its own power (such as through a broad delegation of power to administrative agencies) or that restrained the power of another branch (such as by limiting the president's power to dismiss agency administrators), the Court permitted the innovation. On the other hand, if Congress gave itself new ways to exercise power (such as by creating a legislative veto), the Court struck down the arrangement. Greene's suggestion reconciles many of the Court's separation of powers cases and it has intuitive appeal.[17] It is unseemly for an agent to use power for her own benefit, and that seems at first to be what Congress was doing when it created the legislative veto. One might think that the legislative veto takes legislators off the hook for tough choices. Instead of making the choices that voters elected them to make, legislators punt those choices to agency officials. Normally, legislators would run a risk that agencies would use this discretion in ways that would upset the legislators, but the legislative veto enables Congress to keep the administrators on a short leash. Congress has thus helped itself, quite possibly at the people's expense.

The anti–self-aggrandizement principle sounds sensible, but it is an unsatisfactory foundation for judicial action. The problem is simple: the mere fact that some new mechanism benefits Congress does not tell us anything about whether it is desirable from the standpoint of democracy. For example, in light of the volume and complexity of the problems facing the national government, it might be desirable for Congress to make broad delegations to administrative agencies—not because legislators thereby make their own lives easier, but because agency decision-making is (for some issues) the most effective mechanism by which to solve problems. On the other hand, even if agencies are useful, they might misbehave. The legislative veto provides a way in which elected lawmakers can supervise the activity of the unelected officials who populate the nation's bureaucracy. Of course, the president can also play that supervisory role, but it is possible that increased congressional supervision serves democratic values. The people might be better off with a stronger Congress. If so, legislative vetoes reinforce democracy precisely because they enable Congress to augment its own power.

As in *Timmons*, so too in *Chadha*: the fact that some measure enhances the institutional position of the legislature which passed it does not tell us whether that measure is in the people's best interests. In the case of *Chadha* and the legislative veto, the strategic questions are even more vexing than with *Timmons* and the fusion ballot. Even after decades of experience with the legislative veto, there is no way for the Court (or professional political scientists) to say with confidence whether it is beneficial or detrimental to the American separation of powers.[18] Neither constitutional text nor moral argument provides the Court with any guidance in this pragmatic quagmire, and the *Chadha* Court erred by announcing a broad proscription upon all legislative vetoes.

The Court might nevertheless have had good grounds for striking down the particular veto at issue in *Chadha*. *Chadha* was an immigration case. Congress had given the attorney general discretion to permit otherwise deportable aliens to remain in the United States. Congress also provided, however, for a legislative veto: if the attorney general allowed an alien to stay in the country, either house of Congress could override that decision and cause the alien to be deported. In a concurring opinion, Justice Powell correctly observed that this particular veto allowed Congress not to supervise agency rule-making but to pass judgment upon particular individuals: Congress was reviewing judgments about the fate of persons, and deciding that some of them, like Mr. Chadha, should face the grievous penalty of deportation. Powell said that when the House voted to deport Mr. Chadha and five other persons, its action was "clearly adjudicatory." He argued that when Congress "decides the rights of specific persons, those rights are subject to 'the tyranny of a shifting majority.'"[19] For example, unlike in standard adjudicative proceedings, Mr. Chadha had no right to counsel, and Congress was not subject to the procedural rules that constrain courts.

In two different ways, Powell's rationale for judicial intervention improved upon the majority's. First, Powell identified a discrete moral principle that might constrain the adjustment of the boundaries among the various branches: namely, that when laws are applied to particular facts and persons, that application ought to be constrained by procedural rules designed to protect the rights of individuals. Indeed, one might regard Powell's argument as an interpretation of the Fifth Amendment—one might say that the way in which Congress adjudicated Mr. Chadha's rights deprived him of liberty without due process of law. Second, Powell pointed out that *Chadha* raised issues about the adjudicative process in addition to issues about the relationship between the legislative and executive branches. As we noticed earlier, there is less reason to counsel judges to be cautious about resolving strategic issues when those issues deal with judicial processes. Judges may have little clue about how best to ensure that bureaucrats are accountable to the people, but they presumably know something about which procedures are most likely to produce fair adjudications of statutory rights.

Electoral Fairness: Proportional Representation for Racial Minorities

Many constitutional scholars have suggested that the Court should abstain from determining the boundary between legislative and executive power.[20] Commentators have, however, been more bullish about the

Court's intervention in cases about the electoral process. Indeed, people concerned with the "countermajoritarian" character of judicial review often regard cases about voting rights and elections as paradigmatic instances of legitimate judicial action: one might ordinarily tell people unhappy with policy to take their complaints to their legislators rather than to judges, but one cannot sensibly ask them to do that if they have been deprived of electoral power by unfair laws.[21]

Cases like *Reynolds v. Sims*[22] are undoubtedly among the Court's greatest achievements, and eliminating unfair election laws is an important part of the Court's constitutional job. But which laws are "unfair"? There is no single, right way to aggregate people's preferences, and choices among voting rules will inevitably help some people at the expense of others. It will therefore be impossible for the Court to identify any particular voting scheme as ideal. To carve out a role for itself, the Court must identify side-constraints that (although they will leave open a substantial number of crucially important choices) rule out certain arrangements as impermissible. The resulting role is by no means trivial. The Court has done much good in the domain of election law because there are discrete moral principles that prohibit practices which now exist, or have recently existed, in American politics. For example, even though there are multiple ways to define the "majority" in any representative system, and even though there are multiple legitimate ways for a democratic government to give minorities a share of power, it is impermissible for a minority to enjoy entrenched control of the legislature. That principle is sufficient justification for decisions like *Reynolds*, in which the Court struck down grotesque malapportionments.[23]

On the other hand, discrete moral principles will not always be available to guide judges when constitutional litigants clamor for electoral reform. When such principles are lacking, issues about election law are no different from issues about the separation of powers: they pose murky, intractable issues of democratic design, and there is no reason to think that courts will be able to sort the wheat from the chaff. Unfortunately, as others have observed,[24] some of the courts' successes in the area of voting rights are so dazzling that they have led judges and commentators to feel a misplaced confidence in the ability of courts to reform electoral institutions.

The hottest controversies in American voting rights law deal with how to give racial minorities effective influence upon government policy. Because democracy requires that government be impartial, the government must try to structure electoral processes in ways that encourage legislatures to be sensitive to the interests of all the people, including those who are in the minority. It is especially important that Americans design incentives to make legislatures responsive to the interests of racial minorities, since racial divisions in the United States have been deep and durable. Some people believe that these considerations yield a discrete side-constraint on the design of electoral systems. They believe, in particular, that racial minorities enjoy a right to "proportional representation." They say that the majority will not respect racial minorities unless those minorities have an effective voice in the legislature. Therefore, they continue, racial minorities should enjoy a share of legislative power equal to their share of the electorate. If, for example, blacks constitute 20 percent of a state's population, then they should control 20 percent of the seats in the state legislature, 20 percent of the state's congressional delegation, and so on.[25]

The principle of "proportional representation" leaves many strategic questions unanswered.[26] Still, if we found the principle appealing, we might regard it as sufficiently discrete to warrant judicial enforcement. The principle of "proportional representation" does not require judges to evaluate the fairness of the electoral system as a whole; they need only ask whether racial minorities have a share of the legislature equal to their share of the electorate. In a dissenting opinion in *Mobile v. Bolden,*[27] Justice Thurgood Marshall pretty much endorsed "proportional representation" as a constitutional principle. Marshall said that racial minorities enjoyed a constitutional right to cast meaningful votes.[28] In his view, the votes of racial minorities were rendered meaningless if the candidates whom they supported had no chance to prevail in the election. Marshall concluded that the Court should hold apportionment schemes unconstitutional if they had a disparate impact upon the voting power of racial groups.[29] The disparate impact standard inevitably pushed in the direction of proportional representation: any apportionment scheme that precluded a racial minority from controlling a share of legislative seats equal to its share of the electorate would have a "disparate impact" on that minority.[30]

Yet, a system of proportional representation might actually *diminish* the power of black voters.[31] Indeed, one way to implement proportional representation is to cluster black citizens into a small number of legislative districts.[32] Black voters might control a majority of the votes in these districts even if they are in the minority statewide. By creating such "majority-minority" districts, states could guarantee that black voters would have the power to elect some black representatives. But an apportionment scheme that packs black voters into majority-minority districts will likely reduce their influence in other districts. Those districts may become more hospitable to candidates who are unpopular among blacks. As a result, the legislature as a whole may become less sympathetic to black interests.[33] Majority-minority districts might do nothing more than produce token representatives doomed to lose in hostile assemblies.[34]

These risks are not merely theoretical. During the 1980s, the Republican Party campaigned aggressively to increase the number of majority-minority congressional districts. The party's rationale was simple and explicit. An overwhelming percentage of black votes go to Democratic Party candidates; by packing blacks into a small number of districts, Republicans could enhance their chance to win the remaining districts.[35] Many commentators believe that the Republican plan succeeded, producing more Republican congressmen than would have been elected without the "majority-minority" districts.[36]

Some commentators have accordingly suggested that black Democrats are best off if they spread their power over many districts, where they can try to ally themselves with white Democrats.[37] This strategy has its own risks, however. Most obviously, blacks may find themselves out-voted in majority white districts—either because Republicans have enough votes to win against the alliance between black Democrats and white Democrats, or because white Democrats have so many votes that they do not need to share power with blacks. There is also a more subtle, and uglier, risk. Political scientists have found that white voters sometimes become more hostile to black interests when black voters become more numerous.[38] Black voters in majority-white districts may therefore find themselves facing a kind of catch-22: either they will lack any power to influence the election, or, if they acquire such power, they will see white voters flee to the opposing party.

It is thus hard to say whether majority-minority districts increase the power of black Americans. These short-term strategic puzzles are, however, only the tip of an enormous iceberg. The most important question about majority-minority districts is how they will affect the long-term tendency of Americans to vote along racial lines. To see why that is so, consider the obstacles that face any effort to give racial minorities an effective voice in legislative policy-making. At present, American voters often divide along racial lines.[39] So long as that is true, majority-minority districts can have only a marginal impact on the well-being of racial minorities. Any minority with well-defined and distinctive interests will be a consistent loser in a majoritarian political process unless the majority identifies with or cares about the minority. White majorities will eventually out-vote minorities; they may do so either when choosing representatives or when those representatives vote in the legislature. We can alter the point at which the majority prevails, but it will prevail.

Majoritarian legislatures are likely to govern impartially only if at least one of two conditions holds. The first possibility is that interests vary greatly from person to person, so that everybody is in the majority on some issues. If that were so, everybody would occasionally benefit from majoritarian procedures, and majoritarianism might be a sensible way to implement democracy. Alternatively, citizens might take an interest in one another. They might, in other words, believe that their own well-being depended upon the well-being of their fellow citizens, including citizens in the minority. Members of the minority would then enjoy virtual representation through the concerns of the majority, and majoritarianism might serve democratic ideals.

Both conditions are put in jeopardy by the existence of enduring, cohesive, and self-conscious political factions. When such factions exist, interests vary from group to group, rather than from person to person, and people in one faction are unlikely to identify with those in competing factions.[40] In the United States racial divisions—and especially the division between black and white Americans—have always been the most potent and dangerous source of political division. The most crucial strategic question about majority-minority districts therefore pertains not to their short-term impact upon the ability of minorities to elect sympathetic representatives, but to their long-term consequences for America's tendency toward racial factionalism. We can formulate at least three hypotheses about the latter question. Perhaps majority-minority districts will have no impact whatsoever upon how Americans think about race. Or perhaps majority-minority districts will nurture the careers of black politicians who will later be able to attract the support of white voters in other jurisdictions. On this view, majority-minority districts perform a kind of "affirmative action" function: they integrate American politics by recruiting racial minorities into legislative positions and acclimating white Americans to the idea of black political leaders. Finally, majority-minority districts might reinforce and legitimate racial divisions. Voters might come to believe that the job of white politicians is to represent white voters, and that the job of black politicians is to represent black voters—just as the job of Wyoming senators is to represent Wyoming voters, and the job of New Jersey senators is to represent New Jersey voters.

In *Shaw v. Reno*[41] and its successors, five Supreme Court justices endorsed the last of these three hypotheses. They accordingly limited the discretion of legislators to create highly visible majority-minority districts. Justice O'Connor, writing for the Court, argued that such districts "bea[r] an uncomfortable resemblance to political apartheid." In her view, race-sensitive apportionment schemes "reinforce the perception that members of the same racial group . . . think alike, share the same political interests, and will prefer the same candidates at the polls." For that reason, "a racial gerrymander may exacerbate the very patterns of racial bloc voting that majority-minority districting is sometimes said to counteract." She concluded that "[r]acial gerrymandering, even for remedial purposes, may balkanize us into competing racial factions."[42]

Justice O'Connor is right to think that democratic principles condemn "political apartheid." When the government supports segregation, it supposes that Americans live better if they divide into multiple, distinct sub-communities. That supposition is at odds with the preconditions for democracy, which require that Americans identify with one another and share a common interest. We can express this idea in terms of a judicially enforceable, morally discrete, side-constraint: government must not deliberately create jurisdictions or institutions segregated on the basis of race, religion, or ethnicity. Moreover, Justice O'Connor is also right to think that majority-minority districts *might* damage political unity. That, however, is where her argument runs out of steam. It is equally possible that majority-minority districts might instead promote political unity. Indeed, there is something odd about O'Connor's suggestion that majority-minority districts smack of "political apartheid." She made that remark in a case dealing with the disputed boundaries of North Carolina's 12th Congressional district, which was only 53 percent black.[43] Far from being segregated, this was one of the most racially *integrated* political districts in the nation. Moreover, the effect of the majority-minority districts was to produce a more *integrated* congressional delegation. Indeed, the reapportionment plan that the Court condemned in *Shaw* enabled North Carolina voters to send a black representative to Congress for the first time since Reconstruction.

None of this means that O'Connor was wrong to suppose that majority-minority districts could have bad effects upon America's tendency toward racial factionalism. Her worries may be well-founded. They do not, however, constitute an appropriate foundation upon which to build a judicially enforceable constitutional doctrine. As Justice Stevens has said, there is no "workable constitutional principle . . . that can discern whether the message conveyed [by majority-minority districts] is a distressing endorsement of racial separatism, or an inspiring call to integrate the political process."[44] In light of America's sad racial divisions, proportional representation might either be essential to create impartial government, or it might forever entrench factions that are still miserably deep.

In the domain of democratic theory, there is no shortage of tempting principles—ones that seem to state clear, moral truths rather than empirically contingent judgments of institutional strategy. One might say, with the *Shaw* Court, that race-sensitive proportional representation is undemocratic, because it balkanizes the nation and so encourages "political apartheid." Or one might say, with Thurgood Marshall in *Mobile*, that race-sensitive proportional representation is highly democratic, because it guarantees that minorities will have a fair share of political power. On reflection, though, we can see that both principles are misleading. The connection between proportional representation and impartiality turns out (like most things about democracy) to be messy and pragmatic. The merits of majority-minority districts depend upon speculative judgments about political sociology and comprehensive judgments about the operation of the political system. Despite their stark differences, the majority's opinion in *Shaw* and Marshall's dissent in *Mobile* were wrong for much the same reason. In effect, both demanded that the United States structure its electoral institutions to pursue racial equality as effectively as possible. That is an attractive principle, but it immediately dissolves into systemic judgments of institutional strategy that are beyond the competence of judges.[45]

The Court's Curious View of Federalism

Like cases about the separation of powers and electoral fairness, federalism cases raise issues about the judicial maintenance of democratic institutions. The dispersion of authority between state and national decision-makers is a device for improving the quality of democratic government. To interpret ambiguous constitutional language about the scope of national power, we will have to answer a series of functional questions. What sorts of things can state governments do well? What sorts of things can national governments do well? And to what extent is the judiciary capable of making reliable judgments about the comparative competencies of the state and national governments?

That is not, however, the way American lawyers usually conceptualize constitutional principles of federalism. Instead of emphasizing pragmatic considerations about how to design effective institutions, they view federalism in terms of almost mystical ideas about "state sovereignty." Lawyers suppose that state governments enjoy inherent prerogatives which impose discrete side-constraints upon what the national government can do. People who take this view believe that the states have some presumptive entitlement to govern and that claims on behalf of national power should be greeted with suspicion. This attitude has two sources. One is originalist: in federalism cases, commentators and judges seem especially concerned with arguments about the framers' intentions. The second is normative: some Americans believe that the states are entitled to special respect because they are "close to the people" in a way that the national government cannot be.

The originalist argument is especially prominent in the Court's recent cases. A majority of the justices on the Court treat federalism as a sacred inheritance from past generations endowed with mystical authority, rather than as a practical mechanism for implementing self-government. The Court's opinions about federalism are filled with reverent homages to the wisdom and authority of the framers in general and to James Madison in particular.[46] Madison and his colleagues, we are told, believed that protection for federalism and state sovereignty was one of the Constitution's greatest achievements. We must honor their noble vision even if we could "prove that federalism secures no advantages to anyone."[47]

This is an Alice-in-Wonderland kind of originalism. In his Pulitzer Prize–winning book about the founding, Jack Rakove reports that Madison arrived at the Constitutional Convention profoundly distrustful of state governments. He thought that state legislatures were prone to unwise and corrupt legislation, and he insisted that Congress should have the power to veto any state legislation whatsoever. Madison tried unsuccessfully to persuade other delegates to support the veto he wanted. He left the Convention disappointed; indeed, he wrote Thomas Jefferson that the Constitution was destined to fail because it provided Congress with too little power to prevent the states from acting unjustly.[48] Madison also thought the Constitution was too kind to the states in other ways. For example, he opposed the apportionment plan for the Senate; he thought that giving two senators to each state, regardless of their population, was an inappropriate concession to state sovereignty.

Rakove writes that the "central conviction" at the heart of Madison's constitutional analysis was that "neither state legislators nor their constituents could be relied upon to support the general interest of the Union, the true public good of their own communities, or the rights of minorities and individuals."[49] Rakove's assessment is controversial,[50] but it seems safe to say that Madison was ambivalent about the power the states retained under the Constitution. To present American federalism as his greatest legacy is to distort history. Nor was Madison alone in doubting the competence and virtue of state governments. According to Martin Flaherty, between 1776 and 1787 "innumerable observers came to the reluctant conclusion that the state governments had proven themselves to be sinkholes of demagoguery, faction, and localism that infringed individual right[s]."[51]

We find even deeper ironies if we consider why Madison's proposals were defeated. Madison himself eventually concluded that the crucial division at the Constitution was between free states and slave states. Delegates from both sides feared that if the national government became too powerful, it might interfere with local control over slavery— either by abolishing it nationwide, or by extending it into previously free states. These fears discouraged the Convention from assaulting state sovereignty directly.[52] If this analysis was correct, then federalism, far from being one of the founders' greatest achievements, is yet another aspect of the Constitution that (like the omission of any reference to the idea of equality) reflects the shameful taint of race slavery. In any event, by design or not, constitutional federalism became an obstacle to the national government's efforts to restrict and abolish slavery and to repair its effects. Defenders of slavery and racial discrimination from John C. Calhoun to Orville Faubus invoked the idea of state sovereignty on behalf of their sordid causes.[53]

The connection between slavery and federalism points to the greatest irony of all in the Court's rose-tinted account of federalism and the founding. Rather than the Constitution's greatest achievement, the founders' treatment of federalism was a self-evident failure. Within less than a century, the compromises over federalism disintegrated, and the nation fought one of history's bloodiest civil wars. The war was prosecuted by two armies named after competing conceptions of federalism: "Union" and "Confederate." After the victory of the Union Army, the nation was reconstructed—constitutionally and ideologically—around a changed understanding of federalism. Our federalism today is Lincoln's legacy, as much or more than Madison's.[54] Whatever the framers managed to sort out in the eighteenth century, whatever we might have inherited from them, modern American federalism is not their handiwork.

In order to make eighteenth-century ideas about federalism a functional guide for twenty-first-century policy, the Court has therefore had to pile implausibilities on top of one another. Notable among the epicycles is what Bruce Ackerman has called "the myth of rediscovery."[55] According to that myth, almost all of the powers exercised by Congress since the New Deal had been available to the national government under the Commerce Clause from the very beginning. Those powers had, in fact, been identified by Chief Justice John Marshall in the great case of *Gibbons v. Odgen*,[56] but, later justices lost sight of Marshall's wisdom. They began to construe the Commerce Clause too narrowly. So the New Deal Court had to "rediscover" Marshall's wisdom, and with it the Constitution's original, breathtakingly expansive grant of power to Congress.[57] Hence it is Madison's federalism—as incorporated into the Constitution, and interpreted by Marshall—that now prevails in the United States. This story is, as Ackerman points out, profoundly unsatisfying. American federalism today is different than it was at the founding. The myth of rediscovery provides no useful way to recognize and conceptualize those changes.

What Does the Constitution Say about Federalism?

Of course, the most fundamental defect in the originalist account of federalism is not that it uses so much bad history, but that it is originalist in the first place. Issues about federalism are no different from other tough constitutional questions, and we have no reason to depart from the general conclusions of Chapter 1. Insofar as the Constitution states rules relevant to federalism, later generations must abide by them. Insofar as the Constitution describes abstract principles of federalism, later generations should interpret them on the basis of their own best judgments about justice.

So what does the text say? Remarkably enough, it is not obvious whether the Constitution contains any general principles of federalism. An American reading her Constitution for the first time might expect to find some provision saying, more or less, "The People shall enjoy the advantages of a federal government, in which neither the national government nor the states shall disrespect the prerogatives justly retained by the other." If the Constitution contained an abstract provision of this kind, it would invite debates about which prerogatives were "justly retained" by state governments.

Many people suppose that the Tenth Amendment articulates this kind of broad principle of federalism. But that's not so. The Tenth Amendment says, "The powers not delegated to the United States by the Constitution, nor prohibited by it to the States, are reserved to the States respectively, or to the people." Chief Justice Harlan Fiske Stone said the Tenth Amendment was tautological.[58] Stone's claim has (remarkably enough) been controversial, but it is hard to dispute if one reads the amendment carefully. Of course political powers are vested either in the United States or in the states or in the people—where else would they be? They might, I suppose, vest in cities or counties, and one might read the Tenth Amendment to deny that the Constitution recognizes or protects the autonomy of local governments.[59] But if one is interested only in the relationship between the states and the nation, Stone was undoubtedly correct: the Tenth Amendment is a tautology. The amendment is satisfied so long as American political authority is divided among the nation, the states, and the people. The amendment tells us nothing whatsoever about whether the states have a lot of power or very little, much less anything about what kind of powers they have. It's a rather extreme possibility, to be sure, but the Tenth Amendment could remain inviolate even if the states ceased to exist!

Justices sympathetic to state sovereignty have reacted to this difficulty in a peculiar way. They have suggested that both the Tenth Amendment and the Eleventh Amendment, which renders the states immune from certain suits, allude to principles broader than the ones they actually articulate.[60] This argument puts astonishing weight on the Tenth and Eleventh Amendments. If the Constitution incorporates broad principles of federalism, it is hard to believe that it does so only through the addition of two crabbed amendments which do not themselves state such principles. One might more plausibly argue that the Court is free to infer judicially enforceable principles of federalism from the general structure of the Constitution.

We need not dwell on the merits of such "structural" interpretations of the Constitution,[61] however, for there is a simple way to provide textual roots for federalism principles. Article I, Section 8 authorizes Congress to "make all laws which shall be necessary and proper for carrying into execution" any of the power of the national government. Like all the Constitution's abstract clauses, the Necessary and Proper Clause must be interpreted in light of the American people's best judgments about the political principles to which it refers. In particular, it must be interpreted by reference to what the American people judge "necessary" in light of the goals of the national government and by reference to what they judge "proper" in light of other political principles. As several scholars have recently observed, those "other" political principles will include principles of federalism.[62]

The Necessary and Proper Clause can thus function as (among other things) an abstract reference to federalism. Congressional legislation is proper only if it respects basic principles of federalism. So the "myth of rediscovery" is not wholly wrong—the Necessary and Proper Clause was part of the original Constitution, and the most famous construction of the clause is Marshall's.[63] Perhaps one could defend today's federalism as a reinterpretation of the abstract principles that Marshall announced.[64] But the "myth of rediscovery" is nevertheless hugely misleading. If the original Constitution and Marshall's jurisprudence are consistent with the basic features of American federalism today, that is only by virtue of their extraordinary abstraction, not because Madison or Marshall had prophetic visions of the distant future. The Necessary and Proper Clause provides a vehicle by which to conceptualize how the Civil War and the New Deal changed American federalism. The Civil War and the Depression altered the American people's understanding of federalism, and hence about what it was "proper" for the national government to do. The "myth of rediscovery" ignores these changes, and it thereby presents a distorted account of constitutional development.

Stuck in the Middle

The Necessary and Proper Clause raises the following question: "What is it proper for Congress to do in light of the American people's best judgment about basic principles of federalism?" The resulting analysis will be an exercise in practical political theory. It will demand that we consider how best to structure the diffusion of power between the state and national governments in order to facilitate the project of self-government in the United States.

We now encounter the second source of sentiment on behalf of "state sovereignty." Many people believe that state governments should enjoy special constitutional solicitude because they are somehow "closer to the people" than is the national government.[65] Americans who adhere to this view endorse concerns about state sovereignty not for their pedigree, but on the merits. Judges and law professors who believe that state governments are "closer to the people" sometimes wax poetic about the distinctive character of each American state.[66] Insofar as these arguments take on a communitarian tinge, they are implausible. Texans may take great pride in their state's heritage, but Texas today is bigger and more ethnically diverse than many nations. Oregon is much less populous, but it is extremely dubious to think that Portland, a cosmopolitan urban center, and Klamath Falls, a small town 280 miles away, combine to form a single cohesive community.[67]

Still, there are real differences between, say, Texas, Oregon, and Massachusetts. On many issues, Americans may be better off if the citizens of each state are free to choose their own laws, rather than having to live under a single, uniform rule. "[D]ecentralized government . . . [may] be more sensitive to the diverse needs of a heterogenous society"[68] even if the states do not consist of anything resembling cohesive communities. The argument for state autonomy fares best if cast in the pedestrian language of interest-group politics rather than in the lofty rhetoric of political community.

Yet, even when put in these pragmatic terms, the case for a judicially enforceable constitutional presumption in favor of state power is not convincing. To begin with, any such presumption must yield with regard to policy questions that have a substantial interstate dimension.[69] So, for example, air and water pollution will drift across state boundaries, and it would be perverse to suggest that residents of each state should be able to choose their own anti-pollution policies.[70] States that want a clean environment will find themselves at the mercy of other states that are upstream and have different preferences. Nobody denies this point; indeed, fans of "state sovereignty" generally presume that all exercises of congressional power should be justified in more or less this fashion, as grudging exceptions carved out from state sovereignty to accommodate interstate effects of one kind or another. But all sorts of things cross state lines: trucks, trains, products, jobs, travellers, felons, schoolchildren, unborn children, bacteria, money, information, married couples, unmarried couples, guns, and deadbeat dads, to name only a few. Capital can move instantaneously in response to small changes in the law. Even if judges were omniscient, an "interstate effects" exception might swallow any presumption favorable to state sovereignty. And since judges are not omniscient, it may be utterly impossible for them to determine which congressional policies in fact bear a substantial connection to "interstate effects."

There are other, equally fundamental problems with the idea that states are especially "close to the people." To begin with, the most significant geographic divisions exist *within* states, not *between* them. For example, whatever traits may set New Yorkers in general apart from Pennsylvanians in general,[71] those differences are certainly no greater than the ones that distinguish Manhattanites, upstate New Yorkers, and Long Islanders.[72] What's more, intrastate variation, in addition to being more pronounced than interstate variation, is also more useful. As Edward Rubin and Malcolm Feeley point out, "[T]elling wheat farmers in Kansas that they can obtain the kinds of schools they want by moving to New Jersey is unlikely to provide an increase in their overall utility function. What would help them . . . is a choice of jurisdictions with different educational policies within their own region or city."[73]

Ironically, many commentators suppose that "the very essence of American federalism is that the national government is forbidden to interfere with state policies for managing and controlling local governments."[74] If the Supreme Court were really interested in facilitating local variation, it would have to develop a jurisprudence that protected cities *against* the intrusive power of the states. The Colorado gay rights controversy illustrates the point nicely. Some liberal Colorado municipalities—such as Aspen, Boulder, and Denver—passed ordinances protecting gay rights. Voters elsewhere in the state took offense. They passed a ballot measure that amended Colorado's constitution to prohibit all such ordinances throughout the state. From the standpoint of local autonomy, it is hard to see why this law should be more attractive because imposed by the state of Colorado rather than by the United States government: the imposition upon local governments is identical. One might therefore regard the Supreme Court's decision in *Romer v. Evans*,[75] which struck down the Colorado amendment, as, among other things, a victory for local autonomy.[76]

There remains one last reason to doubt whether state governments are in any sense "close to the people." State governments may in fact be more anonymous, obscure, and unaccountable than either their local or national counterparts. Martin Flaherty makes this point to his students through a series of questions. Flaherty asks his students whether they know who represents them in Congress. He asks whether they know who represents them on their local city council. And he asks whether they know who represents them in their state legislature. The annual results of Flaherty's informal survey are clear and consistent: the students know less about their state representatives than they do about national and local ones. Of course, Flaherty's survey is unscientific, and law students are a non-representative sample of the American people. So reflect, for a moment, on your own attitude toward state government. You are obviously unusually interested in American government—otherwise, you would never have made it through six chapters of this book! If I asked you to list twenty United States senators, and to give a brief description of their political platform or ideology, you would probably have no trouble. Could you do the same if I asked you for a list of twenty state legislators? Five state legislators? My guess is that, unless you have professional reasons for studying or dealing with state legislatures, Flaherty's point will hold: you follow what happens in Congress and your local city council much more closely than what happens in your state's legislature.[77]

There are good reasons why citizens would pay more attention to local and national governments than to state governments. Monitoring politics takes time. Time invested watching local or national government can pay a reasonable return. Nearly everything your local government does will have an impact upon you. The issues may not be momentous (e.g., whether to impose a new tax to finance repairs on city streets), but they involve your money and your roads. The national government repays attention for exactly the opposite reason: some national issues may seem remote from your daily life, but the national government has the last word on the biggest issues of economic and social policy. State governments, by contrast, occupy an awkward middle ground in the political system. On the one hand, much of the state government's legislative docket may seem to deal with issues that are both mundane and remote from your own life—issues about, for example, soil erosion in areas of the state far from where you live. On the other hand, when state governments deal with large economic or social issues—such as health care—their policies are frequently subject to preemption by federal law. Indeed, some of the most innovative state law programs in recent years (such as Oregon's health-care rationing system and Wisconsin's welfare reforms) were the result of state efforts to implement federal programs, and so were subject to federal veto. Moreover, there are fifty states, and it may not be clear *which* state any given citizen should watch—many Americans cross state lines every day when they commute to work.

If indeed most voters do not monitor state legislatures, then we should doubt whether those legislatures will be especially sensitive to the interests of their constituents. Of course, this problem is by no means unique to the states. The ignorance of American voters is legendary, and they may do a terrible job monitoring any of their representatives—local, state, or national. But the problem may be especially severe with regard to state governments. And if voters monitor Congress more carefully than they monitor their own state legislatures, it is possible that Congress might choose a rule more satisfactory to the people of Colorado and Massachusetts than would either state's legislature.

Do Electoral Processes Protect the States?

In the end, it is hard to say whether state governments are more accountable to the people than is the national government. Perhaps, then, judges should not try to identify limits on congressional authority over the states. Many people have taken that view. They claim that, to the extent that states govern well, electoral processes will provide Congress with incentives to protect the states. Every senator, after all, must answer to the voters of an entire state, and every representative must stand for election in some particular state. If congressional legislators depart from what the people of their state want, then they will lose their offices. Hence the states can protect themselves, and judicial intervention is unnecessary.[78]

This argument has considerable force. If voters prefer to see some topic (say, education) regulated locally rather than nationally, then voters can express that preference on election day. In this regard, the benefits of federalism are no different from the benefits of sound fiscal planning or environmental foresight or any other policy judgment: we have to trust voters to protect their own interests. Of course, voters cannot protect their interests perfectly. Voters may sacrifice local autonomy in favor of other considerations—they may, for example, return a senator to office because they agree with her position on health care and social security even if they disagree with her views about federalism. But this fact does not distinguish local autonomy from any of the other issues contested in the political arena.[79] Moreover, state and local governments enjoy some other structural protections. For example, in Chapter 3, I emphasized the relationship between gridlock and local autonomy: the Constitution makes it hard to put together effective national policy coalitions, and it thereby creates political space in which state and local governments can operate. Larry Kramer has identified another mechanism that helps to implement federalism principles. He observes that the national government will often depend upon the cooperation of state and local officials to implement policies; moreover, national politicians will depend upon state and local party organizations to help them when they run for reelection.[80]

Still, there is at least one reason why we might think voters less able to monitor congressional policies regarding federalism than other, more substantive policies about (for example) environmental law or education. Although voters share a general interest in the quality of local government, that interest is probably too diffuse to motivate electoral behavior. Interest groups may be able to goad their membership to write checks or vote in reaction to policies that threaten (say) the environment or civil liberties, but it is hard to believe that many voters have the same sort of hot-button response to issues such as "local autonomy in zoning" or "the procedural integrity of the state budgetary process." Congress may therefore try to capitalize on the anonymity and complexity of state government in order to escape responsibility for its actions. Congress may, for example, try to hide the costs of legislation by imposing new burdens and obligations upon state governments. If Congress disguises its policies effectively, voters will not be able to protect themselves. In principle, state officials could publicize the costs of congressional policy, and ask voters to discipline national representatives at the polls. Yet, if voters do not pay attention to state government, state officials may not be able to get voters' attention or respect.[81]

Ironically enough, then, one of the best reasons for judges to police the boundaries between state and national institutions is exactly the reverse of the one commonly cited. Scholars sympathetic to "states rights" typically suggest that judges should protect the states because state government is especially close to the people. In fact, a good reason for judges to protect state government is that most people feel little connection to it. If they did, the electoral process might well be an adequate safeguard for the benefits of federalism.

Can Judges Do Any Better?

Should judges worry about congressional self-dealing that hurts the states? By now the answer should be familiar. In the ordinary case, judges will find it nearly impossible to distinguish blameworthy self-dealing from laudatory innovation. Consider *Printz v. United States*[82] and *New York v. United States*,[83] in which the Supreme Court launched a doctrine explicitly aimed at protecting state government against congressional self-dealing. In these cases, the Court held that Congress had no power to "commandeer" state officials to implement federal programs. For example, *Printz* dealt with provisions in the Brady Handgun Violence Prevention Act; the provisions required state and local law enforcement officers to run certain background checks on prospective purchasers of handguns. In *New York*, Justice O'Connor explained the fundamental premise underlying the Court's decisions in that case and in *Printz:* "where the Federal Government directs the states to regulate, it may be state officials who will bear the brunt of public disapproval, while the federal officials who devised the regulatory program may remain insulated from the electoral ramifications of their decision."[84]

The Court in *New York* and *Printz* thus seems to be doing exactly the sort of job envisioned in the preceding section: the Court was attempting to prevent Congress from hiding its decisions in a complex lattice of federal institutions. But the doctrine created by the Court for these purposes was an odd one. The Court insisted that Congress could not command state officials directly, but that it was free to secure their cooperation in other ways. For example, Congress could offer states a choice between helping to implement federal law or else losing federal funds. That is a powerful lever: few states can afford to pass up federal funds in order to protect the autonomy of their bureaucrats.[85] In effect, *Printz* and *New York* assumed that voters might be confused if Congress issued instructions to state officials, but not if Congress bribed the states. That is not very convincing; if anything, the opposite seems true.[86] More generally, federal laws contain all kinds of hidden costs, and voters will often find it difficult to figure out what Congress has done. It is not obvious that these difficulties increase when Congress calls upon state officials to help enforce federal laws. Indeed, neither *Printz* nor *New York* appears to have involved a congressional effort to conceal the costs of federal policies. In *Printz*, the challenged provisions were temporary; the law provided for a wholly federal system of background checks to take effect by the end of 1998. In *New York*, the challenged law was enacted at the request of state governments, which wanted federal help enforcing interstate agreements about waste disposal.

The Court's doctrine in *Printz* and *New York* runs smack into the strategic difficulties which bedevil any recommendation that calls upon judges to maintain the integrity of democratic institutions. It is difficult to formulate principles that reliably prevent congressional self-dealing but do not deprive Congress of the flexibility it needs to legislate effectively. The problem that faces us in *Printz* is the same one that confronted us when we analyzed *Timmons* and *Chadha*. One cannot assume that a measure is irresponsible or self-serving simply because it improves the position of the legislature which enacted it. In general, asking judges to police congressional self-dealing will not be much different than asking judges to ensure that Congress makes the best of American federalism. There are undoubtedly a wide variety of ways to make federalism work, and the choice among these ways will turn upon all sorts of highly contingent factual judgments and preferences.

Once we cast aside ideas about "state sovereignty" or inherent state prerogatives, it becomes clear that federalism issues are no different from separation of powers issues. Judges should limit congressional intrusions upon state autonomy only in two circumstances: when judges are able to identify a relevant, liberty-protecting side-constraint, or when the challenged congressional policy deals with matters in which the judiciary has special competence. A jurisprudence restricted to these two exceptional circumstances might prove surprisingly robust. Two recent cases illustrate how. *United States v. Lopez*[87] was the first Supreme Court decision in more than fifty years to hold that Congress had exceeded the scope of its power under the Commerce Clause. *Lopez* dealt with the Federal Gun-Free School Zones Act of 1990. The act prohibited any person from carrying a gun within 1,000 feet of a school. Most people have viewed *Lopez* as a case about the substantive reach of congressional power: the Gun-Free School Zones Act was ultimately about crime control and education, which are often regarded as a local matters, rather than about interstate commerce, which is conceded to be a national matter legitimately regulated by Congress. The *Lopez* Court suggested that its decision rested upon concerns of this kind; it treated the dispute as a case about the boundary between national and local concerns. That rationale was not an appropriate basis for judicial intervention. States enjoy no inherent authority over education or any other policy domain. We should count upon voters, not judges, to pass upon the wisdom of particular congressional policy initiatives.

But there is another way to defend the outcome in *Lopez*. The Gun-Free School Zones Act had two crucial features: it was a criminal law, and it was largely duplicative of state legislation. Even if Texans regard guns more favorably than do other Americans, they do not want them in their schools. Lopez had originally been arrested for violating a Texas state law against bringing guns into schools. Texas authorities dropped their prosecution when the federal government indicted Lopez for breaking its statute. Duplicative state and national criminal laws put special burdens upon individual liberty. According to the Supreme Court's interpretation of the Double Jeopardy and Due Process Clauses, each jurisdiction gets a shot at enforcing its laws: if Texas had failed to convict Lopez, for example, the United States could have stepped in and taken a second shot—and, when doing so, it could have taken into account everything it learned from watching Lopez defend himself at the first trial. The Supreme Court might treat this problem by revising its interpretation of the Double Jeopardy or Due Process Clauses. But it would not be unreasonable for the Court to subject federal criminal laws to special scrutiny on the ground that Congress ought not to manipulate the federal system to subject individuals to multiple prosecutions. That would be a more confined holding than the one announced in *Lopez;* in some respects, it would resemble Justice Powell's approach to *Chadha*, which likewise emphasized principles of individual liberty.

City of Boerne v. Flores[88] provides a second, more complex example of how the Supreme Court might legitimately claim the strategic competence necessary to justify intervening on behalf of federalism. *Boerne* dealt with the Religious Freedom Restoration Act of 1993 (RFRA),[89] in which Congress provided religious believers with exemptions from state and local laws. Under RFRA, all levels of government (state, local, and national) were required to grant exemptions whenever any law imposed a "substantial burden" upon the exercise of religion. This requirement was subject to only one exception: governments could deny exemptions if doing so was the "least restrictive means" by which to achieve some "compelling government interest."[90] That test is very demanding. RFRA thus created valuable privileges for religious believers. RFRA did not provide any comparable privileges for persons whose non-religious commitments were burdened by generally applicable laws. For example, if zoning regulations prohibited charities from operating soup kitchens in residential neighborhoods, religious charities might qualify for an exemption under RFRA, but secular charities would not. I and others have argued that this feature of RFRA made it an establishment of religion,[91] and, in a concurring opinion in *Boerne*, Justice Stevens said RFRA was unconstitutional for that reason.[92]

The *Boerne* majority, however, decided the case on federalism grounds without reaching the Establishment Clause issue. Justice Kennedy wrote the opinion of the Court, and he said that even if RFRA did not violate the Establishment Clause, Congress would still have no power to impose RFRA's restrictions upon state and local government. Congress had claimed to find such power in Section Five of the Fourteenth Amendment, which authorizes Congress to enforce the rights set forth elsewhere in that amendment. The *Boerne* Court rejected that theory. The Court said that "[t]he stringent test RFRA demands of state law reflects a lack of proportionality between the means adopted and the legitimate end to be achieved."[93]

In one sense, it is easy to see how RFRA impaired federalism. RFRA threatened what Lawrence G. Sager and I have called "a catastrophe of misgovernment."[94] It constrained state regulatory authority in every imaginable area and in highly unpredictable ways—the diversity of religious practices and beliefs is, after all, virtually unlimited. Under RFRA, states faced demands for exemptions from (among other things) child support laws, school disciplinary rules, prison regulations, anti-discrimination laws, and zoning ordinances. Congress did not itself take responsibility for any of these domains. It did not, for example, make zoning or education into a national responsibility, for which Congress itself would take credit or blame. The states were still charged with the primary responsibility for negotiating among the demands of property owners, parents, and taxpayers with diverse and often inconsistent interests. But Congress demanded that the states comply with a vague test which the Supreme Court had recently abandoned as unworkable. Congress could thereby take credit for doing God's work, while leaving the states and the courts to execute a nearly impossible assignment. "State judgment [was] ousted along a broad frontier, and the only federal judgment put in its place is Congress's imposition on the federal judiciary of a test that . . . the Court [had] repudiated" as unworkable.[95] The federal system and the separation of powers, which normally invite multiple independent policy judgments, were perverted so that no institution made any independent policy judgment.

Yet, why should that be the Court's concern? Cynics would suggest that "catastrophe of misgovernance" is the standard mode of operation for Congress. In any event, "Congress should avoid catastrophes of misgovernance" is not a discrete moral principle. Nor would it be desirable for the Court routinely to review congressional exercises of power in order to determine whether they lack "proportionality between the means adopted and the legitimate end to be achieved." I would not, for example, recommend that the Court do that when reviewing laws passed under the Commerce Clause. Why should matters be any different when Congress uses Section Five of the Fourteenth Amendment? Questions of this kind led many commentators to conclude that the *Boerne* Court should have shown greater deference to Congress.[96]

Yet, there is a difference between RFRA and ordinary Commerce Clause legislation. RFRA deals with an area in which courts have a claim to special competence.[97] Congress used its Fourteenth Amendment powers because legislators believed that the Court had made a mistaken judgment about religious liberty, and Congress wanted to correct that mistake. There is no reason for the justices to defer to Congress on questions about what religious liberty requires; on the contrary, the case for judicial review depends on the idea that the Court is likely to represent the people better than Congress on questions of moral principle. Of course, as we have noticed throughout this chapter and the last one, the Court must also make strategic judgments to generate legal doctrines, and Congress may actually be better at those judgments than is the Court. The *Boerne* Court acknowledged as much. It said that Congress was entitled to broad deference with regard to the formulation of procedures or prophylactic rules for the vindication of constitutional principles. The Court concluded, however, that RFRA was a dispute about ends, not means. That judgment is certainly contestable, but in my view it was correct.[98]

The crucial point is this: the Court must usually defer to other decision-makers with regard to questions about how federalism limits congressional power, but the need for deference does not entail the absence of relevant constitutional principles. The government is obliged to arrange its institutions so as to maximize the extent to which the government is impartial, effective, and so on. The problem is that although relevant principles exist, the judiciary lacks the competence to determine which arrangements satisfy those principles. Federalism principles are destined to be, in Sager's terminology, "judicially under-enforced."[99] In the case of RFRA, however, Congress made only judgments of a sort that the judiciary could make at least as well. Under those circumstances, there was no reason for the Court to defer to Congress about federalism.[100]

One might reasonably quarrel with these conclusions about *Boerne,* or with the reconstruction of *Lopez* offered earlier. They are both hard cases. What matters is not the outcome, but the character of the arguments. First, judicial arguments about federalism should be pragmatic and functional, rather than derived from some notion about "state sovereignty." Second, the Court should intervene only if it can point to some discrete liberty-regarding side-constraint upon Congress, or if it can make some plausible claim to have special competence with regard to the issues underlying the congressional action under review. Outside of those special cases, the Court ought to trust the electoral process to police congressional disrespect for the value of state government—not because that process is perfect, but because judges cannot reasonably hope to do better.

The Dormant Commerce Clause

Most of the Supreme Court's federalism cases deal not with the scope of congressional power, but with limitations on the power of the states to intrude upon matters that are national in character. Much, though not all, of this jurisprudence proceeds under the curious label of "dormant Commerce Clause doctrine": it purports to interpret restrictions upon state power that are thought to be dormant (in the sense of "latent") within the Commerce Clause's grant of power to Congress. The Supreme Court's jurisprudence in this area is openly pragmatic: it depends to a great extent upon balancing the strength of state and federal interests. One might think, in light of the themes pursued in this chapter, that the Court has no business enforcing restrictions of this kind. What's sauce for the goose is sauce for the gander, after all: if the Court cannot be trusted to determine whether some novel congressional intrusion upon state power is pro-democratic, then surely the Court cannot be trusted to determine whether some novel state intrusion upon interstate commerce is desirable. The stakes and the issues are the same.

In fact, though, the stakes are not the same. Dormant Commerce Clause jurisprudence is unlike most other parts of constitutional law because the Court allows Congress the last word. Under well-established doctrine,[101] Congress may permit the states to take actions that, in the absence of congressional authorization, would violate the dormant Commerce Clause. That fundamentally alters the relationship between Court and Congress. What the Court does under the dormant Commerce Clause is more analogous to what it does under the Voting Rights Act than to what it does under the Commerce Clause or the Equal Protection Clause. Dormant Commerce Clause jurisprudence is a quasi-statutory, quasi-constitutional domain in which the Supreme Court devises provisional rules subject to statutory revision by congressional enactment.

These observations do not tell us whether the Court's dormant Commerce Clause jurisprudence is defensible, either as a textual matter or as a functional matter. But they do yield two conclusions. The first is that, whatever else we may think of that doctrine, it raises questions different from those we have been discussing thus far. We may be willing to allow judges to make strategic assessments about the comparative merits of state and federal regulatory power if those assessments are subject to congressional override, but not if they are unrevisable except by constitutional amendment or court-packing. The second conclusion is that dormant Commerce Clause jurisprudence might provide a model for a new, more general form of judicial involvement in questions of institutional design. If we want the benefits of judicial involvement in questions of political structure, but worry that judges will make strategic errors, we might encourage judges to impose restrictions subject to congressional revision—just as they do under in dormant Commerce Clause jurisprudence. Some scholars have proposed innovations of this kind;[102] they pose complexities beyond what we can explore here.

Conclusion

When people reform political institutions, there is always a risk they will stack the deck. Legislators may protect their own seats, or they may augment the legislature's power at the expense of other institutions that serve valuable democratic purposes. Voters will not always be able to prevent this kind of self-serving behavior. Moreover, voters themselves may have incentives to corrupt democratic institutions—majorities may try, for example, to consolidate power at the expense of minorities. It is therefore tempting to ask judges to help maintain the democratic integrity of American political institutions.

Unfortunately, that assignment involves strategic difficulties of an especially daunting kind. There is no recipe that prescribes how democratic governments should draw electoral districts, or distribute power among national institutions, or allocate power between national and local bodies. Democracy will require a pragmatic mix of institutions, and the desirability of any particular mix will depend upon a host of empirically contingent judgments.[103] Judges cannot evaluate the democratic merits of contested reforms without assessing the fairness of the American political system as a whole. That kind of comprehensive strategic judgment is not something judges can do well. Judges should therefore enforce constitutional restrictions on institutional reform only in relatively exceptional cases, such as when there exists a morally justifiable side-constraint on the government's institutional options, or when the reform deals with an area in which the judiciary has special expertise.

Conclusion

༄

AMERICANS OFTEN ASSUME that the hallmark of constitutional interpretation is its capacity to derive important conclusions from text and history. They expect constitutional theory to identify ways to "squeeze more meaning from the document that inscribes our highest . . . law."[1] If a theory takes an openly forward-looking approach to constitutional adjudication (as mine does), it risks being branded "non-interpretive"—which is pretty much the kiss of death for any constitutional theory, since almost everybody concedes that the Constitution is supreme law and that judges are bound to interpret it faithfully.

But there is no good reason to suppose that constitutional interpretation should be characterized by obsessive efforts to milk normative conclusions from delphic text and unruly history. That supposition rests upon a radical misunderstanding of the United States Constitution. It views the Constitution as a set of textual and historical constraints that limit the capacity of Americans to govern themselves. That picture of the Constitution is neither practical nor attractive. It is impractical because the Constitution's most controversial provisions do not, either on their own or when supplemented by history, yield determinate rules about how judges or other political officials should behave. It is unattractive because if the Constitution consisted of simple constraints inherited from the past, it would hold democratic politics hostage to the views of generations now long dead.

There is a better way to understand the Constitution, and hence a better way to understand the mission of constitutional theory. The Constitution should be regarded as serving a pro-democratic purpose:

it creates a range of institutions to represent a people who would otherwise have no satisfactory way to act collectively. Constitutional theory should accordingly be intensely concerned with how institutions work in practice. Large-scale polities can pursue democratic ideals only by choosing among a variety of institutions, all of which are imperfect representatives of the people. Neither "voters" nor "legislators" nor "judges" are the same thing as "the people"; each is a political office, subject to particular incentives, constructed in order to provide a representation of the people. Constitutional thinkers must also recognize the complexity and variety of political institutions. We cannot, for example, analyze judicial review in terms of a simple choice between courts and legislatures; we must take into account the fact that the American political structure involves local, state, and national legislative bodies. We must also consider how these legislatures are structured. We must contend with (among other things) the fact that congressional legislation becomes law only if it passes two differently constituted houses and either avoids or overcomes a presidential veto.

The job of American constitutional theory is to describe how Americans should conceive and inhabit their institutions so that they can govern themselves on the basis of their own best judgments about justice. Constitutional reasoning will then differ from political theory in general not so much by its delicate sensitivity to text or history, but by its special concern with the institutional structure of the United States. More often than not, "interpreting the American Constitution" will involve interpreting American political institutions, rather than constitutional language or the psyche of the founding generation.

I do not, of course, mean to say that judges or other constitutional interpreters should ignore the text. Any theory that made that recommendation would deserve both to be classified as "non-interpretive" and to bear the opprobrium which accompanies that label. The text will matter in multiple ways. To begin with, the text specifies the institutions that constitutional theory must explicate and construe. It is important what institutions the text establishes, and it is also important what the text omits. The case for judicial review in the United States would be much weaker if judges chose their own successors. It would also be weaker if the Constitution created a body that was (arguably) better constituted to perform some of the functions now handled in the United States by the Supreme Court—for example, a "Council of Constitutional Revision," composed of members who had life tenure and the authority to review and revise legislation, but not to adjudicate courtroom disputes.

More generally, the Constitution facilitates democracy in part by providing specific procedures—constitution-writing and constitutional amendment—that simultaneously enable Americans to settle the institutional details of their government and encourage Americans to deliberate about the long-term consequences of their choices. To preserve this feature of the Constitution, Americans must respect the specific rules which it lays down—such as the rule stipulating that each state will enjoy equal representation in the Senate, or the rule providing that presidents will serve four-year terms. But it does not follow that Americans must treat the Constitution's abstract moral and political concepts as comparably constraining. On the contrary, Americans can, and should, view those provisions as inviting them to deliberate about, and act upon, the best version of the ideals specified therein.

Far from being "non-interpretive," a forward-looking approach to constitutional adjudication is the only way for interpreters to respect the Constitution's democratic purpose, and hence the only legitimate way for interpreters to resolve the meaning of the Constitution's abstract moral language. This understanding of the Constitution imposes a complex burden upon the United States Supreme Court. It assigns the Court two distinct, and not entirely compatible, functions. Because Supreme Court justices enjoy life tenure and stand at the apex of their profession, they are able to carry out their duties relatively untainted by material self-interest or professional ambition. The Court has therefore become what Ronald Dworkin has aptly termed America's "forum of principle:"[2] in the American political system, the Supreme Court is the institution best suited to engage in principled, disinterested constitutional interpretation. But the Court is also America's forum of last resort for all issues of federal law. As such, it is the institution charged with overseeing what Richard Fallon has called the "implementation" of federal law, both constitutional and non-constitutional.[3] The Supreme Court must interpret federal statutes and regulations in addition to the Constitution, and it must devise doctrinal mechanisms to ensure that federal law (whether constitutional or not) is uniformly and effectively applied throughout the nation's courts. The Constitution thus hard-wires a connection between constitutional interpretation and the legal profession.

Commentators tend to assume that the Court's responsibilities are mutually reinforcing. People suggest, for example, that because the Supreme Court acts in the context of particular legal disputes, justices can glean insight from concrete facts. Or people suppose that the threat of judicial tyranny is tamed by the fact that judges cannot act unless presented with an appropriate case or controversy. Or people assume, in a variation upon Marshall's argument in *Marbury v. Madison*, that constitutional interpretation is defensible precisely because (and, hence, only insofar as) it is incidental to the Court's task of implementing federal law. There is some truth to these conventional opinions. Yet, there is also a darker side to the Court's dual role: there is real tension between the Court's responsibility for implementing federal law and its responsibility for interpreting the Constitution. Technical legal skill is much more relevant to the former than the latter. Supreme Court justices have a natural, and destructive, tendency to iron out the complexities in their role by conceiving of constitutional interpretation as a technical legal exercise. That is, after all, what lawyers do best, and people like to exaggerate the importance of things they do well.

This problem may have been exacerbated by changes in the legal profession. The profession itself has become more technical. At the time of America's founding, American lawyers were men of letters. By the time of the Civil War, the profession had changed.[4] American law was more complex; its study and application more consuming. This trend has continued. Today, most American lawyers specialize within the law: they are labor lawyers or securities litigators or criminal lawyers and so on. Much of the law—to say nothing of human letters more generally—is outside the scope of their learning and experience.[5]

It is hard to say whether these changes in legal culture help to explain the timid, technical style preferred by most of the justices on the Supreme Court today. This much, though, seems clear: Supreme Court justices have persistently treated the Constitution like a legal code, accessible only to those with special skill and training. In particular, they have interpreted its abstract provisions not by referring to the best understanding of the political and moral ideas expressed therein, but by searching for hidden textual harmonies and endowing historical facts with sovereign authority. They have thereby magnified the Constitution's shortcomings—and those defects are far from insignificant. However great were the men who framed the Constitution, and however glorious their achievements, their work was sullied by the terrible evil of slavery. That evil is most evident, of course, in provisions like the Fugitive Slave Clause, which explicitly acknowledge and accommodate the rights of slave-owners. But slavery's taint upon the Constitution is more pervasive and hence more durable. The original Constitution contained no mention of equality, the ideal that inspired the American Revolution. It contained no guarantee of citizenship. To this day, the Constitution omits any specific reference to the right of people to travel freely, or to marry whom they wish, or to care for their children. The original Constitution, moreover, created a profoundly unsatisfactory mix of state and national authority, one which (as Madison realized and regretted) left the nation with too little power to supervise the injustices of the states. Eventually, the framers' awkward and inadequate compromises collapsed, and the nation plunged into civil war.

The unreconstructed American Constitution was filled with serious, and ultimately fatal, flaws. Yet, the original Constitution also contained grand abstractions—including the Commerce Clause, the Necessary and Proper Clause, and the Ninth Amendment—that permitted visionary interpreters like John Marshall and Abraham Lincoln and Frederick Douglass to read it as an instrument by which a democratic people could do justice. The reconstructed Constitution, which abolished slavery, guaranteed national citizenship, and restrained the states in the name of liberty and equality, improved greatly upon the original. But the justices have responded perversely, construing the Fourteenth Amendment's abstractions by reference to the flawed details of the unreconstructed Bill of Rights, and analyzing federalism by reference to a founding plan that Madison himself thought unsatisfactory and that history proved unsustainable.

Unfortunately, scholarly commentators have reinforced the Court's love for technical jurisprudence. Law professors have nurtured the fallacious idea that constitutional interpretations should always be derived from text and history. They have joined forces with politicians and journalists to condemn the "politicization" of the Court (as if it had ever been apolitical!). Stimulated by such rhetoric, Supreme Court justices occasionally suggest that the public will punish them if they admit to making political judgments. Justice Scalia, dissenting from the Court's decision not to overrule *Roe v. Wade*, wrote, "As long as this Court thought (and the people thought) that we Justices were doing essentially lawyers' work up here—reading text and discerning our society's traditional understanding of that text—the public pretty much left us alone."[6] According to Scalia, "Texts and traditions are facts to study, not convictions to demonstrate about."[7] If ever the Supreme Court were to render decisions on the basis of "value judgments," then, Scalia claimed, the American people would cease to respect the Court.[8]

It is hard to believe that the American public is so naive.[9] Americans know that some judges, like Scalia, have a conservative political philosophy, and that others, like Ginsburg, are more liberal. They recognize that conservative judges tend to protect conservative values while liberal judges tend to protect liberal ones. Americans realize, for example, that Justice Scalia invoked his own, relatively conservative political values when he voted to prohibit affirmative action programs and when he voted to limit the means by which the federal government could regulate guns. Of course, Americans know that Scalia studied legal texts and traditions before reaching his decision, and I am sure they are glad that he did. But Americans also understand that other justices on the Court studied the same texts and traditions, and that some of these justices reached exactly the opposite conclusions from the ones Scalia endorsed. And Americans know that the best way to predict which judges will reach which conclusions is to know something about their political leanings.

American citizens and their leaders should acknowledge and welcome this feature of their political system. There is nothing wrong with the fact that unelected justices decide questions about (for example) federalism or gay rights or economic justice on the basis of controversial judgments of moral principle. When other political institutions have pandered to the American people's baser selves, the Court has frequently had backbone enough to stand up for the people's values. Despite their proclivity to hide behind legalistic formulae and exaggerate the Constitution's deficiencies, the justices have often represented what is best in the American people. The institution of judicial review is a sensible way to promote non-majoritarian representative democracy; not surprisingly, it is becoming increasingly popular in democratic political systems throughout the world.

Judicial review works well in the United States, but it can work better. Americans should find it embarrassing that their Supreme Court sometimes decides fundamental issues neither on the basis of political principle, nor on the basis of explicit textual provisions, but on the basis of dubious intentions and opinions that were popular with generations now long dead. Americans should insist that the Court resist the temptations of technical jurisprudence. The justices' job is not merely to "play the game by the rules." Their job includes a responsibility to identify principles of liberty and equality; to justify those principles on the basis of moral reasons; and to fashion doctrines that will implement the principles. That responsibility is difficult. It will require the justices to endure vitriolic criticism, and it will put them in the middle of heated controversies. The justices will not be able to take any comfort from the reassuring but delusive idea that their decisions are the product of neutral legal expertise. But they will be able to take heart from the fact that by speaking about justice on behalf of the American people, they make a crucial contribution to constitutional self-government in the United States.

Notes

Introduction

1. See, e.g., Robert Bork, *The Tempting of America: The Political Seduction of the Law* 159 (1990).

2. For example, Ronald Dworkin emphasizes the importance of "constitutional *integrity*," which requires judges to respect "the dominant lines of past constitutional interpretation by other judges." Dworkin, *Freedom's Law: The Moral Reading of the American Constitution* 10 (1996). In Dworkin's view, "[t]he Constitution is a tradition as well as a document," and judges must "interpret that tradition in a lawyerlike way." Dworkin accordingly urged the Senate to reject Robert Bork's nomination on the ground that Bork's reading of the Constitution failed to respect the demands of "integrity," and hence was not only "radical" but "antilegal." Id. at 265. See also David A. Strauss, "Common Law Constitutional Interpretation," 63 *University of Chicago Law Review* 877, 932 (1996).

3. According to Professor Laurence Tribe, what "makes constitutional interpretation truly a legal enterprise" is that it is "genuinely disciplined by widely shared canons of the interpretive arts and by stubborn truths of text, structure, and history." Laurence Tribe, "Taking Text and Structure Seriously: Reflections on Free-Form Method in Constitutional Interpretation," 108 *Harvard Law Review* 1221, 1225 (1995).

4. The analogy between constitutional interpretation and religious interpretation is elaborated in Sanford Levinson, *Constitutional Faith* (1988).

5. Studies by political scientists confirm that American judges are selected "through a political process controlled by politicians and emphasizing partisanship and ideology." Terri Jennings Peretti, *In Defense of a Political Court* 85 (1999).

6. Here again, empirical political science backs up what common sense would suggest; see Jeffrey A. Segal and Harold J. Spaeth, *The Supreme Court and the Attitudinal Model* (1993); see also Peretti, *A Political Court*, at 101–131.

7. Bush v. Gore, 121 S. Ct. 525 (2000). The case is discussed in Chapter 2.

8. 418 U.S. 683 (1974).

9. 520 U.S. 681 (1997).

213

10. John Hart Ely, *Democracy and Distrust: A Theory of Judicial Review* (1980).

11. Id. at 73.

12. Ronald M. Dworkin, *Taking Rights Seriously* 149 (3d ed. 1981).

13. For a confrontation between these schools of thought, see Ronald Dworkin, "In Praise of Theory," 29 *Arizona State Law Journal* 353 (1997); Richard A. Posner, "Conceptions of Legal 'Theory': A Response to Ronald Dworkin," 29 *Arizona State Law Journal* 377 (1997); Cass R. Sunstein, "Response: From Theory to Practice," 29 *Arizona State Law Journal* 389 (1997); and Ronald Dworkin, "Reply," 29 *Arizona State Law Journal* 431 (1997).

14. My views on these points have been greatly influenced by the work of my colleague Lawrence G. Sager. See, e.g., Sager, "Justice in Plain Clothes: Reflections on the Thinness of Constitutional Law," 88 *Northwestern University Law Review* 410 (1993).

1 The Democratic Functions of Inflexible Constitutions

1. Article V of the Constitution provides the Senate with special protection against amendment; it stipulates that "no State, without its Consent, shall be deprived of its equal Suffrage in the Senate."

2. On the role of constitutional concepts in the impeachment debate, see Michael J. Klarman, "Constitutional Fetishism and the Impeachment Debate," 85 *Virginia Law Review* 631 (1999); see also Cass R. Sunstein, "Impeaching the President," 147 *University of Pennsylvania Law Review* 279 (1998), and Neal Devins, "Bearing False Witness: The Clinton Impeachment and the Future of Academic Freedom," 148 *University of Pennsylvania Law Review* 163 (1999). My co-author and I have taken issue with some of Klarman's claims; see Christopher L. Eisgruber and Lawrence G. Sager, "Impeachment and Constitutional Structure," 5 *Widener Law Symposium Journal* 249, 249–252 (2000).

3. See, e.g., Michael J. Klarman, "Antifidelity," 70 *Southern California Law Review* 381 (1997). See also Mark V. Tushnet, "Following the Rules Laid Down: A Critique of Interpretivism and Neutral Principles," 96 *Harvard Law Review* 781, 787 (1983) and Daniel Lazare, *The Frozen Republic: How the Constitution is Paralyzing Democracy* (1996).

4. The various paths to constitutional amendment are discussed and distinguished in William F. Harris, *The Interpretable Constitution* 174–175, 197–201 (1992).

5. Bruce Ackerman, *We the People: Transformations* 3–31 (1998); Akhil Reed Amar, "Philadelphia Revisited: Amending the Constitution Outside Article V," 55 *University of Chicago Law Review* 1043 (1988); Akhil Reed Amar, "The Consent of the Governed: Constitutional Amendment Outside Article V," 94 *Columbia Law Review* 457 (1994).

6. See Harris, *The Interpretable Constitution*, and Jed Rubenfeld, "Reading the Constitution as Spoken," 104 *Yale Law Journal* 1119 (1995).

7. See, e.g., Walter F. Murphy, "Constitutions, Constitutionalism, and Democracy," in *Constitutionalism and Democracy* 1–7 (Douglas Greenberg and Stanley Katz, et al., eds., 1993). Cf. Lawrence G. Sager, "The Incorrigible Constitution," 65 *New York University Law Review* 893, 894 (1990), in which Sager suggests that the Constitution may be democratic, but cannot be reconciled with "popular sovereignty."

8. My approach shares much in common with the one pursued by Stephen Holmes in "Precommitment and the Paradox of Democracy." See Stephen Holmes, *Passions and Constraints* 134–177 (1995).

9. Id. at 167–169. See also Harris, *The Interpretable Constitution*, at 192 and n. 20.

10. Stephen Holmes puts the point in hyperbolic but illuminating terms when he suggests that constitutional provisions "are not restrictions; the[y] *are* the people." Holmes, *Passions and Constraints*, at 166.

11. See, e.g., Giovanni Sartori, *Comparative Constitutional Engineering: An Inquiry into Structures, Incentives, and Outcomes* 27–79 (2d ed. 1997).

12. On the importance of stability to democracy, see Russell Hardin, *Liberalism, Constitutionalism and Democracy* 233–236 (1999); see also Harris, *The Interpretable Constitution*, at 193.

13. See, e.g., Hardin, *Liberalism, Constitutionalism, and Democracy*, at 82–140; Holmes, *Passions and Constraints*, at 173.

14. See Sartori, *Comparative Constitutional Engineering*, at 197; Donald S. Lutz, "Toward a Theory of Constitutional Amendment," in *Responding to Imperfection: The Theory and Practice of Constitutional Amendment* 260–265 (Sanford Levinson, ed., 1995).

15. Andras Sajo, one of Europe's leading constitutional theorists, has remarked that "[t]he U.S. Constitution has proved one of the most stable texts in legal history." Andras Sajo, *Limiting Government: An Introduction to Constitutionalism* 40 (1999).

16. Sheldon S. Wolin, *The Presence of the Past: Essays on the State and the Constitution* (1989).

17. See, e.g., Lloyd N. Cutler, "To Form a Government," in *Separation of Powers— Does It Still Work?* 1–17 (Robert A. Goldwin and Art Kaufman, eds., 1986); James L. Sundquist, *Constitutional Reform and Effective Government* (1986). For a critique of such complaints, see Thomas O. Sargentich, "The Limits of the Parliamentary Critique of the Separation of Powers," 34 *William and Mary Law Review* 679 (1993).

18. See, e.g., Lynn Baker, "Direct Democracy and Discrimination: A Public Choice Perspective," 67 *Chicago-Kent Law Review* 707, 716, and n. 21 (1991).

19. Political inertia is not all bad, of course; indeed, as we saw in the preceding subsection, institutional stability is indispensable to democratic politics. An optimist might hope that the tendency toward political inertia would alleviate the need for constitution-makers to worry about stability: they could rely upon inertia to produce institutional stability, and then design flexible amendment procedures to minimize inertia's undesirable side-effects. That happy arrangement is certainly possible in theory, but there is no reason to assume that it will apply in the general case. To begin with, the problems of stability and inertia may arise sequentially rather than simultaneously. Stability is most likely to be a problem when the constitution is young, and inertia's effects will be most powerful after the constitution matures. The two problems may also coexist. A people might engage in time-consuming debate about minor changes to the political system even though political inertia protects its basic features.

20. "The dead should not govern the living; but they can make it easier for the living to govern themselves." Holmes, *Passions and Constraints*, at 177.

21. Even when a polity manages to repeal an unsuccessful constitutional provision, the repeal itself may introduce new defects into the constitution. For example, the Twenty-First Amendment to the United States Constitution did not simply eliminate the Eighteenth (which had enacted prohibition); it also made peculiar alterations to American federalism. See Laurence H. Tribe, "How to Violate the Constitution Without Really Trying: Lessons from the Repeal of Prohibition to the Balanced Budget Amendment," in *Constitutional Stupidities, Constitutional Tragedies* 98–100 (William N. Eskridge and Sanford Levinson, eds., 1998).

22. Sager, "Incorrigible Constitution," at 893, 951–953. See also Dennis Mueller, *Constitutional Democracy* 62–63 (1996).

23. Sager, "Incorrigible Constitution," at 939–940; see also id. at 896, 936, 945.

24. Sager recognizes that "[t]he bulk of the document is devoted to a description of the composition, selection, powers, terms of office, and mandated procedures of the executive, legislative, and judicial branches of the federal government." He analogizes them to the Constitution's "liberty-bearing provisions" on the ground that both "attend to . . . matters which are seen as necessary to the sound functioning of government" and hence "are conceptually prior to the play of popular preference over governmental outcomes." Id. at 936.

25. "[A] constitution without a declaration of rights still is a constitution, whereas a constitution whose core and centerpiece is not a frame of government is not a constitution." Sartori, *Comparative Constitutional Engineering*, at 196; see also Sajo, *Limiting Government*, at 21.

26. Human beings would require "perfect wisdom and perfect self-control to recognize and follow a government by a criterion as general as 'that which best serves the ends of government.'" People are, of course, far from perfect; as a result, they need "relatively noncontroversial rules as at least a partial basis for recognizing authority in the presence of their inability to grasp and act upon what was simply beneficial and right." Sotirios A. Barber, *On What the Constitution Means* 50 (1984).

27. The Eighteenth Amendment is perhaps the most salient counter-example. The classic account of the highly factionalized politics surrounding the amendment is Joseph R. Gusfield, *Symbolic Crusade* (2d ed. 1986).

28. The classic statement of British constitutional theory is Albert Venn Dicey, *Introduction to the Study of the Law of the Constitution* 39–85 (10th ed. 1960). For discussion of recent debates about parliamentary sovereignty in Britain, see Michael L. Principe, "Albert Venn Dicey and the Principles of the Rule of Law: Is Justice Blind? A Comparative Analysis of the United States and Great Britain," 22 *Loyola of Los Angeles International and Comparative Law Review* 357 (2000).

29. The draft constitution for Albania would have allowed the People's Assembly to amend the constitution by ordinary legislation. Stephen Holmes and Cass R. Sunstein, "The Politics of Constitutional Revision," in *Responding to Imperfection* (Levinson, ed.), at 292. For the most part, however, even easily amendable constitutions require either a super-majority vote, or a "cooling off" period, or both, before an amendment can be ratified. For example, in Sweden, Article 15 of "The Instrument of Government" stipulates that the Riksdag must pass any proposed fundamental law twice, and that the votes must be separated by a period of not less than nine months, during which a general election must have been held. Constitution of Sweden, in Gisbert H. Flanz, ed., *Constitutions of the Countries of the World* (1996).

30. Some political theorists reduce democracy to majority rule by stipulation. Perhaps the most venerable example is John Locke, who stipulated that if the "Majority . . . may employ all [of its] power in making Laws for the community from time to time, and Executing those Laws by officers of their own appointing . . . then the *Form* of the Government is a perfect *Democracy*." John Locke, *Second Treatise on Government* §132. For a modern example, see Jon Elster, Introduction, in *Constitutionalism and Democracy* 1, 1 (Jon Elster and Rune Slagstad eds., 1988). The best argument for this strategy is that it "leaves little doubt about what democracy is," and so focuses discussion upon "whether and when democracy is a good thing." Frederick Schauer, "Judicial Review of the Devices of Democracy," 94 *Columbia Law Review* 1326 (1994). That might be a sensible approach if there were no other way to give operational content to the concept of democracy. There are, however, better ways to explain what democracy is *and* why so many people consider it an attractive goal.

31. One especially elegant elaboration of this idea appears in Ronald M. Dworkin, *Freedom's Law: The Moral Reading of the Constitution* 15–38 (1996).

32. In describing my arguments as "pragmatic," I do not mean to suggest that they are in any way connected to the philosophical position called "pragmatism." Indeed, my approach is inconsistent with at least one prominent version of "legal pragmatism." According to Daniel Farber, "legal pragmatism" maintains that it is neither necessary nor even possible to "provid[e] a theoretical foundation for constitutional law," and that in law "the ultimate test is always experience." Daniel Farber, "Legal Pragmatism and the Constitution," 72 *Minnesota Law Review* 1331, 1332 (1988). Unlike Farber's argument,

my position assumes that we must test experience against moral criteria, such as "impartiality." We should acknowledge the importance of practical, institutional questions without denying that it is both possible and necessary to identify "theoretical foundations" for constitutionalism. See Sager, "The Incorrigible Constitution," at 944–946.

On the other hand, "pragmatism" is a difficult concept to define; it encompasses a variety of positions. See, e.g., Steven D. Smith, "The Pursuit of Pragmatism," 100 *Yale Law Journal* 409 (1990); Richard Warner, "Why Pragmatism? The Puzzling Place of Pragmatism in Critical Theory," 1993 *University of Illinois Law Review* 535, 538–543. "Sometimes [pragmatism] connotes little more than taking a serious interest in practical politics and the realities of human well-being and suffering; at other times it seems to mean simply being practical, 'pragmatic' in the colloquial, nonphilosophical sense." Id. at 538. Obviously, if "pragmatism" entails nothing more than being practical, then I would be happy to have my theory called "pragmatist"—but I do not think that label would usefully distinguish my approach from anybody else's.

33. Stephen M. Griffin, "The Nominee Is . . . Article V," in *Constitutional Stupidities* (Eskridge and Levinson, eds.), at 52–53. See also Stephen M. Griffin, *American Constitutionalism* 38, 40–41 (1996); Lutz, "Toward a Theory of Constitutional Amendment," at 265–266.

34. According to *The Times* of London, in 1991 "black and Asian people" made up less than 5.6 percent of the British population, and, as of 1994, no British town had "an ethnic minority population of more than 50 per cent, and in only 29 of 459 local authority districts d[id] ethnic populations make up more than 14 per cent of the population." Richard Ford, "UK's Ethnic Minorities Will Double in 40 Years," *The Times*, Jan. 20, 1994, at 5, col. 1.

35. A British political scientist, Vernon Bogdanor, has recently written that "[w]hat was an example to be imitated has become a warning of what to avoid. In the 1990s, not one of the new democracies of Central and Eastern Europe contemplated adopting the British system." Vernon Bogdanor, *Power and the People: A Guide to Constitutional Reform* 11 (1997).

36. Donald Lutz developed a statistical index for measuring constitutional inflexibility; he concluded that "the U.S. Constitution has the second most difficult amendment process" in the world. Lutz, "Toward a Theory of Constitutional Amendment," at 260. Lutz gave first prize to the now-defunct constitution of Yugoslavia. Id. at 261.

37. Griffin, "The Nominee Is . . . Article V," at 51–53.

38. Gary Jacobsohn, *Apple of Gold: Constitutionalism in Israel and the United States* 152 (1993).

39. On the other hand, some commentators have suggested that American majorities may soon become impatient with Article V's restrictions on their power. See David S. Broder, *Democracy Derailed: Initiative Campaigns and the Power of Money* 242 (2000). If Broder is correct, then questions of constitutional reform will acquire great urgency, and it will matter enormously whether American public opinion can absorb and respect the distinction between democracy and majority rule.

40. Robert Bork, *The Tempting of America: The Political Seduction of the Law* 75–76, 81–83 (1990). Originalists have taken a variety of positions about *Brown*. Earl Maltz states flatly that "*Brown* . . . cannot be derived from the original understanding of the Fourteenth Amendment." Earl M. Maltz, "*Brown v. Board of Education*," in *Constitutional Stupidities* (Eskridge and Levinson, eds.), at 207. Michael McConnell has suggested that *Brown* is more consistent with the framers' intentions than either Bork or Maltz would allow. Michael W. McConnell, "Originalism and the Desegregation Decisions," 81 *Virginia Law Review* 947 (1995). For debate about McConnell's historical claims, see Michael J. Klarman, "*Brown*, Originalism, and Constitutional Theory: A Response to Pro-

fessor McConnell," 81 *Virginia Law Review* 1881 (1995); Michael W. McConnell, "The Originalist Justification for *Brown:* A Reply to Professor Klarman," 81 *Virginia Law Review* 1937 (1995).

41. Antonin Scalia, "Originalism: The Lesser Evil," 57 *University of Cincinnati Law Review* 849, 864 (1989).

42. Michael McConnell, "The Importance of Humility in Judicial Review: A Comment on Ronald Dworkin's 'Moral Reading' of the Constitution," 65 *Fordham Law Review* 1269, 1292 (1997).

43. Not all abstract constitutional concepts are moral or political in character. For example, the Seventh Amendment provides, "In Suits at common law, where the value in controversy shall exceed twenty dollars, the right of trial by jury shall be preserved." The concept of a "suit at common law" is an abstraction, but it is probably best viewed as describing a technical legal convention, not a moral, political, or jurisprudential ideal. For that reason, someone might believe that "suits at common law" should be defined pursuant to some historical test (e.g., a suit is "at common law" if it would have been treated as a common-law action at the time when the Seventh Amendment was written and ratified) without thereby becoming, under my definition, an originalist.

44. For a "soft" originalism of this kind, see Michael C. Dorf, "Integrating Normative and Descriptive Constitutional Meaning: the Case of Originalism," 85 *Georgetown Law Review* 1765 (1997).

45. "[T]o apply an unintended meaning is no different from introducing a principle that has no textual basis whatsoever. The only difference between the unintended meaning and the extratextual principle is verbal happenstance." Michael McConnell, "The Role of Democratic Politics in Transforming Moral Convictions into Law," 98 *Yale Law Journal* 1501, 1528 (1989). See also Keith Whittington, *Constitutional Interpretation: Textual Meaning, Original Intent and Judicial Review* 59–60, 93–99, 177–179 (1999); Jack N. Rakove, *Original Meanings: Politics and Ideas in the Making of the Constitution* 368 (1996); Earl M. Maltz, *Rethinking Constitutional Law: Originalism, Interventionism, and the Politics of Judicial Review* 26–27 (1994). A similar thought may be at work in Justice Sutherland's dissent from West Coast Hotel v. Parrish, 300 U.S. 379, 403 (1937), where he opined that "to say . . . that the words of the Constitution mean today what they did not mean when written—that is, that they do not apply to a situation now to which they would have applied then—is to rob that instrument of the essential element which continues it in force as the people have made it until they . . . have made it otherwise."

46. Thomas Nagel, "The Supreme Court and Political Philosophy," 56 *New York University Law Review* 519–520 (1981). See also Whittington, *Constitutional Interpretation,* at 45–46.

47. Dworkin, *Freedom's Law,* at 291.

48. The Eighth Amendment to the Constitution reads, "Excessive bail shall not be required, nor excessive fines imposed, nor cruel and unusual punishments inflicted."

49. Dworkin, *Freedom's Law,* at 291.

50. Id.

51. Id. at 291–292.

52. Some people who call themselves originalists seem to accept Dworkin's distinction (at least in principle). For example, Christopher Wolfe writes that "extrinsic sources" should be consulted only to determine "what the framers meant by the principles they embodied in the Constitution," and not to determine "what the framers thought of given, concrete issues, what might be called their 'expectations.'" Christopher Wolfe, *The Rise of Modern Judicial Review* 50 (1994).

53. Michael W. McConnell, "The Role of Democratic Politics," at 1529. See also Whittington, *Constitutional Interpretation,* at 110–159.

54. Some originalists try to solve this problem via a theory of "dualist democracy," in which constitution-making bodies are regarded as authentic representatives of the people and ordinary legislatures are treated as second-best substitutes. See, e.g., Bruce Ackerman, *We the People: Foundations* 3–33 (1991); Whittington, *Constitutional Interpretation*, at 135–142. In such a scheme, the constitutional text is regarded as the best (and perhaps the only true) expression of the will of the "sovereign people." In my view, such theories are mistaken to identify constitution-making bodies and "the people" so closely: like all other political institutions, constitution-making bodies are merely imperfect procedural representations of the people. See Harris, *The Interpretable Constitution*, at 191–192. But even if we take "dualist democracy" at face value, it cannot render originalism democratic: the Constitution's key provisions may be uniquely authentic expressions of *a people*, but they are not expressions of *today's people*.

55. Walter Berns, "Taking Rights Frivolously," in *Liberalism Reconsidered* 51, 59–64 (Douglas MacLean and Claudia Mills, eds., 1983); see also Walter Berns, *Taking the Constitution Seriously* 171–190 (1987). For a non-originalist example, see Larry Alexander and Frederick Schauer, "On Extrajudicial Constitutional Interpretation," 110 *Harvard Law Review* 1359, 1371–1377 (1997). For criticism of Berns, see Sotirios Barber, *The Constitution of Judicial Power* 10–18 (1993).

56. See Christopher L. Eisgruber, "Disagreeable People," 43 *Stanford Law Review* 275, 287–290, 297–298 (1990).

57. Of course, no text is self-interpreting. In theory, people might disagree about the meaning of any constitutional provision, including Article I, Section 3, which stipulates that "[t]he Senate of the United States shall be composed of two Senators from each State." People might, for example, argue that the constitutional rule is subject to implied exceptions—just as some distinguished constitutional theorists now contend that the apparently clear rules specified in Article V are subject to implied exceptions. See Ackerman, *We the People: Transformations* 3–31; Amar, "The Consent of the Governed." Article I, Section 3's meaning seems "plain" only because two conditions hold: first, it immediately suggests an identical rule to virtually every American reader and, second, we think it plausible, under the circumstances, that the provision settles the number of senators each state should have. Both aspects of the provision's context—the fact that it suggests a single meaning to American readers and the fact that settlement is a plausible goal for the provision—are essential to its apparent lack of ambiguity.

58. William E. Nelson, *The Fourteenth Amendment: From Political Principle to Judicial Doctrine* (1988).

59. For example, Antonin Scalia believes that the Free Speech Clause prohibits the government from criminalizing flag-burning, Texas v. Johnson, 491 U.S. 397 (1989), whereas Robert Bork believes the opposite, Robert H. Bork, *Slouching Towards Gomorrah: Modern Liberalism and American Decline* 99–101 (1996). Michael McConnell believes that the Free Exercise Clause requires government to exempt religiously motivated conduct from some neutral and generally applicable laws, Michael W. McConnell, "The Origins and Historical Understanding of Free Exercise of Religion," 103 *Harvard Law Review* 1409 (1990), whereas Scalia believes the opposite, City of Boerne v. Flores, 521 U.S. 507, 537 (1997) (concurring opinion). Clarence Thomas believes that the Free Speech Clause protects anonymous political speech, McIntyre v. Ohio Elections Commission, 514 U.S. 334, 358 (1995) (concurring opinion), whereas Scalia believes the opposite, id. at 371 (dissenting opinion). Indeed, as noted earlier, originalists cannot even agree about whether Brown v. Board of Education, 347 U.S. 483 (1954), is rightly decided under their theory. See note 40, *supra*, of this chapter.

60. Antonin Scalia, *A Matter of Interpretation: Federal Courts and the Law* 40–41 (1997). See also Christopher Wolfe, *How to Read the Constitution: Originalism, Constitutional Interpretation, and the Judicial Power* 14 (1996), in which Wolfe argues that "the

whole point of the written constitution was to provide a *fixed reference point* by which to preserve—even against the legislature—a government of laws rather than men" (emphasis added). Cf. Akhil Reed Amar, "Our Forgotten Constitution: A Bicentennial Comment," 97 *Yale Law Journal* 281, 293 (1987) ("Because the Constitution was written and ratified in the past, in one sense it is almost by definition a 'conservative' document").

61. Scalia, *A Matter of Interpretation*, at 40–41. Sanford Levinson, whose interpretive and political convictions are very different from Scalia's, has nevertheless expressed a somewhat similar view about the Constitution's purpose: "the very existence of written constitutions with substantive limitations on future conduct is evidence of skepticism, if not outright pessimism, about the moral caliber of future citizens." Sanford Levinson, "Law as Literature," 60 *Texas Law Review* 373, 375 (1982).

62. Thomas Jefferson, Letter to James Madison (December 20, 1787), in Thomas Jefferson, *Writings* 916 (Merrill D. Peterson, ed., 1984).

63. Letter to James Madison, September 6, 1789, in Jefferson, *Writings*, at 959–964.

64. Article VII makes the Constitution binding only upon the states that ratified it. For discussion, see Harris, *The Interpretable Constitution*, 175–197.

65. See, e.g., Herbert Storing, "Slavery and the Moral Foundations of the American Republic," in Robert H. Horwitz, ed., *The Moral Foundations of the American Republic* 313–332 (1990).

66. Abraham Lincoln, Speech at Springfield, Illinois, July 17, 1858, in *Created Equal? The Complete Lincoln-Douglas Debates of 1858* 76 (Paul Angle, ed., 1958).

67. On the treatment of paupers in the period after the founding, see Gerald Neuman, *Strangers to the Constitution* (1996).

68. Michael S. Moore, "The Dead Hand of Constitutional Tradition," 19 *Harvard Journal of Law and Public Policy* 263 (1996).

69. See, e.g., Bork, *Slouching Towards Gomorrah*.

70. Americans have long been noted for their faith in progress. See, e.g., Alexis de Tocqueville, 2 *Democracy in America* 33–34 (1945). There is some evidence, however, that their faith in moral progress (if not scientific progress) has waned. See, e.g., the survey responses described by Robert Putnam, *Bowling Alone: The Collapse and Revival of American Community* 139 (2000).

71. Scalia, *A Matter of Interpretation*, at 40–41 (emphasis added).

72. Joseph M. Bessette and Jeffrey Tulis, "The Constitution, Politics, and the Presidency," in *The Presidency in the Constitutional Order* 3, 10–13 (Bessette and Tulis, eds., 1981).

73. See, e.g., Bork, *The Tempting of America*, at 160, 251–259; Scalia, "The Lesser Evil," at 863–864.

74. See, e.g., Mark V. Tushnet, *Taking the Constitution Away from the Courts* 126 (1999).

75. See, e.g., James Bradley Thayer, "The Origin and Scope of the American Doctrine of Constitutional Law," 7 *Harvard Law Review* 129, 144–150 (1893). Keith Whittington's defense of originalism contains elements of a "clear mistake" theory: he contends that the judiciary should enforce the Constitution when and only when its meaning is "knowable" through a process of interpretive "discovery" that "is not essentially creative." Whittington, *Constitutional Interpretation*, at 6, 36. In Whittington's view, however, some important "parts of the constitutional text have no discoverable meaning," and should be elaborated by other branches through a creative process he calls "construction." Id. at 7. These elements of Whittington's theory are not originalist;

he contends, however, that constitutional meaning is "knowable" or "discoverable" only through originalism. Id. at 50–61, 78.

76. Sartori, *Comparative Constitutional Engineering*, at 199.

2 Judicial Review and Democratic Legitimacy

1. See, e.g., Barry Friedman, "The History of the Countermajoritarian Difficulty, Part One: The Road to Judicial Supremacy," 73 *New York University Law Review* 333 (1998).

2. The paradigmatic example is John Hart Ely, *Democracy and Distrust: A Theory of Judicial Review* (1980). See also Ronald M. Dworkin, *Freedom's Law: The Moral Reading of the Constitution* 17–18, 23–25 (1996) and Frank Michelman, "Law's Republic," 97 *Yale Law Journal* 1493 (1988).

3. See, e.g., Rebecca L. Brown, "Accountability, Liberty, and the Constitution," 98 *Columbia Law Review* 531 (1998); James E. Fleming, "Securing Deliberative Autonomy," 48 *Stanford Law Review* 1 (1995); Sotirios A. Barber, *The Constitution of Judicial Power* (1993); David A. J. Richards, *Toleration and the Constitution* (1986); Michael Perry, *The Constitution, the Courts and Human Rights: An Inquiry into the Legitimacy of Constitutional Policymaking by the Judiciary* (1982). Cf. Lawrence G. Sager, "The Incorrigible Constitution," 65 *New York University Law Review* 893, 894 (1990), which treats judicial review as inconsistent with "popular sovereignty" but not "democracy."

4. The Supreme Court protected the right to make decisions about the upbringing of one's children in Pierce v. Society of Sisters, 268 U.S. 510 (1925), and the right to procreate in Skinner v. Oklahoma, 316 U.S. 535 (1942).

5. The Supreme Court protected flag-burning in Texas v. Johnson, 491 U.S. 397 (1989), and hate-speech in R.A.V. v. City of St. Paul, 505 U.S. 377 (1992).

6. For Supreme Court doctrine regarding commercial speech, see, e.g., 44 Liquormart, Inc. v. Rhode Island, 517 U.S. 484 (1996); for doctrine regarding pornography, see, e.g., Miller v. California, 413 U.S. 15 (1973).

7. Michelman, "Law's Republic," at 1531–1535.

8. Lawyers and judges sometimes suggest that judges have authority to limit the power of elected officials simply because the Constitution is law and judges must enforce the law. The most famous articulation of this argument is John Marshall's: "It is emphatically the province and duty of the judicial department to say what the law is." Marbury v. Madison, 5 U.S. (1 Cranch) 137, 177 (1803). As many have pointed out, Marshall's argument involves a non sequitur. See, e.g., William Van Alstyne, "A Critical Guide to *Marbury v. Madison*," 1969 *Duke Law Journal* 1. For our purposes, the most basic problem is this: courts have a responsibility to decide cases according to law, but it does not follow that the law authorizes courts to grant relief on the basis of their own, controversial interpretations of substantive constitutional provisions. The law might require courts to honor reasonable constitutional judgments by legislatures—just as, in the field of administrative law, courts defer to reasonable statutory interpretations made by administrative agencies. Chevron U.S.A. Inc. v. Natural Resources Defense Council, Inc., 467 U.S. 837 (1984). In order to defend the practice of judicial review, we need to provide some reason why it would be undesirable for the court to defer. For further discussion of the point, see Christopher L. Eisgruber, "The Most Competent Branches: A Response to Professor Paulsen," 83 *Georgetown Law Journal* 347, 350 (1994).

9. Jeremy Waldron, *Law and Disagreement* 264 (1999).

10. Terri Jennings Peretti likewise defends the Supreme Court as a "representative and responsive institution." See generally Terri Jennings Peretti, *In Defense of a Political*

Court 236 and *passim* (1999). Peretti describes the Court as "one of many redundant are-
nas for interest group access and pressure," id. at 220, in a pluralist democratic "system
of numerous and diverse (i.e., differently representative) institutions, which are addi-
tionally deliberately arranged in a nonhierarchical manner." Id. at 212. I largely agree
with Peretti's non-majoritarian, pluralist account of American democracy, but not with
her characterization of the Court as an "arena for interest group access and pressure."
Nevertheless, whether or not one agrees with Peretti's theory, her book provides a valuable empirical study of evidence relevant to any conception (including my own) of the
Court as a representative institution.

11. In the words of Dieter Grimm, a German law professor and a former justice of
the German Constitutional Court, "the decision pro or contra judicial review is not one
of principle but one of pragmatics. The choice has to be made between different types
of democracy, not between democracy and judicial review." Dieter Grimm, "Constitutional Adjudication and Democracy," 33 *Israel Law Review* 193, 201 (1999).

12. See, e.g., James S. Fishkin, *Voice of the People: Public Opinion and Democracy* 17–
26, 54–57 (1995).

13. Id. at 55–56. For extensive empirical analysis of New England town meetings,
see Joseph F. Zimmerman, *The New England Town Meeting: Democracy in Action* (1999).

14. Early works applying this insight to analyze the democratic legitimacy of judi-
cial review include Robert Dahl, "Decision-Making in a Democracy: The Supreme
Court as a National Policy-Maker," 6 *Journal of Public Law* 279 (1957) and Martin
Shapiro, *Freedom of Speech: The Supreme Court and Judicial Review* (1966).

15. Perhaps the stunningly close Florida presidential contest of 2000 will cause
voters to believe that their ballots really matter, but the opposite inference seems at least
equally plausible: voters might conclude that when an election is really close, the winner
is likely to be determined by court battles and procedural snafus, not by anybody's ballot.

16. On the distinction between "voters" and "citizens," see, e.g., Benjamin R. Barber, *A Passion for Democracy* 98 (1998); Robert D. Putnam, *Bowling Alone: The Collapse
and Revival of American Community* 37 (2000); and Fishkin, *Voice of the People*, 84–89,
141–154.

17. See, e.g., Aristotle, *Politics*, Book IV.vii.3 (1294b); id. at Book VI.i.8 (1317b).

18. Admittedly, "senator" is a problematic example: Aristotle assumed that legislative decisions in a democracy would be made by an assembly of all citizens operating
pursuant to the principle of majority rule. Id. at Book VI.i.6 (1317b). There was hence
no need to consider how legislators would be elected; Aristotle dealt only with "magis-
tracies," by which he appears to have meant executive and judicial positions. Id. at Book
VI.i.6 (1317b). One can therefore only speculate about what Aristotle would have said
about the election of legislators in a democracy. Nevertheless, at least one commentator
has concluded that because "voting for candidates is aristocratic rather than democratic
. . . modern democracy would have to be described . . . from Aristotle's point of view as a
mixture of democracy and aristocracy." Leo Strauss, *The City and Man* 35 (1964).

19. Benjamin R. Barber, *Strong Democracy: Participatory Politics for a New Age* 290–
293 (1984). Moreover, "until the American and French revolutions, the lot was considered an integral tool of republican government." Samuel Issacharoff, Pamela S. Karlan,
and Richard Pildes, *The Law of Democracy: Legal Structure of the Political Process* 765–769
(1998).

20. The numbers are from Carol Swain, "Women and Blacks in Congress: 1870–
1996," in *Congress Reconsidered* (Lawrence C. Dodd and Bruce I. Oppenheimer, eds., 6th
ed. 1997).

21. See, e.g., Ely, *Democracy and Distrust*, at 179 ("the choosing of values is a prerogative appropriately left to the majority").

22. In recasting my arguments to fit the majoritarian paradigm of the Supreme Court's critics, I do not mean to claim that the elected branches in fact behave in "majoritarian" fashion. There are two powerful reasons to doubt such claims. First, empirical political science suggests that the American institutions in general are nonmajoritarian. See, e.g., Peretti, *A Political Court*, at 192–198, 209–216. Second, social choice theorists have raised profound theoretical questions about the coherence of the idea of "majoritarianism" in a diverse society. See, e.g., Kenneth Arrow, *Social Choice and Individual Values* (2d ed. 1963); William H. Riker, *Liberalism Against Populism* (1982). For a critical comment on Riker's position, with attention to the implications for judicial review, see Ian Shapiro, *Democracy's Place* 16–52 (1996).

23. Ronald Dworkin suggests that "checkerboard solutions," which split the difference on moral questions, may actually be worse than either of the pure, uncompromised alternatives. Ronald M. Dworkin, *Law's Empire* 182 (1986). My claim is weaker: I claim only that, unlike the practice of sharing resources, the practice of "splitting the moral difference" has no inherent appeal from the standpoint of democracy.

24. This requirement resembles one that Frank Michelman proposes: according to Michelman, judicial review can be consistent with democratic ideals only if the constitutional structure "include[s] arrangements for exposing the basic-law interpreters to the full blast of sundry opinions and interest-articulations in society, including on a fair basis everyone's opinions and articulations of interests, including your own." Frank I. Michelman, *Brennan and Democracy* 60 (1999).

25. Cf. Amy Gutmann and Dennis Thompson, *Democracy and Disagreement* 16 (1996). Gutmann and Thompson argue that in order for citizens to govern themselves democratically in circumstances of persistent moral disagreement, "citizens and accountable officials" must seek "deliberative agreement" and must aim to "achiev[e] provisionally justifiable policies that all can mutually recognize as such." Id. The requirements specified by Gutmann and Thompson are more demanding than my own; in particular, they insist that citizens as well as public officials must participate in public deliberation. I include participation as an aspect of democratic flourishing, which is treated in Chapter 3, but not as a condition of democratic legitimacy.

26. Lawrence G. Sager and I elaborate the idea of a partnership between Court and Congress in Christopher L. Eisgruber and Lawrence G. Sager, "Why the Religious Freedom Restoration Act is Unconstitutional," 69 *New York University Law Review* 437, 462–464 (1994).

27. I have discussed issues pertaining to judicial supremacy in Christopher L. Eisgruber, "The Most Competent Branches." Other useful treatments in the extensive literature on the subject include Mark V. Tushnet, *Taking the Constitution Away from the Courts* 6–32 (1999); Neal Devins, *Shaping Constitutional Values: Elected Government, the Supreme Court, and the Abortion Debate* (1996); Michael Stokes Paulsen, "The Most Dangerous Branch: Executive Power to Say What the Law Is," 83 *Georgetown Law Journal* 217 (1994); Sanford Levinson, "Constitutional Protestantism in Practice: Two Questions for Michael Stokes Paulsen and One for his Critics," 83 *Georgetown Law Journal* 373 (1994); Geoffrey P. Miller, "The President's Power of Interpretation: Implications of a Unified Theory of Constitutional Law," 56 *Law and Contemporary Problems* 35 (1993); and Louis Fisher, *Constitutional Dialogues: Interpretation as Political Process* (1988). On extra-judicial constitutional interpretation more generally, see Keith E. Whittington, *Constitutional Construction: Divided Power and Constitutional Meaning* (1999).

28. 497 U.S. 261 (1990).

29. Id. at 293 (concurring opinion).

30. The incentives facing other judges, including federal circuit court judges, may be quite different, since such judges may be interested in pleasing political officials in order to obtain appointment to higher courts. Cf. Richard Revesz, "Environmental

Regulation, Ideology, and the D.C. Circuit," 83 *Virginia Law Review* 1717, 1720–1721 (1997).

31. Lisa Belkin, "Missouri Seeks to Quit Case of Comatose Patient," *New York Times*, Oct. 12, 1990, at A15. David Moutin, one of Nancy Cruzan's court-appointed guardians, suggested that Missouri's attorney general, William Webster, withdrew from the case for partisan, strategic reasons: "I think they probably don't feel they have as much politically to gain at this point." Id. Webster denied the charge.

Almost immediately after Cruzan's death, however, Webster began waging a new battle in an almost identical case, this time involving a woman named Christine Busalacchi. The attorney general fought the woman's father, who wanted to disconnect his daughter from life support machinery. The Busalacchi case became a campaign issue in 1992. Jay Nixon became Missouri's new attorney general after promising to let Busalacchi's family decide her fate. Staci Kramer, "Woman Dies After Years as Focus of Feeding-Tube Court Battles," *Chicago Tribune*, March 8, 1993, at 3. The St. Louis Post-Dispatch editorialized that "Miss Busalacchi was kept alive for years after it was abundantly and painfully clear that she would never recover—ironically because she had ceased to be a person and had become a cause. Activists willfully distorted the issue, claiming speciously that Miss Busalacchi was simply disabled and that removing her feeding tube was equivalent to murder." "The Long Death of Christine Busalacchi," *St. Louis Post-Dispatch*, March 9, 1993, at 2B.

32. Id. at 356–357 (Stevens dissenting).

33. 121 S. Ct. 525 (2000).

34. Not only could the result in *Bush v. Gore* have altered the balance of power between the liberal and conservative wings of the Court, but it might have influenced the personal retirement plans of at least one justice: Sandra Day O'Connor had been upset by predictions of a Gore victory because she and her husband "wanted to retire to Arizona and a Gore presidency meant they would have to wait another four years because she did not want a Democrat to name her successor." "O'Connor Bemoaned News of Gore Victory," *Houston Chronicle*, December 18, 2000, at A10.

35. Justice Breyer elaborated this point nicely in his dissent, 112 S. Ct. at 557–558.

36. Some commentators have been less kind. When the Supreme Court stayed the Florida recount, "Terrance Sandalow, a law professor and a former dean of the University of Michigan Law School, . . . called the stay 'an unmistakably partisan decision without any foundation in law.'" Linda Greenhouse, "The Justices' Dangerous Foray: They Wade into Politics and Put Legitimacy at Risk," *New York Times*, December 12, 2000, at Sec. 1, p. 1. See also Jeffrey Rosen, "Disgrace," *The New Republic*, December 25, 2000, at 18.

37. Justice Stevens was probably correct when he wrote that although "[t]ime will one day heal the wound," the greatest casualty of the *Bush* decision was "the Nation's confidence in the judge as an impartial guardian of the rule of law." 121 S. Ct. at 542 (dissenting opinion).

38. I am inclined to believe that the Court was wrong both to take the case and to decide it in Bush's favor. When this book went to press, however, academic commentators had produced only a trickle of writing on *Bush*; that trickle will undoubtedly swell to a flood. The issues in *Bush* still strike me as rather novel, and it is possible that some clever defender of the Court will offer a justification I have not yet imagined or appreciated.

39. Some years ago, Mark Tushnet said that if he were ever appointed to the Supreme Court, he would decide cases by asking "which result is, in the circumstances now existing, likely to advance the cause of socialism." Mark V. Tushnet, "The Dilemmas of Liberal Constitutionalism," 42 *Ohio State Law Journal* 411, 424 (1981).

Tushnet's proposal is shocking for several reasons, one of which pertains directly to judicial disinterestedness. Tushnet's reference to "the cause of socialism" smacks of ideological partisanship: a man dedicated to a cause sounds like one who has little inclination to consider new arguments and little patience with anything that stands in the way of his program.

40. On the political character of the American judicial appointments process, see, e.g., Peretti, *A Political Court*, 85–100, 111–130; Henry J. Abraham, *Justices and Presidents* (3d ed. 1992); Sheldon Goldman, "Judicial Appointments and the Presidential Agenda," in *The Presidency in American Politics* 19–47 (Paul Brace, Christine B. Harrington, and Gary King, eds., 1989).

41. For a survey of the mechanisms used to appoint judges to constitutional courts, see European Commission for Democracy Through Law, *The Composition of Constitutional Courts* (1997). On Italy and Turkey in particular, see id. at 51–52, 63.

42. Of course, a politicized appointment procedure is not the only mechanism by which to impose a democratic discipline on a constitutional court. The same end might be achieved in other ways (e.g., by creating the possibility for a legislative override of judicial decisions, or by relaxing the rules for constitutional amendment). In a political system that contained such devices, it might be appropriate for elected officials to have less control over the appointments process.

43. Donald P. Kommers, *The Constitutional Jurisprudence of the Federal Republic of Germany* 21 (2d ed. 1997).

44. Some commentators have suggested that the United States would be better off if Supreme Court justices served a limited term. See L. H. Larue, "Neither Force Nor Will," in *Constitutional Stupidities* (Eskridge and Levinson, eds.), at 57–60; L. A. Powe, Jr., "Old People and Good Behavior," in *Constitutional Stupidities*, at 77–80.

45. Some European constitutions expressly permit non-lawyers to serve on the nation's constitutional court. European Commission for Democracy Through Law, *Constitutional Courts*, at 11–12.

46. Jack N. Rakove, *Original Meanings: Politics and Ideas in the Making of the Constitution* 257–258, 261–262 (1996).

47. John Bell, *French Constitutional Law* 29–33 (1992); Alec Stone, *The Birth of Judicial Politics in France: The Constitutional Council in Comparative Perspective* 8, 231–253 (1992).

48. As of 1992, eleven of the forty-eight persons who had served on the French *Conseil Constitutionnel* since 1959 were non-lawyers. Bell, *French Constitutional Law*, at 36. See also Stone, *Birth of Judicial Politics*, at 50–53.

49. I discuss this problem in the Conclusion to this book.

50. For example, in a famous book that shaped thinking about judicial review for at least one generation, Alexander Bickel wrote that judges "have . . . the leisure, the training, and the insulation to follow the ways of the scholar in pursuing the ends of government." Alexander M. Bickel, *The Least Dangerous Branch* 25–26 (1962). More recently, Anthony Kronman has asserted that traditional techniques of legal education "strengthen[] [students'] capacity for sympathetic understanding." Anthony Kronman, *The Lost Lawyer* 115 (1993).

51. For reflections on these divergent assessments of the profession, see, e.g., Robert Post, "On the Popular Image of the Lawyer: Reflections in a Dark Glass," 75 *California Law Review* 379 (1987).

52. See, e.g., Sager, "Incorrigible Constitution," at 958–959.

53. On the tendency of judges and their law clerks to hide controversial judgments behind citations, see Richard A. Posner, *The Federal Courts: Challenge and Reform* 140–157 (1996).

54. Two political scientists have recently concluded, on the basis of an empirical study, that "precedent rarely influences United States Supreme Court Justices." Harold J. Spaeth and Jeffrey A. Segal, *Majority Rule or Minority Will: Adherence to Precedent on the U.S. Supreme Court* 287 (1999). That extreme conclusion strikes me as implausible; on the other hand, the political science literature as a whole strongly suggests that Supreme Court justices not only can, but do, vote on the basis of their political values. See Peretti, *A Political Court*, at 101–111.

55. See Planned Parenthood of Southeastern Pa. v. Casey, 505 U.S. 833, 868–869 (1992); cf. Thornburgh v. American College of Obstetricians and Gynecologists, 476 U.S. 747, 771 (1986).

56. See, e.g., Robert Bork, "Styles in Constitutional Theory," 1984 *Supreme Court Historical Society Yearbook* 53, 60.

57. Thus, for example, Lucas A. Powe points out that in the Court's McCarthyism cases, its two most sophisticated justices—Harlan and Frankfurter—invented theories to justify acquiescence in the government's behavior. On the other hand, Justices Douglas and Black, whom legal scholars regularly dismissed as jurisprudential clods, stood courageously against Senator McCarthy and for free speech. L. A. Powe, Jr., "Justice Douglas After Fifty Years: The First Amendment, McCarthyism and Rights," 6 *Constitutional Commentary* 267 (1989).

58. 60 U.S. (19 How.) 393 (1851) (holding the Missouri Compromise unconstitutional).

59. 109 U.S. 3 (1883) (holding federal civil rights legislation unconstitutional).

60. 198 U.S. 45 (1905) (holding state maximum hours legislation unconstitutional).

61. 247 U.S. 251 (1918) (holding federal child labor laws unconstitutional).

62. 261 U.S. 525 (1923) (holding minimum wage laws unconstitutional).

63. 347 U.S. 483 (1954).

64. 377 U.S. 533 (1964).

65. 403 U.S. 713 (1971).

66. 418 U.S. 683 (1974).

67. 323 U.S. 214 (1944).

68. 341 U.S. 494 (1951).

69. 350 U.S. 891 (1955).

70. "Few" is not the same as "none." Critics from both the right and the left have insisted that we would be better off if the Court's authority over constitutional interpretation were eliminated or drastically curtailed. For the right-wing critique, see, e.g., Mitchell S. Muncy, ed., *The End of Democracy? The Judicial Usurpation of Politics: The Celebrated First Things Debate With Arguments Pro and Con* (1997) and Robert Nagel, *Constitutional Cultures: The Mentality and Consequences of Judicial Review* (1989). For the left-wing critique, see, e.g., Mark V. Tushnet, *Taking the Constitution Away from the Courts* 129–194 (1999); the Court's decision in *Bush v. Gore* will probably earn it some more left-wing critics. Yet, even Tushnet thinks that judicial review would "surely be a good thing" if it were confined to securing certain basic voting rights, rights to free expression, privacy rights, and relief from "real crises" in which a "determined political majority" repudiates "fundamental constitutional principles." Id. at 157–158. Moreover, Tushnet admits that his proposal "swim[s] upstream" because although "[d]ifferent people disagree about when the courts abuse their power, [Americans] seem to think that an institution pretty much like the one we have is good for us." Id. at 173.

71. Some people have suggested that judicial intervention is an ineffective means by which to protect these values. There is, for example, a raging debate about how much Brown v. Bd. of Education, 347 U.S. 483 (1954), improved the position of African-Americans in the United States. The centerpiece of that debate is Gerald Rosenberg,

The Hollow Hope: Can Courts Bring About Social Change? (1991), which contends that courts are rarely effective vehicles for social change. For a critical comment, see David J. Garrow, "Hopelessly Hollow History: Revisionist Devaluing of *Brown v. Board of Education*," 80 *Virginia Law Review* 151 (1994). The questions raised by Rosenberg's book are relevant to, but distinct from, the questions raised in this chapter. Rosenberg's central thesis is that social activists should not rely upon litigation as the primary mechanism for achieving reform. That might be true even if judicial review makes, on balance, a beneficial contribution to self-government.

72. In a Gallup Poll released on July 10, 2000, 47 percent of Americans said they had either "a great deal of confidence" or "quite a lot of confidence" in the Supreme Court. Marks for the other two branches of the national government were lower: 42 percent for the president, and only 24 percent for Congress. Those numbers are typical of the Gallup Poll results for the last decade: the Court has occasionally trailed the president in Gallup's measurements of public support for institutions, but it has always led Congress, usually by large margins. Chris Chambers, "Military Number One in Public Confidence, HMO's Last," *Gallup News Service*, July 10, 2000. For an analysis of variations in the Court's support, see Gregory A. Caldeira, "Neither the Purse nor the Sword: Dynamics of Public Confidence in the Supreme Court," 80 *American Political Science Review* 1209 (1986). However, few Americans pay much attention to the Court, and whatever support it has may be rather soft. For discussion, see, e.g., Gregory A. Caldeira and James L. Gibson, "The Etiology of Public Support for the Supreme Court," 36 *American Journal of Political Science* 635 (1992); see also Peretti, *A Political Court*, at 163–176.

73. "Today, no sitting Justice is a consistent advocate of judicial restraint . . . [T]he real dispute in modern constitutional law is not between advocates of activism and restraint, but between advocates of liberal and conservative activism." Louis Michael Seidman, "Romer's Radicalism: The Unexpected Revival of Warren Court Activism," 1996 *Supreme Court Review* 67, 87–88.

74. 410 U.S. 113 (1973).

75. 505 U.S. 833 (1992).

76. See United States v. Lopez, 514 U.S. 549 (1995); Printz v. United States, 521 U.S. 898 (1997); and Shaw v. Reno, 509 U.S. 630 (1993).

77. For discussions, see, e.g., Alec Stone Sweet, *Governing with Judges: Constitutional Politics in Europe* (2000); Herman Schwartz, *The Struggle for Constitutional Justice in Post-Communist Europe* (2000); Bruce Ackerman, "The Rise of World Constitutionalism," 83 *Virginia Law Review* 771 (1997).

78. See, e.g., Peter W. Hogg, *Constitutional Law of Canada* 759–769 (4th ed. 1999); Scott Reid, "Penumbras for the People: Placing Judicial Supremacy Under Popular Control," in *Rethinking the Constitution: Perspectives on Canadian Constitutional Reform, Interpretation, and Theory* 200–209 (Anthony Peacock, ed., 1996).

79. See, e.g., Upendra Baxi, *Courage, Craft and Contention* 64–110 (1985).

80. See generally Gary Jacobsohn, *Apple of Gold: Constitutionalism in Israel and the United States* (1993).

81. See generally European Commission for Democracy Through Law, *Constitutional Courts.*

82. For a pessimistic assessment of judicial policy-making, see Rosenberg, *The Hollow Hope*; for a more optimistic account, see Malcolm Feeley and Edward L. Rubin, *Judicial Policy-Making and the Modern State: How the Courts Reformed America's Prisons* (1998).

83. See, e.g., Bruce Cain, John Ferejohn, and Morris Fiorina, *The Personal Vote: Constituency Service and Electoral Independence* 212–219 (1987).

84. Stone Sweet, *Governing with Judges*, at 1.

85. According to *The Economist*, "EU membership has blown a hole through the middle of Dicey's theory of parliamentary sovereignty." *The Economist*, October 14, 1995, at 25. On the impact of devolution, see Michael Burgess, "Constitutional Change in the United Kingdom: New Model or Mere Respray?," 40 *South Texas Law Review* 715 (1999).

86. Many state court judges are elected. For discussion of that practice, see Steven P. Croley, "The Majoritarian Difficulty: Elective Judiciaries and the Rule of Law," 62 *University of Chicago Law Review* 689 (1995).

3 Judicial Review and Democratic Flourishing

1. Amy Gutmann and Dennis Thompson register a complaint of this kind when they say that "judges listen only to citizens who happen to appear before them as parties in the cases before them . . . They are not supposed to listen to voices beyond the instant case because their office seems to requires [sic] a kind of independence that prevents them from taking into account much of the normal controversy of public life." Gutmann and Thompson, *Democracy and Disagreement* 46–47 (1996).

2. See, e.g., Anthony Downs, *An Economic Theory of Democracy* 265–271 (1957).

3. The Internet offers new opportunities for individuals to reach a large audience: it is possible to mount a webpage cheaply. Yet, the fact that somebody creates a webpage does not mean that others will learn of it, much less pay attention to it. On both the promise and the limits of the Internet as a means for democratic deliberation, see Benjamin R. Barber, *A Passion for Democracy* 258–282 (1998).

4. Candidates for office have sometimes claimed that neither they nor the voters have the power to set the agenda for public discussion. A recent article reported that "[s]o many independent interest groups are poised to spend large sums on advertising to influence elections this year that Republicans and Democrats alike fear the candidates may find themselves playing bit parts in their own campaigns." Richard L. Berke, "Interest Groups Prepare to Spend on Campaign Spin," *New York Times*, Jan. 11, 1998, Sec. 1, p. 1.

5. Kathleen Hall Jamieson, *Everything You Think You Know About Politics . . . and Why You're Wrong* xiii, 8–10, 106, 211–212 (2000) argues persuasively that campaign discourse is not quite so vapid as its critics sometimes claim. Even if Jamieson is correct, however, it does not follow that elected officials discuss issues more candidly, deeply, or accessibly than do judicial opinions.

6. Robert Post, for example, offers a theory of democracy centered upon the concept of "public discourse." Post emphasizes that his concept of democracy "does not specifically address systems of representation, voting mechanisms, interest groups, and the like. Its essence lies instead in the hermeneutic apprehension of the meaning of our democratic institutions." Robert C. Post, *Constitutional Domains* 187 (1995). For a constructive critique of Post's position, see generally Frank I. Michelman, *Brennan and Democracy* (1999).

7. For a skeptical treatment of dialogic conceptions of democracy, see James A. Gardner, "Shut Up and Vote: A Critique of Deliberative Democracy and the Life of Talk," 63 *Tennessee Law Review* 421 (1996).

8. Some people have suggested that democratic governments must be faithful to the stronger goal of actual participation by "a significant proportion of the citizenry." See, e.g., Benjamin R. Barber, *Strong Democracy: Participatory Politics for a New Age* (1984); see also James S. Fishkin, *The Voice of the People: Public Opinion and Democracy* 34, 44–48 (1995).

9. Many scholars have noted that in large polities, meaningful political participa-

tion by ordinary citizens is most achievable in local units of governments. See, e.g, Gerald Frug, "The City as a Legal Concept," 93 *Harvard Law Review* 1057 (1980); Clayton Gillette, "Plebiscites, Participation, and Collective Action in Local Government Law," 86 *Michigan Law Review* 930, 952 (1988); Jane Mansbridge, *Beyond Adversary Democracy* (1980); Robert Dahl and Edwin Tufte, *Size and Democracy* 41–66 (1973). A critique of localist theories of democracy appears in Richard Briffault, "Our Localism: Part II— Localism and Legal Theory," 90 *Columbia Law Review* 346 (1990).

10. Robert Putnam reports that "social capital" is greater in small towns and rural areas than in large cities. Robert D. Putnam, *Bowling Alone: The Collapse and Revival of American Community* 119, 138, and 205–207 (2000).

11. These points have long been recognized and analyzed by positive political theorists. See, e.g., Charles M. Tiebout, "A Pure Theory of Local Expenditures," 64 *Journal of Political Economy* 416 (1956), and Albert O. Hirschman, *Exit, Voice, and Loyalty: Responses to Decline in Firms, Organizations, and States* (1970). For an application to American constitutional jurisprudence, see Michael W. McConnell, "Federalism: Evaluating the Founders' Design," 54 *University of Chicago Law Review* 1484, 1503–1504 (1987).

12. Thoughtful treatments of both the problems and potential for local governance appear in Martha Derthick, ed., *Dilemmas of Scale in America's Federal Democracy* (1999). See also, e.g., Paul E. Peterson, *City Limits* (1981); Stephen L. Elkin, *City and Regime in the American Republic* (1987); and Dennis P. Judd and Todd Swanstrom, *City Politics* (1994).

13. In 1994, Macks Creek, Missouri, netted about $165,000 from traffic tickets— approximately 75 percent of the annual revenue for the town, which had a population of less than 300. In 1995, however, the town's police officers ticketed the wrong man: a state legislator, who successfully sponsored a bill prohibiting Missouri municipalities from raising more than 45 percent of their revenue from traffic tickets. Three years later, Macks Creek was in bankruptcy; some of the town's police cruisers were repossessed. John Rogers, "Missouri Town, Undone By Its Own Speed Trap, Is Broke and Bewildered," *Newark Star-Ledger,* July 17, 1998, at 22.

14. James Madison, "Federalist 10," in *The Federalist Papers* 77 (Clinton Rossiter, ed., 1961).

15. In general, discussions of judicial review too often focus upon grand clashes between Court and Congress; the twists introduced by federalism are unjustifiably neglected. For discussion of this point in connection with historical arguments, see Jack N. Rakove, "The Origins of Judicial Review: A Plea for New Contexts," 49 *Stanford Law Review* 1031, 1041–1050 (1997).

16. The classic quotation is from Oliver Wendell Holmes: "I do not think that the United States would come to an end if we lost our power to declare an act of Congress void. I do think the Union would be imperiled if we could not make that declaration as to the laws of the several states." Oliver Wendell Holmes, "Law and the Court," in *Collected Legal Papers* 295–296 (1920).

17. A famous example is Colorado's Amendment Two, which deprived local communities of the power to prohibit discrimination on the basis of sexual orientation. Amendment Two was held unconstitutional in Romer v. Evans, 517 U.S. 620 (1996). On state initiatives and referenda more generally, see, e.g., Thomas E. Cronin, *Direct Democracy: The Politics of Initiative, Referendum, and Recall* (1989).

18. John Hart Ely, *Democracy and Distrust: A Theory of Judicial Review* 87 (1980).

19. Edward Rubin and Malcolm Feeley observe that, under the standard view of constitutional doctrine, "the very essence of American federalism is that the national government is forbidden to interfere with state policies for managing and controlling

local governments." Edward L. Rubin and Malcolm Feeley, "Federalism: Some Notes on a National Neurosis," 41 *U.C.L.A. Law Review* 903, 919 and n. 66 (1994). In practice, matters are a bit more complex. See, e.g., Richard Briffault, "Our Localism: Part I—The Structure of Local Government Law," 90 *Columbia Law Review* 1 (1990); David J. Barron, "The Promise of Cooley's City: Traces of Local Constitutionalism," 147 *University of Pennsylvania Law Review* 487 (1999).

20. See S. E. Finer, Vernon Bogdanor, and Bernard Rudden, *Comparing Constitutions* 58–59, 64–65 (1995).

21. Frederick Schauer, "The Constitution of Fear," in *Constitutional Stupidities, Constitutional Tragedies* 84–89 (William N. Eskridge, Jr., and Sanford Levinson, eds., 1998).

22. Lynn Baker, "Direct Democracy and Discrimination: A Public Choice Perspective," 67 *Chicago-Kent Law Review* 707, 716 and n. 21 (1991); Daniel Mandelker, Dawn Clark Netsch, Peter W. Salisch, Jr., and Judith Welch Wegner, *State and Local Government in a Federal System: Cases and Materials* 701–703 (3d ed. 1990).

23. One crucial effect of this gridlock is to decentralize revenue-raising and spending. "In contrast to France, where 99 percent of all revenue is collected and approximately 85 percent of all expenditures are made by the national government, U.S. local governments receive only 33 percent of their revenue from the states and the federal government." Kathryn M. Doherty and Clarence Stone, "Local Practice in Transition: From Government to Governance," in *Dilemmas of Scale* (Derthick, ed.), at 160. Obviously, these differences are not the result of judicially enforced limits; Supreme Court doctrine provides Congress and the states with virtually unlimited authority to preempt local control over raising and spending public money.

24. Robert F. Nagel, "The Last Centrifugal Force," in *Constitutional Stupidities* (Eskridge and Levinson, eds.), at 71–74.

25. Professors Bednar and Eskridge have made this point in a superb article that applies "positive political theory" to analyze the Supreme Court's federalism doctrine. Jenna Bednar and William N. Eskridge, Jr., "Steadying the Court's 'Unsteady Path': A Theory of the Judicial Enforcement of Federalism," 68 *Southern California Law Review* 1447, 1476 (1995).

26. Professors Bednar and Eskridge again make a similar point, id. at 1480; their analysis, however, is concerned principally with "dormant commerce clause" issues (which I shall discuss briefly at the end of Chapter 6) rather than with individual rights issues.

27. An imaginative discussion of the relationship between federalism and national institutions appears in Bruce Ackerman, "The New Separation of Powers," 113 *Harvard Law Review* 633, 671–683 (2000).

28. In practice, however, cultural barriers may be insufficient unless buttressed by formal institutions. In a comparative study of federalism, Bednar, Eskridge, and Ferejohn argue that after 1830 "the system of decentralized administration that had characterized British life became unglued" because "[t]here was nothing in the British constitutional system to stand in the way of highly organized and disciplined parties once they appeared on the scene." Bednar and her co-authors conclude that "fragmentation of national authority might be a necessary condition for a durable federalism." Jenna Bednar, William N. Eskridge, Jr. and John Ferejohn, "A Political Theory of Federalism," in *Constitutional Culture and Democratic Rule* 238, 241 (John Ferejohn, Jack Rakove, and Jonathan Riley, eds., 2001).

29. Of course, it remains possible that judges will do a bad job supervising local government. For arguments that judicial enforcement of individual rights has harmed local governments, see, e.g., James Q. Wilson, "City Life and Citizenship," in *Dilemmas*

of Scale (Derthick, ed.), at 34–35, and Martha Derthick, "How Many Communities? The Evolution of American Federalism," in *Dilemmas of Scale* at 135–149. Both authors seem, however, to want *less* control over localities rather than *legislative* control over localities. Indeed, Derthick's argument is particularly complex; she suggests that the net effect of judicial intervention has been to increase state legislative control over localities. Id. at 142–149.

30. "The Constitution in action at the trial level most frequently involves damage actions seeking to invoke protections of minimal civil decency against street-level bureaucrats who exercise delegated discretion." Seth F. Kreimer, "Exploring the Dark Matter of Judicial Review: a Constitutional Census of the 1990's," 5 *William and Mary Bill of Rights Journal* 427, 429 (1997). See also Matthew D. Adler, "Judicial Restraint in the Administrative State: Beyond the Countermajoritarian Difficulty," 145 *Pennsylvania Law Review* 759 (1997); Barry Friedman, "Dialogue and Judicial Review," 91 *Michigan Law Review* 577, 630–634 (1993).

31. Cass R. Sunstein, "*Dred Scott v. Sandford* and its Legacy," in Robert P. George, ed., *Great Cases in Constitutional Law* 64, 81 (2000). See also Cass R. Sunstein, "Leaving Things Undecided," 110 *Harvard Law Review* 6, 98 (1996); Mary Ann Glendon, *Abortion and Divorce in Western Law* 45 (1987).

32. Ronald Dworkin makes a similar point. Ronald M. Dworkin, *Freedom's Law: The Moral Reading of the American Constitution* 345 (1996).

33. Jeremy Waldron, *Law and Disagreement* 291 (1999).

34. Sunstein, "Leaving Things Undecided," at 98 n. 498.

35. Sunstein's comment about "futility" is directed, in particular, to the "public outcry" that followed "*Dred Scott, Lochner v. New York, Brown v. Board of Education,* and *Roe v. Wade.*" Id. The public reaction to *Scott* included the Lincoln-Douglas debates; it seems odd to characterize Lincoln's argument as "futile." For further discussion of Lincoln's response to *Scott,* see "Judicial Review in Historical Perspective," later in this chapter.

36. One political scientist goes so far as to say that "[f]or the most part, Court decisions are tentative and reversible like other political events." Louis Fisher, "The Curious Belief in Judicial Supremacy," 25 *Suffolk Law Review* 85, 87 (1991). See also Barry Friedman, "Dialogue and Judicial Review," at 643–648; Neil Devins, "The Interactive Constitution: An Essay on Clothing Emperors and Searching for Constitutional Truth," 85 *Georgetown Law Review* 691 (1997).

37. By no means do I wish to claim that legislators *ought* to heed only preferences. It is undoubtedly desirable and important for legislators to deliberate conscientiously about justice. See, e.g., Jeremy Waldron, *The Dignity of Legislation* (1999); see also Gutmann and Thompson, *Democracy and Disagreement,* at 46–47. Nevertheless, legislatures are, for good reason, structured in a way that forces legislators to be sensitive to preferences. The resulting incentives tend to produce various kinds of "interest-group deals."

38. The classic statement of this position is James B. Thayer, "The Origin and Scope of the American Doctrine of Constitutional Law," 7 *Harvard Law Review* 129, 155 (1893). A modern restatement is Mark V. Tushnet, *Taking the Constitution Away From the Courts* 57–65 (1999).

39. Perhaps the best-known statement of this position is Mary Ann Glendon, *Rights Talk: The Impoverishment of Political Discourse* (1991). Glendon complains that "a gradual evolution in the role of courts" has "propelled" American political discourse to take the form of what she calls "rights talk." Id. at 4. She blames this "rights talk" for a bevy of social ills: among other things, it "promotes unrealistic expectations, heightens social conflict, . . . inhibits dialogue that might lead toward consensus, accommodation,

[or] the discovery of common groun[d,] . . . [and] undermines the principal seedbeds of civic and personal virtue." Id. at 14. See also Sunstein, "Leaving Things Undecided," at 19–20.

40. 410 U.S. 113 (1973).

41. Ruth Bader Ginsburg, "Speaking in a Judicial Voice," 67 *N.Y.U. Law Review* 1185, 1205–1209 (1992); Ginsburg, "Some Thoughts on Autonomy and Equality in Relation to *Roe v. Wade*," 63 *North Carolina Law Review* 375, 381–383, 385–386 (1985); Glendon, *Abortion and Divorce in Western Law*, at 40–58; Robert A. Burt, *The Constitution in Conflict* 346–350 (1992); Sunstein, "Leaving Things Undecided," at 50.

42. See, e.g., Ginsburg, "Speaking in a Judicial Voice," at 1208.

43. The Supreme Court held unconstitutional Nebraska's law banning partial-birth abortions in Stenberg v. Carhart, 120 S. Ct. 2597 (2000). The Court's decision, of course, did not end the controversy over the procedure. See, e.g., William Glaberson, "The Supreme Court: The Course Ahead; Foes of Abortion Start New Effort After Court Loss," *New York Times*, June 30, 2000, at A1, col. 6.

44. Ginsburg says that *Roe* "halted a political process that was moving in the direction of reform and thereby . . . prolonged divisiveness and deferred settlement of the issue." Ginsburg, "Speaking in a Judicial Voice," at 1208. Burt speculates that if the *Roe* Court had been more restrained, the nation might have achieved the "rough, tacit accommodation" that he believes is required by the abortion controversy. Burt, *The Constitution in Conflict*, at 351.

45. This ironic faith is shared by people of many different political convictions. For example, Robert Nagel, a conservative, blames lawyers and judges for making "disagreement and instability the norm" with regard to constitutional principles. Robert Nagel, *Constitutional Cultures: The Mentality and Consequences of Judicial Review* 22 (1989). In Nagel's view, the Supreme Court's willingness to intervene regularly in social controversies has tended to break down tacit agreements without which the American political system cannot function properly. Id. at 23–24.

Likewise, Michael Sandel, a progressive communitarian, argues that Americans have attempted to "banish moral and religious argument from the public realm"; this effort is "impoverishing political discourse and eroding the moral and civic resources necessary to self-government." Michael Sandel, *Democracy's Discontent: America in Search of a Public Philosophy* 23 (1996). According to Sandel, the Supreme Court "presides over" this unfortunate quest, and constitutional law is the "clearest expression" of it. Id. at 28. It is not clear whether Sandel thinks the Court can solve this problem. He does, however, blame the Court for having helped to generate it. In Sandel's view, "constitutional discourse has come to define the terms of political discourse in American public life." Id. at 108.

46. During the last forty years, fundamentalist and evangelical Protestant denominations have grown while mainstream Protestant denominations have weakened. See, e.g., Robert Wuthnow, *The Restructuring of American Religion: Society and Faith Since World War II* (1988); Wade Roof Clark and William McKinney, *American Mainline Religion: Its Changing Shape and Future* (1987); and Roger Finke and Rodney Stark, *The Churching of America: 1776–1990* (1992). The conclusions from these studies are crisply summarized in Putnam, *Bowling Alone*, at 75–78. Moreover, beginning in the 1970s, evangelicals became more politically active. Id. at 161–162. Robert Wuthnow attributes this development to a variety of factors, such as changes in the demographics of evangelical faiths; the increasing influence of religious television; and a series of episodes (including Watergate and the *Roe* decision) that blurred traditional boundaries between "morality and public life." Wuthnow, *The Restructuring of American Religion*, at 198–202.

47. Or consider the case of affirmative action. Would affirmative action have been less controversial if the Supreme Court had avoided ruling upon it? That seems un-

likely. Consider the following analysis from a *New York Times* reporter: "[affirmative action] is an easy issue for politicians and the news media to focus on. It lends itself to sound bites and expressions of high moral principle like fairness, equality, color-blindness, and inclusiveness. It avoids vexing questions about what to do about the failure of minority schools, the growing class divide within minority groups and the stereotypes that keep Americans apart." Stephen A. Holmes, "Thinking About Race With a One-Track Mind," *New York Times*, Dec. 21, 1997, Sec. 4, p. 1.

48. I suspect that criticisms of "rights consciousness" in America ultimately have little to do with the distinction between legislatures and courts. At issue are more substantive questions about the government's role. Some scholars believe that local government should have "control over . . . the process of village life on which moral development depends." Wilson, "City Life and Citizenship," at 35. People who take this view will oppose the supervision of local governments by either courts or pluralist legislatures. Other scholars believe that "there is no escaping the fact that we live in a diverse society" and that "[a]ttempting to create small, homogenous and 'pietistic' communities [is] a short-sighted strategy as we move into the twenty-first century." Doherty and Stone, "Local Practice in Transition," at 174–175. People who take this view will insist that some institution should identify and enforce limits upon the discretion of "villages" to influence "moral development." In neither case does the distinction between courts and legislatures matter much.

49. Lincoln, First Inaugural Address, Mar. 4, 1861, in 4 *The Collected Works of Abraham Lincoln* 268 (Roy P. Basler, ed., 1953).

50. Taney issued a writ of habeas corpus instructing the commanding officer of a Baltimore fort to produce John Merryman, a secessionist agitator imprisoned at the fort. The officer refused, and said that he was acting pursuant to Lincoln's instructions. The case, *Ex Parte Merryman*, 17 Fed. Cas. 144 (C.C.D. Md. 1861), and its background are discussed in James M. McPherson, *Battle Cry of Freedom: The Civil War Era* 287–289 (1988).

51. In 1864, Congress added a tenth seat to the Supreme Court, which Lincoln filled with Stephen Field. Charles Fairman, *Reconstruction and Reunion, Part 1* 4 (1971). After Lincoln's death, the Republican Congress shrunk the Court to deny Andrew Johnson any appointments, and enlarged it for the benefit of Ulysses S. Grant. For discussion, see, e.g., Bruce Ackerman, *We the People: Transformations* 274–275 (1998).

52. See Sanford Levinson, *Constitutional Faith* 141–142 (1988).

53. Lincoln's Speech at Chicago, July 10, 1858, in *Created Equal? The Complete Lincoln-Douglas Debates of 1858* 36 (Paul Angle, ed., 1958); Lincoln's Opening Speech at Quincy, in *Complete Debates*, at 333.

54. See, e.g., Sunstein, "*Dred Scott v. Sandford* and its Legacy," at 75–76; Sunstein, "Leaving Things Undecided," at 49.

55. See, e.g., Lincoln's Speech at Chicago, July 10, 1858, in *Complete Debates*, at 41; Lincoln's Reply at Alton, October 15, 1858, in *Complete Debates*, at 386.

56. Lincoln's Speech at Springfield, Illinois, June 16, 1858, in *Complete Debates*, at 2.

57. Lincoln's Speech at Chicago, July 10, 1858, in *Complete Debates*, at 34–35.

58. Lincoln said that Douglas "looks upon this matter of slavery . . . as an exceedingly little thing—only equal to the question of the cranberry laws of Indiana—as something having no moral question in it . . . it so happens that there is a vast portion of the American people who do *not* look upon that matter as being this very little thing. They look at it as a vast moral evil." Lincoln's Speech at Chicago, July 10, 1858, in *Complete Debates*, at 35. See also Lincoln's Reply at Alton, Oct. 15, 1858, in *Complete Debates*, at 387–390.

59. Lincoln's Reply at Galesburg, Oct. 7, 1858, in *Complete Debates*, at 310.

60. Lincoln's Reply at Alton, Oct. 15, 1858, in *Complete Debates*, at 393; Lincoln's Opening Speech at Quincy, Oct. 13, 1858, in *Complete Debates*, at 334–335.

61. Lincoln's Speech at Chicago, July 10, 1858, in *Complete Debates*, at 32. Later, in Alton, Lincoln said he meant in his House Divided Speech "to propose nothing but what has a most peaceful tendency." Lincoln's Reply at Alton, Oct. 15, 1858, in *Complete Debates*, at 386.

62. For discussion of Lincoln's thinking during the Fort Sumter crisis, see McPherson, *Battle Cry of Freedom*, at 271–275 and n. 78. McPherson reports that Lincoln gave the South a choice between backing down at Sumter or firing upon unarmed supply convoys. Id. at 271. When the South elected the latter option, it stood "convicted of a hostile act," id., and the news "galvanized the North." Id. at 274.

63. "Instead of removing the issue of slavery from politics, the Court's ruling became itself a political issue." Id. at 176.

64. Id. at 177–178; Paul M. Angle, "Introduction," in *Complete Debates*, at xxviii–xxx (1958).

65. "Thus instead of crippling the Republican party as Taney had hoped, the Dred Scott decision strengthened it by widening the sectional schism among Democrats." McPherson, *Battle Cry of Freedom*, at 178.

66. James M. McPherson, "Politics and Judicial Responsibility: *Dred Scott v. Sandford*," in *Great Cases* (George, ed.), at 92–93.

67. "In this and like communities, public sentiment is everything. With public sentiment, nothing can fail; without it nothing can succeed." Lincoln's Reply at Ottawa, Aug. 21, 1858, in *Complete Debates*, at 128.

68. Lincoln's Reply to Douglas at Ottawa, in *Complete Debates*, at 128; see also Lincoln's Reply to Douglas at Galesburg, Oct. 7, 1858, in *Complete Debates*, at 307–308.

69. Lincoln's Reply to Douglas at Galesburg, Oct. 7, 1858, in *Complete Debates*, at 308.

70. Lincoln said, "[I]t is my opinion that the Dred Scott decision, as it is, never would have been made in its present form if the party that made it had not been sustained previously by the elections. My own opinion is, that the new Dred Scott decision, deciding against the right of the people of the states to exclude slavery, will never be made, if that party is not sustained by the elections. I believe, further, that it is just as sure to be made as to-morrow is to come, if that party shall be sustained." Lincoln's Reply to Douglas at Galesburg, Oct. 7, 1858, in *Complete Debates*, at 309.

71. "In November 1857 the *Washington Union*, organ of the Buchanan administration, carried an article asserting that the abolition of slavery in northern states had been an unconstitutional attack on property." McPherson, *Battle Cry of Freedom*, at 180.

72. In *Scott*, Taney said that the right of slavery was "distinctly and expressly affirmed in the Constitution." Scott v. Sandford, 60 U.S. (19 How.) 393, 451 (1856). Given that the word "slavery" never appears in the Constitution—and that, indeed, the framers exercised great ingenuity to avoid any express *mention*, much less *affirmation*, of slavery—this claim is remarkable. But that was not Taney's most ambitious exercise in creative interpretation: more astonishing still was his conclusion that when the Declaration of Independence said that "All men are created equal," it meant that *not* all men are created equal. Id. at 410. For discussion, see generally Christopher L. Eisgruber, "*Dred* Again: Originalism's Forgotten Past," 10 *Constitutional Commentary* 37 (1993).

73. "[H]e who moulds public sentiment, goes deeper than he who enacts statutes or pronounces decisions. He makes statutes and decisions possible or impossible to be executed." Lincoln's Reply at Ottawa, Aug. 21, 1858, in *Complete Debates*, at 128.

74. Lincoln's Reply at Galesburg, Oct. 7, 1858, in *Complete Debates*, at 310–311.

75. For example, in the Ottawa debate, Lincoln said: "Judge Douglas is a man of vast influence, so great that it is enough for many men to profess to believe anything, when they once find out that Judge Douglas professes to believe it. Consider also the attitude he occupies at the head of a large party—a party which he claims has a majority of all the voters in the country." *Complete Debates*, at 128. See also id. at 311.

76. Garry Wills calls the Gettysburg Address both a "stunning verbal coup" that amounted to a "'refounding'" of the Republic, and a "daring[] act of open-air sleight-of-hand," which "picked" the "intellectual pocket" of every person who heard the speech. Garry Wills, *Lincoln at Gettysburg: The Words that Remade America* 38–40 (1992).

77. Christopher L. Eisgruber, "Disagreeable People," 43 *Stanford Law Review* 275 (1990).

4 Text and History in Hard Cases

1. For elegant taxonomies of constitutional argument, see Philip Bobbitt, *Constitutional Fate: Theory of the Constitution* (1982) and William F. Harris II, *The Interpretable Constitution* (1993).

2. See, e.g., David Strauss, "Common Law Constitutional Interpretation," 63 U. Chi. L. Rev. 877, 883 (1996).

3. For example, Article II, Section 4 of the Constitution provides that the president "shall be removed from Office on Impeachment for, and Conviction of, Treason, Bribery, or other high Crimes and Misdemeanors." In modern American English, the term "misdemeanors" usually refers to a set of minor criminal offenses; hence, "high crimes and misdemeanors" sounds rather like "felonies and misdemeanors." When the Constitution was drafted, however, "misdemeanors" had a meaning broad enough to encompass some non-criminal forms of "maladministration," and the technical criminal law category of "misdemeanor" was not well developed. See, e.g., Laurence H. Tribe, "Defining High Crimes and Misdemeanors: Basic Principles," 67 *George Washington Law Review* 712, 717 (1999). The Second Amendment's "right to keep and bear arms" may present analogous difficulties; for discussion of the problem, see "Bad Provisions: Ghost Towns and Interpretive Quarantines" later in this chapter.

4. 394 U.S. 557 (1969).

5. 354 U.S. 476, 485 (1957).

6. In Miller v. California, 413 U.S. 15 (1973) and other cases, the Court reformulated the rules defining obscenity. In that respect, *Roth* has been modified. The Court has not, however, retreated from *Roth*'s most basic holding, which was that the First Amendment does not prohibit states from criminalizing the circulation and dissemination of obscene materials.

7. *Stanley*, 394 U.S. at 565.

8. Id.

9. See Paris Adult Theatre I v. Slaton, 413 U.S. 49, 113 (1972) (Brennan, J., dissenting).

10. For further discussion of *Stanley* and other examples of interpretive fetishism, see Christopher L. Eisgruber, "The Fourteenth Amendment's Constitution," 69 *Southern California Law Review* 84–98 (1995).

11. Ronald M. Dworkin, *Life's Dominion: An Argument About Abortion, Euthanasia, and Individual Freedom* (1993) (abortion and the Establishment Clause); Akhil Reed Amar, "Attainder and Amendment 2: Romer's Rightness," 95 *Michigan Law Review* 203 (1996) (gay rights and the Bill of Attainder Clause); Laurence H. Tribe, "Taking Text and History Seriously: Reflections on Free-Form Method in Constitutional Interpretation," 108 *Harvard Law Review* 1221, 1298–1299 n. 247 (1995) (school desegregation

and the Bill of Attainder Clause); and David Cole and William N. Eskridge, Jr., "From Hand-Holding to Sodomy: First Amendment Protection of Homosexual (Expressive) Conduct," 29 *Harvard Civil Rights-Civil Liberties Law Review* 319 (1993) (gay rights and the First Amendment).

12. Akhil Reed Amar, "Intratextualism," 112 *Harvard Law Review* 747, 793–794 (1999).

13. Tribe, "Taking Text and Structure Seriously," at 1236. Tribe goes on to recommend the use of "topologically sound modes of constitutional interpretation," which, he says, are essential in order to preserve the Constitution's "particular architectural configuration." Id. at 1237.

14. Sanford Levinson, *Constitutional Faith* (1988).

15. Michael McConnell, "The Role of Democratic Politics in Transforming Moral Convictions into Law," 98 *Yale Law Journal* 1501, 1525 (1998).

16. Michael McConnell, "Federalism: Evaluating the Founders' Design," 54 *University of Chicago Law Review* 1484, 1486 (1987).

17. Akhil Reed Amar, "The Bill of Rights as a Constitution," 100 *Yale Law Journal* 1131, 1168–1175 (1991).

18. Tribe, "Taking Text and Structure Seriously," at 1270, 1273.

19. Eisgruber, "The Fourteenth Amendment's Constitution," at 62; Christopher L. Eisgruber, "Justice and the Text: Rethinking the Constitutional Relation Between Principle and Prudence," 43 *Duke Law Journal* 1 (1993).

20. For a similar point, made from an historian's perspective, see Jack N. Rakove, "Two Foxes in the Forest of History," 11 *Yale Journal of Law and the Humanities* 191, 199 (1999).

21. Jack N. Rakove, *Original Meanings: Politics and Ideas in the Making of the Constitution* 197 (1996).

22. Amar, "Intratextualism," at 813.

23. 478 U.S. 186 (1986).

24. Id. at 195.

25. Id.

26. Id. at 191.

27. See "The 'Dead Hand' Problem Revisited," in Chapter 1.

28. The Supreme Court found a right to travel implicit in the structure of the Constitution before the Fourteenth Amendment was ratified. Crandall v. Nevada, 73 U.S. 35 (1867). The Court used the Fourteenth Amendment's Due Process Clause to protect parental autonomy. Pierce v. Society of Sisters, 268 U.S. 510 (1925); Meyer v. Nebraska, 262 U.S. 390 (1923). The Court generalized the Equal Protection Clause to reach the federal government by "reverse incorporating" that Clause into the Fifth Amendment's Due Process Clause. Bolling v. Sharpe, 347 U.S. 497 (1954).

29. See, e.g., Peggy Cooper Davis, *Neglected Stories: The Constitution and Family Values* (1997).

30. Ronald M. Dworkin, *Freedom's Law: The Moral Reading of the American Constitution* 73, 78 (1996); John Hart Ely, *Democracy and Distrust: A Theory of Judicial Review* 32 (1980).

31. Buck v. Bell, 274 U.S. 200, 208 (1927).

32. Times v. Sullivan, 376 U.S. 254 (1964).

33. Engel v. Vitale, 370 U.S. 421 (1962).

34. Miranda v. Arizona, 384 U.S. 436 (1966); Dickerson v. United States, 120 S. Ct. 2326 (2000).

35. Lucas v. South Carolina Coastal Council, 505 U.S. 1003 (1992).

36. The obsession with linguistic specificity forces judges to decide cases on "grounds that have nothing to do with these semantic devices, but that are hidden from

view by . . . them. The search for limits on judicial power ends by allowing judges the undisciplined power of the arbitrary." Dworkin, *Freedom's Law*, at 81.

37. Ronald Dworkin takes a more extreme view: he claims that the distinction between enumerated and unenumerated rights is "bogus" and ought to be "shut up with other legal concepts dishonorably discharged for bad philosophy." Dworkin, *Freedom's Law*, at 72.

38. See, e.g., Patrick Lee and Robert P. George, "What Sex Can Be: Self-Alienation, Illusion, or One-Flesh Union," 42 *American Journal of Jurisprudence* 135 (1997). For counter-arguments, see, e.g., Andrew Koppelman, "Is Marriage Inherently Heterosexual?," 42 *American Journal of Jurisprudence* 51 (1997); Stephen Macedo, "Homosexuality and the Conservative Mind," 84 *Georgetown Law Journal* 261, 276 (1995).

39. Linda Greenhouse, "When Second Thoughts in Case Come Too Late," *New York Times*, Nov. 5, 1990, at A14, Col. 5.

40. This idea is gathering momentum in the scholarly literature. The seminal article is Sanford Levinson, "The Embarrassing Second Amendment," 99 *Yale Law Journal* 637 (1989). Other significant treatments include L. A. Powe, Jr., "Guns, Words, and Constitutional Interpretation," 38 *William and Mary Law Review* 1311 (1997); William Van Alstyne, "The Second Amendment and the Personal Right to Arms," 43 *Duke Law Journal* 1236 (1994); Glenn Harlan Reynolds, "A Critical Guide to the Second Amendment," 62 *Tennessee Law Review* 461 (1995); Nelson Lund, "The Past and Future of the Individual's Right to Arms," 31 *Georgia Law Review* 1 (1996); Eugene Volokh, "The Commonplace Second Amendment," 73 *N.Y.U. Law Review* 793 (1998); and Randy E. Barnett and Don B. Kates, "Under Fire: The New Consensus on the Second Amendment," 45 *Emory Law Journal* 1139 (1996).

41. After all, a leading authority maintains that "the power to tax involves the power to destroy." McCulloch v. Maryland, 17 U.S. (4 Wheat.) 316, 431 (1819).

42. On the historical context of the Second Amendment, see, e.g., Michael A. Bellesiles, *Arming America: The Origins of a National Gun Culture* (2000).

43. Dworkin, *Freedom's Law*, at 291. The distinction is discussed at length in Chapter 1, in the section titled, "Originalism as a Theory About What Words Mean."

44. Ely's suggestion about the Ninth Amendment appears in *Democracy and Distrust*, at 39. There is much debate about the significance of "the Second Amendment's 'preamble.' " See, e.g., Eugene Volokh, "The Commonplace Second Amendment"; David C. Williams, "Response: The Unitary Second Amendment," 73 *N.Y.U. Law Review* 822 (1998).

45. On the relationship between the National Guard and militias, see Perpich v. Department of Defense, 496 U.S. 334 (1990).

46. Sugarman v. Dougall, 413 U.S. 634, 651–672 (1972) (Rehnquist, J., dissenting).

47. Schneider v. Rusk, 377 U.S. 163, 165 (1963).

48. For further discussion of "interpretive quarantines," see Christopher L. Eisgruber, "Birthright Citizenship and the Constitution," 72 *N.Y.U. Law Review* 54, 86–95 (1997).

49. The classic citation for this point is Alfred Kelly, "Clio and the Court," 1965 *Supreme Court Review* 119. For more recent commentary by historians on the peculiarities and deficiencies of historical argument by judges and law professors, see, e.g., Laura Kalman, *The Strange Career of Legal Liberalism* (1997); Martin Flaherty, "History 'Lite' in Modern American Constitutionalism," 95 *Columbia Law Review* 523 (1995).

50. 274 U.S. 357, 375 (1927) (concurring opinion).

51. Id. at 378, 377, 375.

52. See Robert F. Nagel, "'Unfocused' Government Interests," in *Public Values in Constitutional Law* 61–62 (Stephen E. Gottlieb ed. 1993).

53. John C. Miller, *Crisis in Freedom: The Alien and Sedition Acts* 114–119 (1951).

54. 300 U.S. 379 (1937).

55. 298 U.S. 587 (1936).

56. See, e.g., Michael Ariens, "A Thrice-Told Tale, or Felix the Cat," 107 *Harvard Law Review* 620 (1994).

57. Cass R. Sunstein, "Lochner's Legacy," 87 *Columbia Law Review* 873 (1987). For further discussion of *Lochner* and "*Lochner*-izing," see the Section in Chapter 5, *infra*, titled, "*Lochner.*"

58. Important recent accounts of the "switch in time" include Barry Cushman, *Rethinking the New Deal Court: The Structure of a Constitutional Revolution* (1998) and Bruce Ackerman, *We the People: Transformations* 279–382 (1998).

59. See, e.g., C. Herman Pritchett, *The Roosevelt Court: A Study in Judicial Politics, 1937–1947* 8–9 (1948). For citations to a variety of other realist accounts of *West Coast Hotel*, see Ariens, "Thrice-Told Tale," at 631–633.

60. For summary, analysis, and critique of the "non-political" theory of *West Coast Hotel*, see Ariens, "Thrice-Told Tale," at 634–666. For a more sympathetic presentation, see Cushman, *Rethinking the New Deal Court*, at 3–92.

61. See Ackerman, *Transformations*, at 3–31, 342–344.

62. For discussion of the exceptional character of the political support enjoyed by the Roosevelt administration, see Ackerman, *Transformations*, at 281–311.

63. On South Africa, see David Dyzenhaus, *Hard Cases in Wicked Legal Systems: South African Law in the Perspective of Legal Philosophy* (1991). On the antebellum United States, see Robert M. Cover, *Justice Accused: Antislavery and the Judicial Process* (1975).

64. The concept of constitutional failure is introduced and analyzed in Mark Brandon, *Free in the World: American Slavery and Constitutional Failure* 3–33 (1998).

5 Liberty, Strategy, and Tradition

1. Lawrence Gene Sager, "Foreword: State Courts and the Strategic Space Between the Norms and Rules of Constitutional Law," 63 *Texas Law Review* 959 (1985).

2. 376 U.S. 254 (1964).

3. Id. at 279–280.

4. This principle tracks the "constitutive" justification for free speech recommended by Ronald Dworkin in his philosophical reconstruction of *Sullivan*. Ronald M. Dworkin, *Freedom's Law: The Moral Reading of the American Constitution* 200 (1996).

5. British libel law, which is much more restrictive than American law, is sometimes said to provide a benefit of this kind. See Sarah Lyall, "Where Suing for Libel Is a National Specialty; Britain's Plaintiff-Friendly Laws Have Become a Magnet for Litigators," *New York Times*, July 22, 2000, at B7, Col. 1.

6. Harry Kalven, Jr., "The *New York Times* Case: A Note on the 'Central Meaning of the First Amendment,'" 1964 *Supreme Court Review* 191, 221 n. 125.

7. Among the most notable of these cases were Brandenburg v. Ohio, 395 U.S. 444 (1969), in which the Court overturned the conviction of Ku Klux Klan leader charged with criminal syndicalism; Cohen v. California, 403 U.S. 15 (1971), in which the Court upheld the right of a protester to enter a courtroom wearing a jacket bearing the words, "Fuck the Draft," and *New York Times* v. United States, 403 U.S. 713 (1971), in which the Court quashed the government's effort to suppress publication of the Pentagon Papers.

8. See, e.g., Sager, "The Strategic Space Between Norms and Rules of Constitutional Law"; David Strauss, "The Ubiquity of Prophylactic Rules," 55 *University of Chicago Law Review* 190 (1988); and Richard H. Fallon, Jr., "Foreword: Implementing the Constitution," 111 *Harvard Law Review* 54 (1997).

9. 347 U.S. 483, 495 (1954).

10. These difficulties, of course, led the Court to adopt its notorious "all deliberate speed" formula. Brown v. Bd. of Education II, 349 U.S. 294, 301 (1955). See Lucas A. Powe, Jr., *The Warren Court and American Politics* 50–74 (2000).

11. Moore v. City of East Cleveland, 431 U.S. 494, 503 (1977).

12. Snyder v. Massachusetts, 291 U.S. 97, 105 (1934).

13. For White, see, e.g., *Moore*, 431 U.S. at 544 (dissenting opinion) and Bowers v. Hardwick, 478 U.S. 186, 191–195 (1986). For Scalia, see, e.g., Michael H. v. Gerald D., 491 U.S. 110, 122–123 (1989) (plurality opinion).

14. This point is well made by Laurence H. Tribe and Michael C. Dorf, *On Reading the Constitution* (1991) and Rebecca Brown, "Tradition and Insight," 103 *Yale Law Journal* 177, 210 (1993).

15. Robin West, among others, has recommended exactly that. West, "The Ideal of Liberty: A Comment on *Michael H. v. Gerald D.*," 139 *University of Pennsylvania Law Review* 1373, 1380 (1991).

16. Palko v. Connecticut, 302 U.S. 319, 325 (1937).

17. Poe v. Ullman, 367 U.S. 497, 541 (1961) (Harlan, J., dissenting), quoting Corfield v. Coryell, 6 Fed. Cas. 546, 551 (C.C.E.D.Pa. 1823) (Washington, J., on circuit) and Calder v. Bull, 3 U.S. (3 Dall.) 386, 388 (1798).

18. 367 U.S. at 542.

19. 505 U.S. 833, 848–849 (1992).

20. The best article published on this question is Brown, "Tradition and Insight." Brown argues that tradition is "essential . . . to the process of constitutional interpretation," Id. at 181. She assigns tradition a kind of epistemic value: she claims that by studying and interpreting tradition, readers of the Constitution can appreciate "principles that will allow society not merely to change but mature—to develop a certain degree of autonomy and capacity for independent judgment while still appreciating the value to be gained from the wisdom and experiences of prior generations." Id. at 180. My treatment of tradition diverges from Brown's, but I have nevertheless learned much from her article.

21. Id. at 179; Frank I. Michelman, *Brennan and Democracy* 101 (1999).

22. See "Justice Brandeis and the Sedition Acts," in Chapter 4.

23. For useful discussions, see Reva B. Siegel, "'The Rule of Love': Wife-Beating as Prerogative and Privacy," 105 *Yale Law Journal* 2117 (1996); Robin West, "Equality Theory, Marital Rape, and the Promise of the Fourteenth Amendment," 42 *Florida Law Review* 45 (1990); Note, "To Have and to Hold: The Marital Rape Exemption and the Fourteenth Amendment," 99 *Harvard Law Review* 1255 (1986).

24. See *Casey*, 505 U.S. 833 (abortion); *Bowers*, 478 U.S. 186 (homosexual sodomy); *Moore*, 431 U.S. 494 (extended family households); Cruzan v. Director, Missouri Dept. of Health, 497 U.S. 261 (1990); Vacco v. Quill, 521 U.S. 793 (1997) (euthanasia); Washington v. Glucksberg, 521 U.S. 702 (1997) (euthanasia); *Michael H.*, 491 U.S. 110 (paternity rights); and Troxel v. Granville, 120 S. Ct. 2054 (2000) (parental autonomy).

25. 262 U.S. 390 (1923).

26. 268 U.S. 510 (1925).

27. 262 U.S. 390, 399–400 (1923).

28. Id. at 400.

29. Bartels v. Iowa, 262 U.S. 404, 412 (Holmes, J., dissenting). *Bartels* was a companion case to *Meyer*; Holmes wrote a single opinion in *Bartels* to express his dissent from both decisions.

30. For discussion of the concerns that motivated the legislation in *Pierce* and *Meyer*, see Barbara Woodhouse, "'Who Owns the Child?': *Meyer* and *Pierce* and the Child as Property," 33 *William and Mary Law Review* 995 (1992).

31. *Bartels*, 262 U.S. at 412 (Holmes dissenting).

32. 367 U.S. 497 (1961).

33. 381 U.S. 479 (1965).

34. *Poe*, 367 U.S. at 554–555 (Harlan dissenting). For more detailed discussion of the political and historical background to the birth control cases, see C. Thomas Dienes, *Law, Politics and Birth Control* (1972).

35. 431 U.S. 494.

36. 431 U.S. at 520 (Stevens concurring).

37. 405 U.S. 438 (1972).

38. 431 U.S. 678 (1977).

39. *Eisenstadt*, 405 U.S. at 448–449; *Carey*, 431 U.S. at 690–691; see also *id.* at 715 n. 3 (Stevens, J., concurring in part and in the judgment).

40. 505 U.S. at 848–849.

41. Gerald N. Rosenberg, *The Hollow Hope: Can Courts Bring About Social Change?* 189–195 (1991).

42. Cass R. Sunstein, "Foreword: Leaving Things Undecided," 110 *Harvard Law Review* 4, 49–50 (1996). See also Ruth Bader Ginsburg, "Some Thoughts on Equality and Autonomy in *Roe v. Wade*," 63 *North Carolina Law Review* 365, 376, 382, 385–386 (1985).

43. *Casey*, 505 U.S. at 870.

44. 431 U.S. at 503.

45. 405 U.S. 645 (1972).

46. 491 U.S. 110.

47. Useful recent treatments and critiques of "substantive due process" and "privacy" jurisprudence include Toni M. Massaro, "Reviving Hugo Black? The Court's 'Jot for Jot' Account of Substantive Due Process," 73 *N.Y.U. Law Review* 1086 (1998); Richard H. Fallon, Jr., "Some Confusions About Due Process, Judicial Review, and Constitutional Remedies," 93 *Columbia Law Review* 309 (1993); Jed Rubenfeld, "The Right of Privacy," 102 *Harvard Law Review* 737 (1989); and Daniel O. Conkle, "The Second Death of Substantive Due Process," 62 *Indiana Law Journal* 215 (1987).

48. 405 U.S. at 453.

49. Doe v. Bolton, 410 U.S. 179, 221 (1973) (White, J., dissenting).

50. 381 U.S. at 486.

51. See Andrew Koppelman, "Sex, Law and Equality: Three Arguments for Gay Rights," 95 *Michigan Law Review* 1636, 1663–1666 (1997) and Richard Posner, *Sex and Reason* 243–266 (1992).

52. Thomas Grey has suggested a social policy rationale that might reconcile *Eisenstadt* with the conservative, marriage-oriented focus of *Griswold*. He argued that *Eisenstadt* and *Roe* were "simply family planning cases." On this view, those decisions "represent two standard conservative views: that social stability is threatened by excessive population growth; and that family stability is threatened by unwanted pregnancies, with their accompanying fragile marriages, single-parent families, irresponsible youthful parents, and abandoned or neglected children." Thomas C. Grey, "Eros, Civilization and the Burger Court," 43 *Law and Contemporary Problems* 83, 88 (Summer 1980).

53. In *Bowers*, Justice Stevens argued that consensual sodomy was protected by extension of whatever principles underlay *Griswold*, *Eisenstadt*, and *Carey*. 478 U.S. 218 (dissenting opinion). He was, in my view, correct, but his argument begs the question of what those principles are.

54. See, e.g., Sylvia A. Law, "Rethinking Sex and the Constitution," 132 *University of Pennsylvania Law Review* 955, 1016–1028 (1984); Catharine A. MacKinnon, "Reflections on Sex Equality Under Law," 100 *Yale Law Journal* 1281, 1309–1324 (1991); Andrew Koppelman, *Antidiscrimination Law and Social Equality* 146–153 (1996);

Cass R. Sunstein, "Sexual Orientation and the Constitution: A Note on the Relationship Between Due Process and Equal Protection," 55 *University of Chicago Law Review* 1161 (1988); and Kendall Thomas, "Beyond the Privacy Principle," 92 *Columbia Law Review* 1431 (1992).

55. *Casey*, 505 U.S. at 876 (opinion of O'Connor, Kennedy, and Souter).

56. See, e.g., Hyman Rodman, Betty Sarvis, and Joy Walker Bonar, *The Abortion Question* 142 (1987).

57. For whatever reasons, the Playboy Foundation has been a consistent supporter of abortion rights. Catharine MacKinnon, "Roe v. Wade: A Study in Male Ideology," in *Abortion: Moral and Legal Perspectives* 51 (Jay L. Garfield and Patricia Hennessey, eds., 1984). See also Michael W. McConnell, "How Not To Promote Serious Deliberation About Abortion," 58 *University of Chicago Law Review* 1181, 1190–1191 and nn. 19–20 (1991).

58. See, e.g., Thomas, "Beyond the Privacy Principle," at 1463–1465.

59. The distinction between status and conduct is, of course, crucial to most efforts to explain how *Bowers* might be consistent with Romer v. Evans, 517 U.S. 620 (1996). In *Romer*, the Court struck down an amendment to the Colorado constitution which would have prevented state and local legislatures from enacting laws that prohibited discrimination on the basis of sexual orientation. For discussion of how the status/conduct distinction matters to *Romer*, see, e.g., Daniel Farber and Suzanna Sherry, "The Pariah Principle," 13 *Constitutional Commentary* 257 (1996). For more general discussion of the relationship between status and conduct, see Janet Halley, "Reasoning About Sodomy: Act and Identity in and after *Bowers v. Hardwick*," 79 *Virginia Law Review* 1721 (1993).

60. This example is not entirely hypothetical; North Carolina, for example, has used its anti-sodomy laws to get around the consent defense in rape cases. See, e.g., North Carolina v. Poe, 40 N.C. App. 385; 252 S.E.2d 843 (1979). The Supreme Court inexcusably ducked the constitutional issue by dismissing Poe's appeal for want of a substantial federal question; Justices Brennan and Stevens would have noted probable jurisdiction. Poe v. North Carolina, 445 U.S. 947 (1980).

61. The typical view, I suspect, is comparable to that of Akhil Amar, who suggests that *Eisenstadt* implies the unconstitutionality of any law prohibiting "male-female anal sex," and that "stone cold logic" plus the Equal Protection Clause entail the unconstitutionality of a wide range of other laws regulating sexual behavior—including laws prohibiting homosexual sodomy. Akhil Reed Amar, "Attainder and Amendment 2: Romer's Rightness," 95 *Michigan Law Review* 203, 231–232 (1996).

62. For an excellent analysis of the possibilities, see David B. Cruz, "'The Sexual Freedom Cases'? Contraception, Abortion, Abstinence, and the Constitution," 35 *Harvard Civil Rights-Civil Liberties Law Review* 299 (2000).

63. To be sure, the Court has repeatedly declined to endorse any libertarian principle of this kind. The relevant cases include not only *Bowers* but Wainwright v. Stone, 414 U.S. 21 (1973), Rose v. Locke, 423 U.S. 48 (1975), and Poe v. North Carolina, 445 U.S. 947 (1980). *Poe* is one of the cases in which North Carolina prosecuted consensual heterosexual sodomy; Thomas Grey has aptly summarized *Wainwright* and *Rose* as cases that "upheld . . . two . . . ludicrous 'crime against nature' sodomy statutes against void-for-vagueness attacks." Grey, "Eros, Civilization, and the Burger Court," at 86. More recently, Janet Halley has noted that "several courts have refused to hold that unmarried cross-sex sodomy is protected, and at least one court has held that sexual 'misconduct' is subject to regulation notwithstanding the marital status of the participants." Janet Halley, "Reasoning About Sodomy," at 1778–1779 (1993) (footnotes omitted).

64. *Bowers*, 478 U.S. at 205 (quoting Paris Adult Theatre I v. Slaton, 413 U.S. 49, 63 (1973)) (dissenting opinion).

65. Id. at 206.

66. Kendall Thomas, who is a harsh critic of *Bowers*, nevertheless observes that "'there need be no necessary relationship between sexual practice and sexual identity'" and that "for many of the individuals who have embraced it, homosexual identity is not primarily erotic, but social and political." Thomas, "Beyond the Privacy Principle," at 1506 (1992) quoting Jeffrey Weeks, "Questions of Identity," in *The Cultural Construction of Sexuality* 31, 47 (Pat Caplan, ed., 1987).

67. Olmstead v. United States, 277 U.S. 438, 478 (1928) (Brandeis, J., dissenting). The quote seems less apt if put in context: for Brandeis, the "right to be left alone" was justified by "man's spiritual nature" and by the fact that "only a part of the pain, pleasure and satisfactions of life are to be found in material things." Id. The right he named protected "Americans in their beliefs, their thoughts, their emotions and their sensations." Id. A right of privacy tailored to man's "spiritual nature" repeats exactly the same set of advantages and disadvantages attendant upon the modern Court's references to reproductive autonomy, intimate association, and committed relationships—it fits easily within the domain of constitutional privilege, but it may not be expansive enough to comprehend the pursuit of sexual pleasure.

68. I am not aware of any such regulation, but restauranteurs have worried that they might be sued by patrons who become ill after eating rare burgers. Jim Carlton, "Some Diners Have a Beef: Pink Burgers Are Now a Rare Find," *Wall Street Journal*, July 15, 1999, at A1.

69. In terminology that Lawrence Sager and I have developed elsewhere, constitutional solicitude for sexual freedom depends upon the modality of "protection," rather than the modality of "privilege": that is, it results from the special vulnerability of sexual conduct to hostile government action, rather than from the special value of sexual conduct to either individual flourishing or community well-being. See Lawrence G. Sager and Christopher L. Eisgruber, "The Vulnerability of Conscience: The Constitutional Basis for Protecting Religious Conduct," 61 *University of Chicago Law Review* 1245, 1250–1251 (1994).

70. 198 U.S. 45 (1905).

71. Cass R. Sunstein, "Lochner's Legacy," 87 *Columbia Law Review* 873, 873–874 (1987).

72. Not everybody thinks *Lochner* was wrongly decided. See, e.g., Richard Epstein, *Takings: Private Property and the Law of Eminent Domain* 5 (1985); Hadley Arkes, "*Lochner v. New York* and the Cast of Our Laws," *Great Cases in Constitutional Law* 94–129 (Robert P. George, ed., 2000).

73. Stephen Macedo, *Liberal Virtues: Citizenship, Virtue, and Community in Liberal Constitutionalism* 192, 197–199 (1990).

74. Cass Sunstein, *The Partial Constitution* 45, 46 (1993).

75. 198 U.S. at 68–72.

76. Of course, economic power and individual liberty will intersect in a number of domains. For an important effort to address that intersection in the context of free speech doctrine, see Yochai Benkler, "Free as the Air to Common Use: First Amendment Constraints on Enclosure of the Public Domain," 74 *N.Y.U. Law Review* 354 (1999).

77. U.S. Const., Art. I., Sec. 10. In Adkins v. Children's Hospital, Oliver Wendell Holmes observed that "[c]ontract is not specially mentioned" in the Fourteenth Amendment. 261 U.S. 525, 568 (1923) (dissenting opinion). True enough: the word "contract" never appears in the Fourteenth Amendment. On the other hand, the Constitution does contain a Contracts Clause, and it contains no comparably specific phrase protecting free speech rights against state governments. From a purely textual stand-

point, it is not clear why challenges to *state* laws based upon "the liberty of contract" should fare worse than those predicated upon "the freedom of speech."

78. Ogden v. Saunders, 25 U.S. 213, 344–353 (1827) (dissenting opinion).

79. See, e.g., Jennifer Nedelsky, *Private Property and the Limits of American Constitutionalism* (1990).

80. See Gary D. Rowe, "*Lochner* Revisionism Revisited," 24 *Law and Social Inquiry* 221 (1999).

81. "I think the word 'liberty,' in the 14th Amendment, is perverted when it is held to prevent the natural outcome of a dominant opinion, unless it can be said that a rational and fair man necessarily would admit that the statute proposed would infringe fundamental principles." 198 U.S. at 76.

6 Judicial Maintenance of Political Institutions

1. 376 U.S. 254 (1964).

2. For general discussions of this point, see, e.g., Richard H. Pildes, "Why Rights Are Not Trumps: Social Meanings, Expressive Harms, and Constitutionalism," 27 *Journal of Legal Studies* 725 (1997); Christopher L. Eisgruber, "Political Unity and the Powers of Government," 41 *U.C.L.A. Law Review* 1297 (1994); Richard H. Fallon, Jr., "Individual Rights and the Powers of Government," 27 *Georgia Law Review* 343 (1993).

3. 520 U.S. 351 (1997).

4. Samuel Issacharoff and Richard H. Pildes, "Politics as Markets: Partisan Lockups of the Democratic Process," 50 *Stanford Law Review* 643, 685 (1998). Issacharoff and Pildes rightly complain that the Court consistently treats claims about the democratic process as though they were claims about individual liberties rather than political structures. Id. at 644–645. For a recent example of the pattern, see California Democratic Party v. Jones, 120 S. Ct. 2402 (2000), in which the Court struck down California's open-primary law on the ground that it violated the constitutional right to freedom of association.

5. Issacharoff and Pildes, "Politics as Markets," at 683–687, 716–717. On the subject of "lockups" or "entrenchment," see also Michael Klarman, "Majoritarian Judicial Review: The Entrenchment Problem," 85 *Georgetown Law Journal* 491 (1997).

6. The literature on party decline in the United States is summarized in John J. Coleman, *Party Decline in America: Policy, Politics, and the Fiscal State* 3–32 (1996). Competing positions on the two-party system are presented in Theodore J. Lowi and Joseph Romance, *A Republic of Parties? Debating the Two-Party System* (1998). Issacharoff and Pildes contend (along with some prominent political scientists) that there is no need for states to protect the two major parties against challenges. See Issacharoff and Pildes, "Politics as Markets," at 668, 674–675, and 680.

7. Of course, *Sullivan* might also be defended on the basis of a comprehensive principle—such as, "the government is obliged to facilitate robust and open public debate." Indeed, any decision on any topic might be defended by reference to a comprehensive principle such as, "the government must do justice, all things considered." For purposes of my argument, the crucial point is that some constitutional claims cannot be defended except by reference to comprehensive principles, whereas others (including *Sullivan*) implicate one or more discrete principles.

8. Hence, while Richard Epstein thinks *Sullivan*'s holding "dubious" because of the assumptions it makes about "certain elusive, empirical issues," he nevertheless believes that "the case was correctly decided on its facts" because the "Supreme Court had to stay the hand of Alabama defamation law." Richard Epstein, "Was *New York Times v. Sullivan* Wrong?," 53 *University of Chicago Law Review* 782, 817 (1986).

9. The classic article is Abraham Chayes, "The Role of the Judge in Public Law Litigation," 89 *Harvard Law Review* 1281 (1976).

10. Indeed, Minnesota elected a third-party candidate—Jesse Ventura—as governor less than a year after the Supreme Court decided *Timmons*. As Pildes himself has noted, Ventura's success was attributable partly to Minnesota's election laws, which are, on the whole, *more* favorable to third parties than the laws of most other states. Richard H. Pildes, "The Theory of Political Competition," 85 *Virginia Law Review* 1605, 1617–1618 (1999). See also Garry Wills, "The People's Choice," *New York Review of Books*, Aug. 12, 1999, at 40–43.

11. Cf. Issacharoff and Pildes, "Politics as Markets," at 679: although "first-past-the-post" electoral procedures are the primary impediment to the success of third parties, "courts would surely find it well beyond their proper role to hold [such procedures] unconstitutional."

12. 5 U.S. (1 Cranch) 137 (1803).

13. Issacharoff and Pildes, "Politics as Markets," at 690–699.

14. 462 U.S. 919 (1983).

15. There is an extensive literature on the legislative veto; see, e.g., Michael Herz, "The Legislative Veto in Times of Political Reversal: *Chadha* and the 104th Congress," 14 *Constitutional Commentary* 319 (1997); William N. Eskridge and John Ferejohn, "The Article I, Section 7 Game," 80 *Georgetown Law Journal* 523 (1992); Louis Fisher, "Micromanagement by Congress: Reality and Mythology," in *The Fettered Presidency: Legal Constraints on the Executive Branch* (Jeremy Rabkin and Gordon Crovitz, eds., 1989).

16. Abner S. Greene, "Checks and Balances in an Era of Presidential Law-Making," 61 *University of Chicago Law Review* 123, 176 (1994).

17. That is all Greene himself claims on behalf of the principle; he has reservations about the sweeping rule announced by the *Chadha* Court. Greene, "Checks and Balances," at 176–177 and 187–195.

18. To make matters more complex, *Chadha*'s impact is less sweeping than lawyers might suppose: Congress continues to insert legislative vetoes into bills, and a significant number escape judicial review. For discussion, see Fisher, "Micromanagement by Congress," at 147–149.

19. 462 U.S. at 919.

20. Perhaps the best known statement of that thesis is Jesse Choper, *Judicial Review and the National Political Process* 263 (1980).

21. A recent affirmation of this theme is the work of Michael Klarman; see, e.g., Klarman, "The Puzzling Resistance to Political Process Theory," 77 *Virginia Law Review* 747 (1991).

22. 377 U.S. 533 (1964).

23. "*Baker* [*v. Carr*, 369 U.S. 186 (1962)] and *Reynolds* drew their greatest strength from malapportionments so dramatic that it was possible to compute meaningful, even shocking, disparities in individual access to representation. When the disparities were as great as 23–1, as in . . . *Baker*, or even 41–1, in . . . *Reynolds*, a rule of equipopulational representation could restore individual claims to representation under a legal regime easily administered by courts." Samuel Issacharoff, "Judging Politics: The Elusive Quest for Judicial Review of Political Fairness," 71 *Texas Law Review* 1643, 1652 and n. 49 (1993).

24. "One person, one vote has encouraged the Court's hubris. And we all know what comes after hubris." Pamela S. Karlan and Daniel R. Ortiz, "Constitutional Farce," in William N. Eskridge and Sanford Levinson, eds., *Constitutional Stupidities, Constitutional Tragedies* 180, 186 (1998). See also Peter Schuck, "The Thickest Thicket:

Partisan Gerrymandering and Judicial Regulation of Politics," 87 *Columbia Law Review* 1325, 1338–1384 (1987).

25. A useful discussion of the concept of proportional representation, and its allure, is Sanford Levinson, "Gerrymandering and the Brooding Omnipresence of Proportional Representation: Why Won't It Go Away," 33 *U.C.L.A. Law Review* 257 (1985).

26. For description of various different ways to implement a scheme of proportional representation, see Samuel Issacharoff, Pamela S. Karlan, and Richard H. Pildes, *The Law of Democracy: Legal Structure of the Political Process* 719–726 (1998).

27. 446 U.S. 55, 103 (1980).

28. Id. at 119.

29. Id. at 134 (Marshall dissenting). Justice Brennan agreed with Marshall's conclusion; id. at 94 (Brennan dissenting).

30. See, e.g., Thornburgh v. Gingles, 478 U.S. 30, 84 (1986) (O'Connor, J., concurring); see also Samuel Issacharoff, "Polarized Voting and the Political Process: The Transformation of Voting Rights Jurisprudence," 90 *Michigan Law Review* 1833, 1850 (1992).

31. This paragraph, and the five that follow it, draw heavily from Christopher L. Eisgruber, "Democracy, Majoritarianism, and Racial Equality," 50 *Vanderbilt Law Review* 347 (1997).

32. Majority-minority districts are not the only way to achieve this result, and some proponents of proportional representation favor much different schemes. See, e.g., Lani Guinier, "[E]racing Democracy: The Voting Rights Cases," 108 *Harvard Law Review* 109, 132–134 (1994) (recommending a system of cumulative voting as a mechanism to implement "universal group representation"). In one respect, though, Guinier's proposal is no different than the majority-minority districts: both mechanisms have the potential to increase overall legislative hostility to minority interests. Guinier recognizes this problem. She suggests altering assembly voting rules in order to address it. Lani Guinier, *The Tyranny of the Majority: Fundamental Fairness in Representative Democracy* 107–108 (1994).

33. Jean-Pierre Benoit and Lewis Kornhauser criticize voting rights doctrine and scholarship for failing to recognize that "[t]hough our electoral institutions are candidate-based, individual preferences [among candidates] are significantly determined by preferences over assemblies or over policy outcomes." Jean-Pierre Benoit and Lewis Kornhauser, "Assembly-Based Preferences, Candidate-Based Procedures, and the Voting Rights Act," 68 *Southern California Law Review* 1503, 1544 (1995).

34. Indeed, "packing" minorities into a small number of districts is a recognized tactic that has been used to disenfranchise black voters. See, e.g., Pamela S. Karlan, "All Over the Map: The Supreme Court's Voting Rights Trilogy," 1993 *Supreme Court Review* 245, 249–250.

35. At a 1990 meeting of the Southern Republican Leadership Conference, the Republican National Committee announced its plan to join forces with civil rights groups to bring suits designed to create majority-black and majority-Hispanic voting districts. Paul Taylor, "GOP Will Aid Civil Rights Groups in Redistricting; Party Sees Additional Minority Legislative Seats Boosting Republican Fortunes Elsewhere," *Washington Post*, April 1, 1990, at A6. For further discussion and citations to related stories, see Eisgruber, "Democracy, Majoritarianism, and Racial Equality," at 353 n. 25.

36. See, e.g., Samuel Issacharoff, "The Constitutional Contours of Race and Politics," 1995 *Supreme Court Review* 45, 55 n. 37; Charles S. Bullock III, "Winners and Losers in the Latest Round of Redistricting," 44 *Emory Law Journal* 944 (1995). The view is by no means unanimously held; for a dissent, see Pamela S. Karlan, "Loss and

Redemption: Voting Rights at the Turn of a Century," 50 *Vanderbilt Law Review* 291 (1997).

37. Perhaps the best known version of the argument is Abigail M. Thernstrom, *Whose Votes Count? Affirmative Action and Minority Voting Rights* 232–244 (1987). Another important treatment is Carol M. Swain, *Black Faces, Black Interests: The Representation of African-Americans in Congress* 207–225 (2d ed. 1995).

38. The evidence is summarized in Richard H. Pildes, "The Politics of Race," 108 *Harvard Law Review* 1359, 1382–1384 (1995) (reviewing Chandler Davidson and Bernard Grofman, eds., *Quiet Revolution in the South* (1994)).

39. Richard H. Pildes makes this claim in emphatic terms: "The arguments that Blacks need not run in 'safe' minority districts to be elected, that White voters increasingly support Black politicians, that racial-bloc voting is now unusual—all turn out to be among the great myths currently distorting public discussion." Pildes, "The Politics of Race," at 1367. See also Keith Reeves, *Voting Hopes or Fears: White Voters, Black Candidates and Racial Politics in America* (1997). On the other hand, Carol Swain contends that "[e]very indication suggests that racial polarization is declining, even in the South." Carol M. Swain, "Not 'Wrongful' By Any Means: The Court's Decisions in the Redistricting Cases," 34 *Houston Law Review* 315, 319 (1997). In Swain's view, "The prospects . . . of electing additional minority candidates from majority-white constituencies is anything but dismal." Id.

40. For a contrasting perspective, see Guinier, "[E]racing Democracy," at 125. Guinier argues that democracy is best realized through a system of group representation, which recognizes and perhaps even reinforces the identities of intermediary groups within society.

41. 509 U.S. 630 (1993).

42. Id. at 647–648.

43. Kenneth Cooper, "Voting Rights and Wrongs; Backers of Odd N.C. District Point to History," *Washington Post*, July 13, 1993, at A1.

44. Shaw v. Hunt, 517 U.S. 899, 925 (1996) (dissenting opinion).

45. My argument applies only to constitutional decisions. The Court retains an important role to play in this area through statutory interpretation. After the Court's decision in *Mobile*, Congress amended Section 2 of the Voting Rights Act to prohibit any election scheme "which results in the denial or abridgment of the right of any citizen to vote on account of race or color." 42 U.S.C. §1973(a) (1994). The statute explicitly provides that Section 2 violations may be inferred from "[t]he extent to which members of a protected class have been elected to office." 42 U.S.C. §1973(b) (1994). The resulting statutory partnership between the courts and Congress is entirely legitimate.

46. See, e.g., Gregory v. Ashcroft, 501 U.S. 452, 457–459 (1991).

47. New York v. United States, 505 U.S. 144, 157 (1992).

48. Jack Rakove, *Original Meanings: Politics and Ideas in the Making of the Constitution* 197 (1996). In Rakove's view, Madison's preferred version of federalism was so relentlessly nationalist that "[o]nly by abolishing the states altogether could Madison have moved to alter the structure of the Union more radically." Id. at 169.

49. Rakove, *Original Meanings*, at 47.

50. The two leading students of Madison's thought in the academy today are Rakove and Lance Banning, who portrays Madison as more sympathetic to the states. See Lance Banning, *The Sacred Fire of Liberty: James Madison and the Founding of the Federal Republic* (1995). Even Banning concedes, however, that a concern with the failures of state government was fundamental to Madison's constitutional theory. Id. at 120.

51. Martin S. Flaherty, "More Apparent Than Real: The Revolutionary Commitment to Constitutional Federalism," 45 *Fordham Law Review* 993, 1009 (1997).

52. Rakove, *Original Meanings*, at 68–69, 74–75, 77–79. Rakove concludes that Madison's effort to apportion the Senate on the basis of population, rather than state by state, was fated to fail once "the specter of sectional conflict [over slavery] legitimated the small states' appeal to [the need for] security for states' rights." Id. at 79.

53. See Robert Cover, "The Origins of Judicial Activism in the Protection of Minorities," 91 *Yale Law Journal* 1287 (1982). See also Rakove, *Original Meanings*, at 93.

54. Garry Wills, *Lincoln at Gettysburg: The Words That Remade America* 37–40, 145–147 (1992).

55. Bruce Ackerman, *We the People: Foundations* 47 (1991).

56. 22 U.S. 1 (1824).

57. Ackerman, *We the People: Foundations*, at 42–43. The post–New Deal Court announced in Wickard v. Fillburne, 317 U.S. 111, 120 (1942), that it was doing no more than following Marshall's lead.

58. United States v. Darby, 312 U.S. 100, 124 (1941).

59. Even this conclusion strikes me as doubtful, since (for example) the powers retained by the people might include the power to form themselves into cities and towns. Still, the Tenth Amendment does seem to require that any constitutional arguments about the autonomy of local government will have a derivative character: the constitutional claims of local government will depend upon more fundamental constitutional rights, powers, or responsibilities attaching to either the national government, the states, or the people.

60. For example, in New York v. United States, 505 U.S. at 156–157, the Court declared, "The Tenth Amendment . . . restrains the power of Congress, but this limit is not derived from the text of the Tenth Amendment itself, which . . . is . . . essentially a tautology. Instead, the Tenth Amendment confirms that the power of the Federal Government is subject to limits that may, in a given instance, reserve power to the States." See also Seminole Tribe v. Florida, 517 U.S. 44, 54 (1996): "'we have understood the Eleventh Amendment to stand not so much for what it says, but for the presupposition . . . which it confirms'" (quoting Blatchford v. Native Village of Noatak, 501 U.S. 775, 779 (1991)).

61. See Charles L. Black, *Structure and Relationship in Constitutional Law* (1965).

62. See Gary Lawson and Patricia B. Granger, "The 'Proper' Scope of Federal Power: A Jurisdictional Interpretation of the Sweeping Clause," 43 *Duke Law Journal* 267 (1993); Stephen Gardbaum, "Rethinking Constitutional Federalism," 74 *Texas Law Review* 795 (1996). Cf. Randy E. Barnett, "Necessary and Proper," 44 *U.C.L.A. Law Review* 745 (1997).

63. McCulloch v. Maryland, 17 U.S. 316 (1819).

64. An effort to do so is Gardbaum, "Rethinking Constitutional Federalism," at 814–819.

65. For a discussion rich with citations to other leading works, see Barry Friedman, "Valuing Federalism," 82 *Minnesota Law Review* 317, 389–397, and 400–402 (1997).

66. See, e.g., Stephen G. Calabresi, "'A Government of Limited and Enumerated Powers': In Defense of *United States v. Lopez*," 94 *Michigan Law Review* 752, 768–769 (1995).

67. Even at the time of the founding, most political thinkers regarded the American states as too large to be genuine communities. Alexander Hamilton wrote, "When Montesquieu recommends a small extent for republics, the extent he had in view were of dimensions far short of the limits of almost every one of these States." Alexander Hamilton, "Federalist 9," in *The Federalist Papers* 73 (Clinton Rossiter, ed., 1961). See also James S. Fishkin, *Democracy and Deliberation* 17–18 (1991); Richard Briffault, "Our Localism: Part II—Localism and Legal Theory," 90 *Columbia Law Review* 346, 414 (1990).

68. *Gregory,* 501 U.S. at 458.

69. See, e.g., Friedman, "Valuing Federalism," at 405–412.

70. For a discussion of this problem that articulates a powerful general model of federalism, see Richard L. Revesz, "Federalism and Interstate Environmental Externalities," 144 *University of Pennsylvania Law Review* 2341 (1996).

71. Stephen Calabresi, an enthusiastic champion of distinctive state identities, declares with gusto (and apparent approval) that "New Yorkers think they are different from Pennsylvanians." Calabresi, "In Defense of *Lopez,*" at 769. Perhaps such a rivalry exists, but, after working in New York City for more than a decade, I've not noticed it.

72. Edward Rubin and Malcolm Feeley argue that "[t]he United States, despite its federal structure and its self-image as a vast and variegated nation, is in fact a heavily homogenized culture with high levels of normative consensus." Edward L. Rubin and Malcolm Feeley, "Federalism: Some Notes on a National Neurosis," 41 *U.C.L.A. Law Review* 903, 922 (1994). In their view, America's "ethnic and cultural differences do not correspond to geographic sections of the country." For example, "African-Americans [may be] a distinct, excluded group, but they are no more so in Denver than they are in Baltimore." Id. at 944–945.

73. Rubin and Feeley, "Notes on a National Neurosis," at 919.

74. Id. at 919 and n. 66. For a nuanced account of the way in which state and federal law, including federal constitutional law, provides some practical protection to local governments, see Richard Briffault, "Our Localism: Part I—The Structure of Local Government Law," 90 *Columbia Law Review* 1 (1990).

75. 517 U.S. 620 (1996).

76. Rubin and Feeley, "Notes on a National Neurosis," at 919–920 and n. 67. David Barron, "The Promise of Cooley's City: Traces of Local Constitutionalism," 147 *University of Pennsylvania Law Review* 487, 586–594 (1999).

77. If you wanted to follow state government, you might find it hard to do. "[J]ournalists have historically paid relatively little attention to state government and politics." Michael X. Delli Carpini and Scott Keeter, *What Americans Know About Politics and Why It Matters* 211 (1996). By contrast, local news coverage tends to be extensive; "[t]he space given to local news is three times as great as that given to cosmopolitan news even in a cosmopolitan newspaper such as the *Los Angeles Times;* it is undoubtedly much greater in less ambitious journals." James Q. Wilson, "City Life and Citizenship," in *Dilemmas of Scale in America's Federal Democracy* 19 (Martha Derthick, ed., 1999).

78. The two classic statements of this position are Choper, *Judicial Review and the National Political Process,* and Herbert Wechsler, "The Political Safeguards of Federalism: The Role of the States in the Composition and Selection of the National Government," 54 *Columbia Law Review* 543, 558–560 (1954). A superb critique of Wechsler's argument, which arrives at similar conclusions but on the basis of better reasons, is Larry Kramer, "Putting the Politics Back into the Political Safeguards of Federalism," 100 *Columbia Law Review* 215 (2000).

79. Rubin and Feeley, "Notes on a National Neurosis," at 913.

80. Larry Kramer, "Understanding Federalism," 47 *Vanderbilt Law Review* 1485, 1528, and 1542–1543 (1994).

81. On the other hand, "[s]tate and local governments are organized into formal lobbying groups inside the Beltway, and the casually empirical evidence found in the legal literature tentatively suggests that these groups have at least as much clout as other groups." Jenna Bednar and William N. Eskridge, Jr., "Steadying the Court's 'Unsteady Path': A Theory of the Judicial Enforcement of Federalism," 68 *Southern California Law Review* 1447, 1476 (1995). For a more systematic study which reaches a similar con-

clusion, see Anne Marie Cammina, *Governments as Interest Groups: Intergovernmental Lobbying and the Federal System* (1995).

82. 521 U.S. 898 (1997).

83. 505 U.S. 123 (1992).

84. 505 U.S. at 169.

85. See, e.g., Thomas R. McCoy and Barry Friedman, "Conditional Spending: Federalism's Trojan Horse," 1988 *Supreme Court Review* 85 (1988).

86. There are a number of other mechanisms that Congress can use to involve the states in the enforcement of federal law. It is not clear why these devices are less objectionable than the ones stricken in *Printz* and *New York*. A thoughtful discussion of the problem is Evan H. Caminker, "Printz, State Sovereignty, and the Limits of Formalism," 1997 *Supreme Court Review* 199 (1997). Creative efforts to refine and defend the anti-commandeering doctrine include Vicki Jackson, "Federalism and the Uses and Limits of Law: Printz and Principle?," 111 *Harvard Law Review* 2180 (1998) and Roderick Hills, "The Political Economy of Cooperative Federalism: Why State Autonomy Makes Sense and 'Dual Sovereignty' Doesn't," 96 *University of Michigan Law Review* 813 (1998).

87. 514 U.S. 549 (1995).

88. 521 U.S. 507 (1997).

89. 42 U.S.C. §§2000bb-2000bb-4 (1994).

90. "Government shall not substantially burden a person's exercise of religion" unless it first demonstrates that "application of the burden to the person" is the "least restrictive means" to further "a compelling government interest." 42 U.S.C. at §2000bb-1(a)-(b).

91. For my views, see Christopher L. Eisgruber and Lawrence G. Sager, "Why the Religious Freedom Restoration Act was Unconstitutional," 69 *N.Y.U. Law Review* 437, 452–460 (1994). For other criticism of RFRA on Establishment Clause grounds, see, e.g., Scott Idleman, "The Religious Freedom Restoration Act: Pushing the Limits of Legislative Power," 73 *Texas Law Review* 247, 285–302 (1994); Marci A. Hamilton, "RFRA is Unconstitutional, Period," 1 *University of Pennsylvania Journal of Constitutional Law* 1, 8–14 (1998); Jed Rubenfeld, "Antidisestablishmentarianism: Why RFRA Really Was Unconstitutional," 95 *Michigan Law Review* 2347 (1997); and William P. Marshall, "The Religious Freedom Restoration Act: Establishment, Equal Protection, and Free Speech Concerns," 56 *Montana Law Review* 227 (1995). RFRA also has many defenders; see, e.g., Thomas C. Berg, "The New Attacks on Religious Freedom Legislation, and Why They Are Wrong," 21 *Cardozo Law Review* 415 (1999). For an overview of the debate about RFRA, with extensive references, see Ira C. Lupu, "Why the Congress Was Wrong and the Court Was Right—Reflections on *City of Boerne v. Flores*," 39 *William and Mary Law Review* 793 (1998).

92. 521 U.S. at 536–537 (concurring opinion).

93. 521 U.S. at 533.

94. Eisgruber and Sager, "Why the Religious Freedom Restoration Act Is Unconstitutional," at 467.

95. Id.

96. See, e.g., Michael W. McConnell, "Institutions and Interpretations: A Critique of *City of Boerne v. Flores*," 111 *Harvard Law Review* 153 (1997); David Cole, "The Value of Seeing Things Differently: *Boerne v. Flores* and Congressional Enforcement of the Bill of Rights," 1997 *Supreme Court Review* 31.

97. One might try to make a similar claim about Seminole Tribe of Florida v. Florida, 517 U.S. 44 (1996) and subsequent Eleventh Amendment cases in which the Supreme Court expanded the states' immunity from private suits in federal court. Inso-

far as those cases dealt with issues about the range of remedies available in lawsuits and about the jurisdiction of the federal courts, it is possible that the judiciary possessed special competence relevant to the strategic issues they posed. That argument is strongest if one believes that Eleventh Amendment doctrine reflects a concern about whether federal courts can be trusted to treat state governments fairly. Federal judges might plausibly claim expertise about what circumstances create a risk of biased adjudication. On the other hand, if Eleventh Amendment doctrine is instead predicated upon a judgment about the relative importance of compensating plaintiffs versus protecting state treasuries, or about the "inherent sovereignty of the states" (whatever that might mean), then it is hard to understand why judges would have any special competence to decide the issue.

Of course, even if judges do have special competence with regard to Eleventh Amendment questions, it does not follow that *Seminole Tribe* and its successors were rightly decided. One might believe that judges have no obligation to defer to Congress about whether the states are entitled to immunity from suit, but also believe, with the dissenters in *Seminole Tribe*, that state immunity ought to be defined very narrowly.

98. Distinguishing "means" from "ends" is a delicate business. My co-author and I interpreted the *Boerne* decision as defining the realm of "means" generously, and hence as leaving ample scope for Congressional power. We suggested, in particular, that the *Boerne* rationale would allow the Court to uphold the authority of Congress to enact legislation under Section Five of the Fourteenth Amendment so long as Congress was "acting in support of the Court's constitutional judgment [about individual liberties], not in conflict [with it]." See Lawrence G. Sager and Christopher L. Eisgruber, "Congressional Power and Religious Liberty After *City of Boerne v. Flores*," 1997 *Supreme Court Review* 79, 92 (1997). Unfortunately, in later cases that invalidated portions of the Age Discrimination Act, Kimel v. Florida Bd. of Regents, 120 S. Ct. 631 (2000), and the Violence Against Women Act, United States v. Morrison, 120 S. Ct. 1740 (2000), the Court refined *Boerne*'s test in a way that was less deferential to congressional authority.

99. Lawrence G. Sager, "Fair Measure: The Legal Status of Underenforced Constitutional Norms," 91 *Harvard Law Review* 1212 (1978).

100. Of course, the question of whether the Court must defer to Congress is not the same as the question of whether the Court should uphold the challenged law. The Court might have decided, for example, that it had no obligation to defer to Congress about RFRA's impact on the states, but might nevertheless have upheld the law on the ground that it did no constitutionally significant damage to state or local government.

101. See, e.g., Prudential Insurance Co. v. Benjamin, 328 U.S. 408 (1946); Northeast Bancorp, Inc. v. Bd. of Governors, 472 U.S. 159 (1985). See also Laurence H. Tribe, *American Constitutional Law* §6–33 (2d ed. 1988).

102. See, e.g., Michael Dorf, "Foreword: The Limits of Socratic Deliberation," 112 *Harvard Law Review* 4, 60–73 (1998) (elaborating a concept of "provisional adjudication").

103. As Frederick Schauer says, "for almost all of the institutions of democratic decision making there are choices, all of which are at least plausibly compatible with the basic contours of representative democracy." Frederick Schauer, "Judicial Review of the Devices of Democracy," 94 *Columbia Law Review* 1326, 1326 (1994).

Conclusion

1. Akhil Reed Amar, "Intratextualism," 112 *Harvard Law Review* 747, 826–827 (1999).

2. Ronald M. Dworkin, *A Matter of Principle* 71 (1985).

3. Richard H. Fallon, Jr., "Foreword: Implementing the Constitution," 111 *Harvard Law Review* 54 (1997).

4. Robert Ferguson, *Law and Letters in American Culture* 202–205 (1984).

5. Anthony Kronman, *The Lost Lawyer* 273–307 (1993).

6. Planned Parenthood of Southeastern Pa. v. Casey, 505 U.S. 833, 1000 (1992) (dissenting opinion).

7. Id.

8. Id. at 1000–1001.

9. The empirical political science literature strongly suggests that public attitudes toward the Court vary according to whether or not people sympathize with the results of the Supreme Court's decisions, not on the basis of judgments about whether the Court was appropriately "legalistic" or "apolitical." See, e.g., Gregory A. Caldeira, "Neither the Purse nor the Sword: Dynamics of Public Confidence in the Supreme Court," 80 *American Political Science Review* 1209 (1986); Terri Jennings Peretti, *In Defense of a Political Court* 161–188 (1999).

Index